BENEDICTINE MONASTICISM

AS REFLECTED IN THE

WARNEFRID-HILDEMAR
COMMENTARIES ON
THE RULE

BY

SISTER M. ALFRED SCHROLL, O.S.B.

AMS PRESS, INC.
NEW YORK
1967

Permissu Superiorum Religiosorum

Nibil obstat

✠ MARTINUS VETH, O. S. B., Abbas
Censor Deputatus

Die 5 Julii 1940

Imprimatur

✠ PAUL C. SCHULTE
Episcopus Leavenworthiensis

Die 5 Julii 1940

Reprinted 1967
with permission of Columbia University Press

AMS PRESS, INC.
New York, N.Y. 10003

Manufactured in the United States of America

STUDIES IN HISTORY, ECONOMICS AND
PUBLIC LAW

Edited by the
FACULTY OF POLITICAL SCIENCE
OF COLUMBIA UNIVERSITY

NUMBER 478

BENEDICTINE MONASTICISM AS REFLECTED IN
THE WARNEFRID-HILDEMAR COMMEN-
TARIES ON THE RULE

BY

SISTER M. ALFRED SCHROLL

PREFACE

St. Benedict wrote his Rule for the guidance of his followers within the first half of the sixth century at Monte Cassino. When, later in the same century, the monastery was plundered by the Lombard invaders, its inmates fled to Rome and were given refuge in a monastery near the Lateran basilica.

Monte Cassino was restored in the early part of the eighth century and in the later part of this century the Lombard historian, Paul Warnefrid, also known as Paul the Deacon, became one of its members. He it is who wrote the first commentary on the Rule, a comparatively detailed exposition based on current interpretation and practice. Of it, Dom Butler writes " it gives us an insight into the earliest phase of Benedictinism, before it was overlaid with ideas and usages of the early Middle Ages, and shows us the working of primitive Benedictinism after it had run its course for two centuries." [1]

Within the first half of the ninth century, several other commentaries appeared. One of them is ascribed to the monk and *Magister* Hildemar, and is preserved in the form in which it was written by his pupils at his dictation.[2] It is largely a reproduction of Paul's commentary, being modified and enlarged somewhat in the process.

Hildemar's commentary has served as the basis of two further versions, the anonymous commentary of Novalese and the commentary ascribed to an Abbot Basil. Thus a family of commentaries is seen to have sprung from the eighth-century exposition made by Paul Warnefrid.

The two oldest manuscripts of this parent commentary date from the tenth century; one of them was published at Monte Cassino in 1880. In the course of the text, however, there are instances in which the lines fail to make sense, and sometimes

1 *Benedictine Monachism* (2d ed., 1924), p. 178.
2 *Cf. infra*, p. 129.

even contain a contradiction. Practically all of these obscurities can be cleared by comparison with the corresponding passage in Hildemar's version; in the majority of cases they are seen to be scribal errors consisting in the omission of the text which, in the more correct form, occurs between repeated words or phrases.

Although these and later commentaries have been drawn from occasionally by writers on asceticism, they have not been made the subject of systematic study. Therefore the commentary of Warnefrid, because of its unique characteristics, and the commentary of Hildemar, because of its worth in correcting and verifying the extant version of Paul's work, have been selected as the chief sources of the present study.

Its aim is to gather from the concrete applications of the general principles of the Rule, from the interpretation of obscure passages, and from the alterations and amplifications of the Rule, a general picture of the monasticism reflected in the commentaries; in particular, to present the aims and ideals set up as the goal, the spirit and means to be utilized in the attainment of the end, and, in as far as is possible, the material, social, and cultural levels in which these ideals are to be striven for.

In referring to the commentaries, when Paul's and Hildemar's contain substantially the same thought, both have been cited, the preference being given to the earlier one. When there is a difference, the commentary used in the text has been cited.

It is a pleasure to acknowledge the unfailing courtesy and helpfulness of the staffs of the various libraries in which I have had occasion to work, particularly that of Columbia University, of the Union Theological Seminary, and of the Library of Congress. The courtesy of the librarians of St. Benedict's Abbey, Atchison, Kansas, and of St. Vincent's Archabbey, Latrobe, Pennsylvania, placed at my disposal commentaries not easily obtainable elsewhere.

To Professors Lynn Thorndike, Dino Bigongiari, and Eugene Byrne, all of Columbia University, I am sincerely grateful for their careful reading of the manuscript and for helpful criticisms. My greatest debt is to Professor Austin P. Evans, also of Columbia University, who directed the research and whose scholarly guidance and kindly interest accompanied the work to its completion.

S. A.

ABBREVIATIONS USED

Albers .... B. Albers, *Consuetudines monasticae.*

Hildemar .... R. Mittermüller, *Expositio regulae ab Hildemaro tradita* (Part III of *Vita et regula SS. P. Benedicti una cum expositione regulae a Hildemaro tradita*).

Mansi .... J. Mansi, *Sacrorum conciliorum nova et amplissima collectio.*

MGH .... *Monumenta Germaniae historica.*

Paul .... *Pauli Warnefridi Diaconi Casinensis in sanctam regulam commentarium.*

PL .... J. P. Migne, *Patrologia Latina.*

TABLE OF CONTENTS

The principles of Benedictinism arise in the Rule; external observances vary with time and place; nature and purpose of the Carolingian commentaries; variation in the aim and viewpoint of the medieval commentators; authenticity of the Warnefrid commentary; of the Hildemar version; biographical sketch of Paul Warnefrid; of Hildemar; when and where each wrote his commentary.

Location of the monastery; the church and oratories; the cloister; the refectory—dishes, food, drink, the abbott's table; the kitchen—equipment, cleaning, laundry; the dormitory—baths, soap, towels, combs; clothing—articles of, quantity, color, quality, procurement; the infirmary—rooms, oratory; guest department—divisions for the nobility, the clergy, the poor; outlying units—garden, cells, villas; lay service—on villas, in domestic ministries.

Number of monks in the community; the abbott—his authority final but limited, difficulty of his position, need of discretion, ordination not essential, canonical abbots; the council—for major matters, for minor matters; the provost and deans; the *camerarius*; the cellarer; the infirmarian; the guestmaster; the doorkeeper; the *magister* of the boys; the admission of novices; the period of probation; profession ceremony and formula; admission of priests; of monks from other monasteries; commendatory letters; *formatae* and their authenticity; admission of the child oblate—ceremony and symbolism, irrevocability of promise, age of admission, attainment to complete monastic status.

Rank; equality; exceptions for merit, talent, or office; proportionate number of priests; impediments to ordination; enclosure rules; the penal code; classification of sins; modifying circumstances; the "seven steps" of correction for lesser faults—tradition, practical application; penalty for grave faults—custody, excommunication; monastic and canonical excommunication; monastic and canonical penances; readmission—in the original text of the Rule, in the *textus receptus*, as interpreted by the commentators; terms of readmission; prevailing practice.

CHAPTER I

INTRODUCTION

OF St. Benedict's Rule it has been well said that it is in its
" emphasis on inner principles, rather than in any enforcement
of a definite organization that we find its secret of power. An
organization would have waxed old and perished; an inner
principle can adapt itself to changing need." [1] Thus it is that
the Rule has, for more than fourteen hundred years, supplied
the principles of Benedictine monasticism. Its adaptability to
changing times and climes, however, has called forth, in the
course of its history, numerous statutes, customaries, and commentaries.

Moreover, the brevity of the Rule and the wisdom of its
author would not permit him to attempt a minute legislation
for the varying circumstances and situations which would in-
evitably arise in the future. In spite of its unusual practicality,
it contains passages which, even today, are not received uniformly by Benedictine scholars.[2] It is not a matter of wonder,
then, that an age which was emerging from the Frankish
conquest of the Lombards, more especially, an age which wit-
nessed the restoration of Monte Cassino after an interruption
of a century and a half in its traditions, should bring forth a
lengthy exposition of the Rule.

The author of that exposition, Paul Warnefrid, writes that
" the Rule contains many things by implication which are not
fully expressed in words." [3] Conciliar and imperial decrees,
alike, prescribe that in the monasteries the abbots read and
explain each sentence of the Rule fully and intelligently.[4] This

1 H. B. Workman, *The Evolution of the Monastic Ideal,* p. 148.

2 *Cf. infra,* p. 186.

3 *In sanctam regulam commentarium,* p. 188; Hildemar, *Expositio regulae,*
p. 255.

4 " Statuta Murbacensia," published in Albers, *Consuetudines monasticae,*
III, 79; " Capitulare monasticum," *MGH, Capitula regum Francorum,* I, 344
(no. 1). The Statutes of Murbach contain a recapitulation of the twenty-

took place, doubtless, at the morning chapter.[5] An early ninth-century capitulary prescribed that if a question arose concerning a chapter of the Rule which the abbots could not define among themselves, its meaning should be discussed by the bishops in council.[6] Thus it appears that the need of an authoritative interpretation of the Rule was frequently felt at this period of monastic history.

Smaragdus, a contemporary biographer of Benedict of Aniane, states that the latter wrote his *Concordia regularum,* a quasi-commentary,[7] to be read aloud at chapter.[8] The *Diadema monachorum,* written by another Smaragdus also of the early ninth century, was designed for reading at the evening conference.[9] It is quite possible that the commentaries of Paul and Hildemar were likewise used for public reading in the monastery.[10] Traube speaks of them as being the subject matter of oral discourses on the Rule delivered by their respective authors to their pupils.[11] Some other recent writers are of opinion that the discourses were delivered chiefly to the oblate pupils, i. e., to the boys destined to become monks.[12] With

seven decrees relating to monastic discipline, which were drawn up, it is thought, by the Synod of Aachen (816); see *infra,* p. 39. The Monastic Capitulary was composed by the Council of Aachen (817), an assembly of the abbots of the empire brought together by Louis the Pious under the influence of St. Benedict of Aniane.

5 *Cf. infra,* p. 115.

6 " Capitulum de inspiciendis monasteriis," Albers, III, 94, no. 3.

7 For a brief analysis of this work, see *infra,* p. 198.

8 *Vita Benedicti abbatis Anianensis et Indensis auctore Ardo,* in *MGH, SS,* XV, i, 217. Smaragdus is also known as Ardo.

9 *Op. cit., PL,* 102, col. 593.

10 C. Cipolla is of opinion that Hildemar's commentary was used for monastic *lettura*; see his article, " Brevi appunti di storia Novaliciense," *Memorie della reale accademia della scienze di Torino,* XLV (1896), 153.

11 *Textgeschichte der Regula S. Benedicti* (2d ed. by H. Plenkers, 1910, in Abhandlungen der königlich bayerischen Akademie der Wissenschaften: Philosophisch-philologische und historische Klasse, XXV), pp. 40, 42.

12 *Cf.* I. Herwegen, *Geschichte der benediktinischen Professformel,* in Beiträge zur Geschichte des alten Mönchtums und des Benediktinerordens, Heft 3 (1912), 40; K. Neff, *De Paulo Diacono Festi epitomatore,* p. 3, n. 1.

reference to Hildemar's commentary, the inscription on the manuscript stating that it was written by his pupils at his dictation, would seem to confirm the two latter opinions.[18]

Regardless of the specific purposes which our Carolingian commentaries served or the immediate audience to which they were addressed, it is obvious that the prime concern of their authors was to prepare a detailed explanation of the Rule, to express with greater fullness the original intention of St. Benedict, not to outline and present the norm of contemporary monasticism. Their purpose was practical, however, and the exposition of the Rule was made with a view to its current observance. Thus the commentators frequently find themselves, or, at least, we find them, making applications and refinements which extend considerably beyond the scope of the Rule; they treat of questions which, doubtless within their own experience, have come up for solution and which, therefore, are deemed worthy to be recorded for future reference. It is chiefly in these practical applications, refinements of the Rule, and attitudes in general that the commentator, indirectly, fills in the picture of contemporary monasticism.

As might be expected, the religious and spiritual elements are given the greater emphasis; nevertheless, the material and social aspects are not ignored. On the contrary, Warnefrid, in describing the ideal abbot, states emphatically that he should be zealous not only for the spiritual welfare of those entrusted to him, but also for their temporal necessities, for "it would avail nothing if he were solicitous only for the spiritual welfare and ignored the temporal; and again, it would be to no avail were he concerned only with the temporal necessities to the exclusion of the spiritual; but [the commentator concludes] he should be more solicitous for the spiritual than for the temporal welfare." [14]

It seems safe to say that Warnefrid's commentary is unique, not only in being the first of its kind, but also in being the

13 *Cf. infra*, p. 129.
14 Page 56.

most revealing of the medieval commentaries from the viewpoint of presenting the life and thought of contemporary monasticism. Hildemar's commentary is even more enlightening but its originality extends only to the small portion which is not taken from Warnefrid's *Expositio*. In some of the medieval commentaries the chief emphasis is placed on the literal interpretation of the Rule; in others, on its moral aspects; still others are devoted largely to the compilation of pertinent material from the writings of the Fathers or from monastic Rules other than that of St. Benedict.

The commentators themselves, beginning with Hildemar, constitute the class of writers who have made the greatest use of the commentaries. Among these, the two learned commentators of the early modern period, Martène and Calmet, have drawn most extensively from the medieval commentaries.[15]

The secondary literature on the commentaries is surprisingly scant. Only one of the commentaries written before the fifteenth century, that of Smaragdus,[16] was printed before 1880. Anyone wishing to use them prior to that date, therefore, was restricted to manuscript copies. Although a number of the commentaries are still in manuscript, several of the important ones have been published since 1880. The lack of easy accessibility to the commentaries has, doubtless, been one of the reasons for their infrequent use by the more general students of monasticism. Furthermore, their very bulkiness tends to make them prohibitive, both to the editor who would undertake to publish them and to him who would seek information from their numerous folios. Moreover, they contain much that is obvious and much that has been taken over from previous commentaries. Nevertheless, in spite of these limitations, the commentaries constitute a literary source with which, as we hope to

15 E. Martène, *Commentarius in Regulam S. P. Benedicti,* Paris, 1690 (reprinted in *PL,* 66, cols. 215-932) ; A. Calmet, *Commentaire littéral, historique, et moral, sur la règle de saint Benoît,* 2 vols. in 1, Paris, 1734 (translated into Latin in 1750 and into Italian in 1751).

16 *Cf. infra,* p. 198.

show in the course of this study, the historian of monasticism cannot well dispense.[17]

Concerning the authenticity of the commentaries of Warnefrid and Hildemar, considerable controversial literature has appeared since the middle of the seventeenth century. The medieval commentators, Peter the Deacon, Bernard of Monte Cassino, and Peter Bohier listed among their predecessors Paul the Deacon, but seemed to know nothing of Hildemar. In the seventeenth century, such Benedictine scholars as Haeften, Mabillon, and Martène knew and made excerpts from the manuscripts of Hildemar's commentary. Martène went so far as to say that the commentary heretofore ascribed to Paul should be attributed to Hildemar, thinking, evidently, that the two expositions were identical.[18]

The tradition of a commentary written by Warnefrid cannot be traced beyond the two extant manuscripts of the tenth century: Codex G. V. 4 at Turin, originating at Bobbio, and the famous Codex 175 at Monte Cassino.[19] Bethmann judged the manuscript at Turin to be a copy of the one at Monte Cassino,[20] but O. Seebass considers both to have been copied from the same source,[21] and Traube confirms this view on the basis of comparisons reported to him.[22] One of the two miniatures contained in Codex 175 has been taken to indicate that the commentary was copied from a manuscript at Capua by the

---

17 *Cf.* Appendix for a brief survey of the medieval commentaries.

18 *Op. cit.*, col. 206. *Cf.* also J. Mabillon, *Annales ordinis S. Benedicti*, II, 619.

19 This manuscript was edited at Monte Cassino in 1880: *Pauli Warnefridi diaconi Casinensis in sanctam regulam commentarium*. Besides being printed in this separate edition, it is published also in *Bibliotheca Casinensis*, IV (*Florilegium Casinense*, folio pages 1-173). In the present study all citations from Warnefrid are taken from the separate edition.

20 L. Bethmann, " Paulus Diaconus, Leben und Schriften," *Archiv der Gesellschaft für ältere deutsche Geschichtskunde*, X (1849), 298 ff.

21 " Ueber zwei turiner Handschriften des Capitulare monasticum," *Neues Archiv für ältere deutsche Geschichtskunde*, XIX (1894), 220.

22 *Textsgeschichte*, p. 102.

monks of Monte Cassino at the request of Abbot John (914-933).[23]

The fact that the inscription on Codex 175 attributing the work to Paul the Deacon was written by a different and perhaps later hand than the one by which the text was written, has been cited by some as an argument against Paul's authorship.[24] Traube has made a careful analysis of the problem, however, and explains that the omission of Paul's name in the original inscription was due to the introduction of a new arrangement in this codex, namely, the combination of the complete text of the Rule with the commentary. He is confident that the original manuscript from which Codex 175 was copied was attributed to Paul.[25] In fine, he considers the authenticity of the Warnefrid commentary no longer a matter of doubt, on the basis of the old manuscripts and also on the basis of linguistic characteristics.

Karl Neff devotes thirty pages of his brief study, establishing Paul as the author of the *Epitome* of Festus, to a comparison of the features of language and style found in Paul's commentary with those of his better known works.[26] He considers the results so conclusive that he frequently cites similarities of style and language between the commentary and the abridgment of Festus as proof that the latter is a genuine work of Paul the Deacon.[27]

Hildemar's version, on the other hand, cannot be thought the work of Warnefrid. It cites events such as the Council of Aachen held in 817, the Council convoked at Rome in 826 by Pope Eugenius II, and a letter written to Bishop Urso of Benevento in 833, which took place after the death of Warne-

23 *Ibid.*, pp. 103-104; Preface to Paul's commentary, p. iii.

24 R. Mittermüller, the editor of Hildemar's commentary, stresses this point in " Der Regel-Commentar des Paul Diakonus (Warnefrid), des Hildemar und des Abtes Basilius," *Studien und Mitteilungen aus dem Benediktiner- und dem Cistercienserorden*, IX (1888), 397.

25 *Op. cit.*, pp. 38, 103.

26 *De Paulo Diacono Festi epitomatore*, pp. 4-33.

27 *Ibid.*, pp. 34-39, 53.

frid. It is becoming more and more recognized that the commentary ascribed to Paul and that ascribed to Hildemar are the work of two distinct authors; that Paul's is the "nucleus around which Hildemar works in modifying, and particularly in enlarging it with new explanations and citations." [28] Mittermüller has retreated somewhat from his earlier position in which he held Hildemar to be the author of both versions: the first as his original or "Grundriss," the second as the result of later additions made to the original in the course of his lectures.[29]

The time and place of Paul's writing have likewise been the subject of some controversy. Being a monk of Monte Cassino and having written his better known works there, he was thought to have written his commentary there also. Were this true, it would follow that the life and thought outlined in the commentary would have special reference to that of Monte Cassino. On the basis of internal evidence contained in the commentary, however, comparatively recent research has altered the earlier view. Although the unknown chronicler of Salerno, writing about 980, recorded that Paul the Deacon entered Monte Cassino about 787 and at the request of his abbot and brethren wrote a commentary entitled *Super regulam*, Traube largely discounts the report. He sees in the similarity between the title and the inscription on the tenth-century manuscripts of the commentary the clue to the chronicler's source of information.[30]

In order to place the writing of the commentary in the proper perspective with the rest of Paul's life, we shall sketch briefly his career, emphasizing particularly the evidence relating to the composition of the commentary. He was born between 720 and 730, probably at Cividale del Friuli, certainly in Friuli.[31] He

28 C. Cipolla, "Brevi appunti," p. 153.

29 "Der Regel-Commentar," pp. 396, 398.

30 *Op. cit.*, p. 38; *Chronicon Salernitanum*, in *MGH, SS*, III, 488.

31 K. Neff, *Die Gedichte des Paulus Diaconus*, Quellen und Untersuchungen zur lateinischen Philologie des Mittelalters, III (1908), iv, 65.

was educated at the Lombard court of Pavia and, at the advice of King Ratchis (744-749), entered the clerical state. At a mature age we find him at Monte Cassino from which in 782 he transferred to the court of Aachen for some years.[32] The intervening years are difficult to account for; nevertheless, several conjectures regarding them have been made by recent writers.[33]. Traube's suggestion, based on internal evidence found in the commentary and in other works of Paul, is that before 774 Paul lived and taught in a cloister situated in the neighborhood of Lake Como and of Monza, and separated some distance from Milan and Pavia; that there he wrote and delivered his *Expositio* before his pupils; and that with the fall of the Lombard state in 774 he transferred to Monte Cassino.[34]

Speaking with greater precision, Traube furthermore suggests that the Lombard monastery in which Paul lived was that of St. Peter situated on a mountain (Monte Pedale) near Civate.[35] He bases this suggestion on a comment made by Hildemar whom Traube proves to have written in a monastery at Civate.[36] Hildemar remarks to his hearers that "a guest who comes from Monte Pedale is your neighbor." [37] Traube notes, moreover, that, in using Paul's exposition, Hildemar found no occasion to make the changes which a different place of writing would necessitate. Thus, according to Traube, Paul wrote his commentary before 774 in a monastery near Civate in the diocese of Milan. This conclusion has been generally accepted

32 Traube, *op. cit.*, p. 40.

33 *Cf.* M. Manitius, *Geschichte der lateinischen Literatur des Mittelalters*, I, 257; P. Paschini, " Paolo Diacono e la sua Expositio super regulam Sancti Benedicti," *Memorie storiche Forogiuliesi*, XXV (1929), 71-72; Neff, *op. cit.*, pp. 13-23; P. De Santi, " Paolo Diacono," *Civilta cattolica*, series 17, X (1900), 414; W. Wattenbach, *Deutschlands Geschichtsquellen im Mittelalter*, I (7th ed., 1904), 181.

34 *Op. cit.*, pp. 39-40.

35 *Ibid.*, p. 42. Traube also notes that the monastery of S. Pietro al Monte was founded, according to tradition, by King Desiderius (759-774).

36 *Cf. infra*, p. 25.

37 Hildemar, p. 503; Traube, p. 43.

by writers on the subject. The noted exception is that of P. Paschini who conjectures that Paul wrote his commentary only after his return from Aachen to Monte Cassino about 786. The arguments, based on the references to place in the commentary, whereby he arrives at this conclusion are not convincing.[38]

The exact time at which Paul entered Monte Cassino is not known but is generally assumed to have been about the year 774. It is certain, however, that he was there before 782. In this year he journeyed to Aachen, as it appears, to plead for the freedom of his brother Arichis, who had been imprisoned for taking part in the revolt of Friuli in 776.

In time a warm friendship developed between Paul and Charlemagne and, through the influence of the emperor, Paul's sojourn was extended to several years. During this time he taught in the palace school making Metz his headquarters. Although he enjoyed the friendship of such noted persons as Angilram of Metz, Adalard of Corbie, and Peter of Pisa, a letter written by Paul to Theodemar, abbot of Monte Cassino, describes his yearning to leave the prison of the court and return to the quiet of the cloister. This he did about the year 786, devoting the remainder of his life to writing. To this period belong, among his major works, a collection of homilies, the biography of Gregory I, and the Lombard history. The last named work was incomplete at the time of his death in the closing years of the eighth century.[39]

Much less is known about Hildemar, and the little that is known has been brought to light in connection with his commentary. The earliest extant copy of it is contained in the eleventh century MS. Lat. 12637 originating at the monastery of St. Benignus of Dijon and preserved now at the Bibliothèque Nationale in Paris. This manuscript was known and used by

38 *Op. cit.*, pp. 78-83.

39 A. Hauck, *Kirchengeschichte Deutschlands*, II (3d and 4th ed., 1912), 165-169; Neff, *Die Gedichte, passim*; Manitius, *Gesch. d. lat. Lit.*, I, 257-258; G. Falco, "Lineamenti di storia Cassinese," *Casinensia*, II, 483-484; Wattenbach, *op. cit.*, I, 181-184.

Mabillon and Martène but, unfortunately, was not used by Mittermüller in preparing his edition of the commentary which he published in 1880 at Metten. He judged from the excerpts printed from the Paris codex by Martène that it did not differ notably from the four manuscripts which he did use.[40] Three of these are in the national library of Munich and the fourth, when used by Mittermüller, was in the library of the monastery of Melk, Austria.[41]

In the course of his commentary, Hildemar occasionally alludes to the customs of the monasteries of the Franks,[42] and once he refers to "my monastery in Francia."[43] Thus it appears that he had formerly been a monk in Frankland but was elsewhere at the time of his writing. In the manuscript attributed to Abbot Basil, which is thought to have originated from Hildemar,[44] there are additions which indicate that Hildemar was once in Corbie.[45]

In general, however, it is evident from the various allusions to place that Hildemar, like Paul, taught in the diocese of Milan. In one instance he adds to the remark of Paul concerning a Milanese practice.[46] His cloister can scarcely be distinguished from that of Paul from the viewpoint of location. Regarding the evidence contained in the commentary relative to the time of its writing, the latest piece cited is a letter addressed to Bishop Rampertus of Brescia in 845.[47]

The meager information concerning Hildemar which can be gleaned from contemporary literature corresponds well with the

40 *Expositio Regulae ab Hildemaro tradita,* Prolegomena, p. xiv. Cipolla ("Brevi appunti," p. 151-152) points out that the printed edition is not, therefore, definitive, but is recognized to contain, substantially, the work of Hildemar.

41 Mittermüller, *Expositio,* xii-xiv.

42 Pages, 369, 572, 582, 611.

43 Page 462.

44 *Cf. infra,* p. 199.

45 Traube, *Textgeschichte,* pp. 44, 109.

46 Page 476.

47 Page 563.

foregoing. From an old document of Bishop Rampertus, we learn that the monk Hildemar and Abbot Leutgar, formerly of France but at the time of the document (841) in the diocese of Milan under Archbishop Angilbert, were sent by the latter to the monastery of Saints Faustinus and Jovita at the request of Rampertus for help.[48] Traube suggests that in 845 Hildemar and Leutgar returned to their Milanese cloister, for in that year Agano, bishop of Bergamo, sent his monk Mainard to be abbot of St. Faustinus.[49] Traube suggests further that after Hildemar's return from Brescia he wrote his lectures on the Rule, among which he quotes two letters from the episcopal archives of Brescia.[50]

In a confraternity book for the year 845, Traube finds the names of Hildemar, priest, and Leutgar, abbot, heading the list of thirty-three monks under the title: "These are the names of the brothers of the monastery of Civate." He concludes that the Hildemar and Leutgar here named are to be identified with those sent to Brescia in 841, and that their Milanese cloister was that of Civate. He also observes that this monastery was founded by Archbishop Angilbert of Milan, and that it was formerly a dependency of the older monastery on Monte Pedale but that in time this monastery was supplanted by the newer foundation.[51]

Thus our evidence ties together and seems to justify the conclusion that Paul wrote his commentary in the monastery of St. Peter near Civate about 770, and that about seventy-five years later in the newly founded monastery of Civate, Hildemar compiled his commentary based, as it is, on Paul's exposition.

48 *Historiae patriae monumenta* (*Codex diplomaticus Langobardia*), XIII, 245-248.

49 *Cf.* Hildemar, p. 563, where this letter is quoted in full; Traube, *op. cit.*, p. 42.

50 *Loc. cit.*

51 Traube, *op. cit.*, pp. 42-43.

CHAPTER II

THE MATERIAL ORGANIZATION

INTEREST in the monastic buildings and equipment is not o
paramount importance in a study of the monasticism of any
age or region. Nevertheless information of this kind should ge
a long way toward reconstructing the state of the arts and the
material civilization in which a given monastery finds itself
Studies have been made which concern themselves with the
plan and architecture of the buildings only. Such studies, however, give little detailed information relative to pre-Cluny
monasteries. The two extant ninth-century drawings of
monasteries are of limited value.[1] The one, sketching the
monastery of St. Riquier, was executed with little perspective
and is, therefore, none too intelligible; the other, purporting to
be a sketch of St. Gall, is thought to be merely a fancifu
representation of an ideal monastery.[2]

It seems worthwhile, therefore, to present the meager information which the commentaries under consideration offer
relative to the material organization of the monastery. Much of
this is given in the form of recommendations as to what the
arrangement should be; however, passing remarks and recur-
rent references to the various departments give the reader of
the commentaries an impression, not altogether vague, as to the
material conditions under which the Carolingian monk lived.

The Rule of St. Benedict prescribes that if possible the
monastery should be so situated that the requisites such as
water, the mill, and the garden may be enclosed and the various
arts may be plied inside the monastery.[3] In discussing this

1 Plates VII and VIII in H. Leclercq, *L'Ordre bénédictine.*

2. A. Dopsch, *Wirtschaftliche und soziale Grundlagen der europäischen
Kulturentwicklung aus der Zeit von Caesar bis auf Karl den Grossen,* II (2d
ed., Vienna, 1924), 406.

3 *Sancti Benedicti regula monachorum,* c. 66. The definitive text of the
Rule was being prepared for the *Corpus scriptorum ecclesiasticorum Lati-
norum* by H. Plenkers before his death in 1931. Until such time as the work

passage, the commentator lays stress on the words, " if possible," saying that should it be necessary to construct a monastery in a place having some but not all of these desirable features, it would be permissible to build in such a place; however, should the site be wholly lacking in these requirements, it would be contrary to the mind of St. Benedict to build thereon.[4]

Moreover, the commentator adds, investigation should be made as to whether the site chosen be such that the future monastery will not suffer hindrance from the king, bishop, or count, because when situated near the court of such persons it is wont to endure hardships through this proximity. Finally, the location should be such that the monks will not be impeded by other seculars—women, clerics, or laymen—who are accustomed to congregate at certain places for religious devotions.[5]

The church or oratory in which the monk spent a considerable portion of his time is not the subject of direct discussion in the commentaries. Indirectly, mention is made of the several altars at which the brothers prayed at stated times.[6] From the references it is clear that these altars were located within the monastery church or main oratory. It is prescribed, moreover, that the house of the infirm have an oratory near the rooms of the sick, so that the sick while lying in bed may hear Mass and receive Holy Communion.[7] And again it appears that the guest-house which was near the gate of the monastery[8] was also provided with an oratory, for it is recommended that monk guests should sleep in a dormitory separated from that of the

---

is completed by another, the most authentic editions are by B. Linderbauer in *Florilegium patristicum*, Vol. 17 (Bonn, 1928), and C. Butler (3d ed., Freiburg, 1935). Dom. Justin McCann has recently made an English translation of the Rule with notes: *The Rule of St. Benedict* (Stanbrook Abbey, 1937).

4 Hildemar, p. 607.

5 *Ibid.*, p. 606.

6 Paul, p. 272. *Cf.* also pp. 232-233, 261, and Hildemar, pp. 296, 322, 333. For this custom, *cf. infra*, p. 158.

7 Paul, p. 340; Hildemar, p. 406.

8 For the location of the guest department, *cf. infra*, p. 89.

lay guests and near the oratory.[9] That this mention of an oratory refers to that of the guest-house seems also to follow from another passage regarding the porter of the monastery: " for in our province there is a *solarium* (balcony) over the door and an oratory in the same place." [10]

The cloister of the medieval monastery was, doubtless, the most characteristic department of the entire institution. The proper size of the cloister and the uses to which it was put are explained in the following passage taken from the commentaries:

Well did he [St. Benedict] call the cloister [11] of the monastery " workshops " because as in workshops the different crafts are carried on by the masters, as we have said, so also in the monastery different works take place in its various parts, i. e., when some read, others chant; others work with their hands, still others work in the kitchen and at similar tasks. . . . Therefore the cloister of the monastery ought to be such that therein these things which we have mentioned can be accomplished without an occasion of sin. However, there are many who, poorly understanding the occasion of sin, either make the cloister smaller, or perhaps larger, than necessary; for the abbot ought so to arrange the size of the cloister that those works which a monk has to do can be performed therein, whether it be to sew, to wash clothes, or to devote himself to reading, to the care of the infirm, and to such like tasks. If the cloister be larger than necessary, when a brother goes about he meets a layman or an outsider with whom he speaks, or gives or receives something without the abbot's permission, and thus is found an occasion of sin. Likewise if it be too small, i. e., small as compared with the needs of the work, then transgression occurs by going outside. The garden, however, is not within the cloister,

9 Hildemar, pp. 611-612.

10 Paul, p. 493; Hildemar, p. 605.

11 It is obvious that in this passage the word " cloister " is not restricted to the narrower sense signifying an inner court, but refers at times to the entire monastic enclosure. Elsewhere, and in a still wider sense, the commentators use it in the abstract to designate limitations of movement varying with the work enjoined on each member. *Cf.* Paul, pp. 498-499, and Hildemar, p. 613.

but no one should enter it except him to whom it has been entrusted. The abbot ought so to adjust the cloister that there can be stability in the congregation and no occasion for wandering about. Now, many say that the cloister of a monastery ought to extend one hundred feet on each side; in no case less, for it would be too small, but if desired, it may be made larger. For the cloister is so called because of that little area or court yard (*curtina*) in which the monks are, and which extends from portico to portico.[12]

The various activities in which the monks engaged within the cloister will be treated in subsequent discussion; concerning the cloister itself other references add nothing to that given in this passage.

The monastic refectory together with its adjunct, the kitchen, constituted another integral part of the institution. In the main, the general provisions of the Rule [13] calling for one or two meals a day varying with the season, and for an additional allowance to the servers and reader prefatory to their service, are accepted unqualifiedly by the commentators. But, in addition, certain details which they offer concerning the kind, quantity, and preparation of the food may be of interest.

The dishes and table service are not described as such, but in another connection these elementary articles are mentioned: a knife, a spoon, and a dish called *cuppa,* probably a cup or bowl.[14] Another reference to the knife leads us to conclude that this utensil was not proper to the table service but was carried about by each monk more or less constantly: " It would be neither charity nor obedience, if, while sitting among the brethren at table, a brother should fail to offer his knife to his neighbor who did not happen to have his own knife." [15] Evidently the same knife was used for all purposes.

12 Hildemar, pp. 183-184. Paul's account is similar but not so complete; *cf.* pp. 117-118 of his commentary.

13 Chapters 35, 38, 41.

14 Hildemar, p. 471, 474.

15 *Ibid.,* p. 388. *Cf.* references to this instrument in the Rule, chapters 22 and 55.

The Rule prescribes that two cooked foods be served at the daily refection, and if there be fruit or fresh vegetables a third may be added. If, however, the abbot should think fit, due to the intensity of the labor, to increase this fare, it is left to his discretion and power to do so. At the same time the use of the flesh of quadrupeds is forbidden except to the infirm.[16] The commentators describe somewhat profusely the contemporary usages relative to the monastic table.

The term for cooked food, *pulmentaria cocta,* as used in the Rule, they write, has been used in the Bible to signify various foods: fleshmeat, legumes, and fish. But the word *pulmentum* is used of anything eaten with bread. If cheese be eaten with bread it is raw *pulmentum,* but if the cheese has been cooked, the food is called cooked *pulmentum.* However, as used in this passage of the Rule, the cooked food refers to herbs, legumes, or any cooked food made from cheese and from grain.[17] The " fresh vegetables " mentioned in the Rule are understood by the commentators to be sprouted legumes. They tell us it was a custom of the region of Monte Cassino, of the Roman and other provinces, to prepare legumes for eating by placing them in water until sprouted.[18]

On days on which only one meal is served, the three dishes, two cooked and one raw, are to be prepared for this refection at None (about 3 o'clock); when two meals are served, the two cooked foods and the one raw are to be prepared for the midday meal (*prandium*), and one cooked food for the evening repast (*coena*). Apples may be served at any of these meals but are not to be eaten in the evening if there is the one meal at None, nor are they to be eaten in the afternoon if there are the noon and evening meals, for in so doing the number of times which

16 Chapter 39.

17 Paul, pp. 358-359; Hildemar, pp. 435-436.

18 Paul, p. 359; Hildemar, p. 436. *Cf.* the letter of Paul Warnefrid to Charlemagne in Albers, III, 55-56; Peter the Deacon in his commentary on the Rule (*Florilegium Casinense* in *Bibliotheca Casinensis,* V, 137) writes that the *germina* are served with vinegar or fruits.

the Rule permits the brothers to eat daily would thereby be exceeded.[19] On this point the commentator adheres closely to the Rule. In contemporary practice, however, exceptions are to be found; in some instances fruit or a drink is served after the chanting of None in summer; in another, a honey drink is served at the fourth hour to those engaged in cutting hay; finally, the twelfth canon of the Council of Aachen (817) provides that when necessary because of strenuous work, even in Lent, and when the Office of the Dead is celebrated, the brothers are to be given a drink after the evening meal and before the reading of Compline.[20]

This menu was not looked upon as a monotonous order not subject to change. Although the Rule speaks of it as the " daily refection," both Paul and Hildemar provide that on the solemnities as well as at times of strenuous labor,[21] three cooked foods and one dish of fresh vegetables be served at Sext and one cooked dish in the evening. They base this *proviso* on that elastic phrase of the Rule in which it is left to the discretion and power of the abbot to add something if he think fit.[22] They further justify their arrangement by interpreting the phrase " daily refection " to refer to week days for as elsewhere " he [St. Benedict] distinguishes between the week days and Sundays, so also here concerning food, he makes the distinction." [23] At Monte Cassino the contemporary practice was to serve three cooked foods for the refection on all days except Wednesdays and Fridays,[24] and to add a fourth dish on Sundays and on the principal feasts.[25]

---

19 Paul, p. 359; Hildemar, pp. 436-437.

20 *Cf.* Albers, III, pp. 16, 57, 102, 109, 118.

21 The labor is considered strenuous when the monks work from Prime until Vespers or even from the second hour until None (Paul, p. 362; Hildemar, p. 439).

22 Paul, pp. 359-360; Hildemar, p. 437.

23 Paul, p. 358; Hildemar, p. 435.

24 For Wednesdays and Fridays as days of special fast, *cf. infra*, p. 173.

25 Letter of Paul to Charlemagne, in Albers, III, pp. 55-56.

Besides these victuals, the Rule also provides that a pound (*libra*) of bread and a portion (*hemina*) of wine be given each monk as a daily allowance; on days of two repasts, a third of this portion is to be reserved for the second meal.[26] Paul Warnefrid states that the measure of bread, the *libra,* should weigh twenty-two *solidi* when in the dough, so that when baked it will weigh twenty *solidi.*[27] Basing his statement on the authority of Isidore,[28] Hildemar writes that the *hemina* weighs one *libra* and that two *heminae* make one *sextarius.* He also refers to the traditional standard wine measure long preserved at Monte Cassino:

In this way did Charlemagne learn about the *hemina,* namely, he sent to the Beneventan monastery of St. Benedict and there he found the ancient *hemina,* according to which measure wine was given the monks; we likewise employ this same measure.[29]

The standard weight for bread has been preserved at Monte Cassino even unto modern times.[30]

26 Chapters 39 and 40.

27 Page 307; *cf.* also *ibid.,* p. 333. This measure does not tally with that decreed by the Council of Aachen (817), namely, that a *libra* of bread should contain thirty *solidi,* each the equivalent of twelve *denarii* (*MGH, Capitularia regum Francorum,* I, 347, can. 57). The Council of Frankfort (794) records that Charlemagne decreed the maximum price of grain, if sold in form of bread, to be one *denarius* for twelve wheaten loaves each weighing two *librae* (*ibid.,* I, 74, can. 4). Thus we see that although the same terms were used for the monetary units as for those of weight, there was no direct correlation between them; and since both fluctuated with time and place, it is difficult to arrive at the exact quantity of bread appointed by Paul, or to compare this quantity with that intended by the sixth century Lawgiver.

28 *Etymologiae,* lib. 16, c. 26, n. 5.

29 Page 445.

30 The editor of Paul's commentary writes at considerable length on these traditional standards in the Preface, pp. ix–xvii. The first mention of them is made by none other than Paul Warnefrid in his *Historia Langobardorum,* lib. iv, c. 18. He did not mention them in his commentary, due, doubtless, to the fact that he became connected with Monte Cassino (where he wrote the Lombard history), sometime after writing his commentary (*cf. supra,* p. 23).

The interpretation of the commentators regarding the prohibition of fleshmeat and the contemporary attitude on this point will be discussed later. Suffice it to say here that both Paul and Hildemar consider the words of the Rule, " Let all abstain from eating the flesh of quadrupeds," to exclude all fleshmeat—that of fowls as well as of quadrupeds—from the monastic table, although this view was not universally held at the time.[31]

There remains one final point in connection with the daily food of the monks. Chapter forty-three of the Rule forbids the taking of food or drink before or after the appointed time, but elsewhere [32] the Rule prescribes that the weekly servers and the table reader should partake of some bread and wine *(mixtus)* an hour before the community refection. The commentators explain this provision in the following manner: The phrase, " an hour before the refection," signifies at a suitable interval; the term *mixtus,* customary at the time of St. Benedict, signifies what was currently called a " bite " or a " snack " *(mordere).* Thus at the proper time all who are to receive the *mixtus* will find a fourth of a *libra* of bread and a cup of drink prepared at their individual places.[33]

From what has just been said and from another remark in passing,[34] it is evident that to each monk was appointed his particular place at table, doubtless in accordance with the order of his entrance into the community, as the Rule (c. 63) ordains. Regarding the abbot's table, at which, according to the Rule (c. 56), guests were to eat, there appears to have been no clearly established practice as to whether it was in the common refectory or in a separate room, due, probably, to the obscurity

31 *Cf. infra,* p. 174.

32 Chapters 35 and 38.

33 Paul, pp. 333, 354; Hildemar, pp. 399, 427. The letter of Paul Warnefrid to Charlemagne (Albers, III, p. 54-55) states that the measure of the goblet *(calix)* which the brothers ought to receive in compliance with the Rule was sent to Aachen along with the standard measures of the *pondus* and the *hemina.*

34 Hildemar, p. 462.

of the Rule on this point. Delatte points out in his modern commentary that " the Rule contains few chapters shorter, and, it would seem, clearer, than this; yet there are few which have given rise to so much controversy." [35] This chapter, the fifty-sixth, reads:

Let the table of the abbot be always with the guests and pilgrims. But as often as there are few guests, it shall be in his power to invite any of the brethren he wishes. Let him take care, however, always to leave one or two seniors with the brethren for the sake of discipline.

After adducing various arguments for each side of the question, Hildemar concludes that the abbot's table should be in the monastic refectory, although he admits that the Rule is not clear on this point; influenced by that passage of the Rule (c. 56) in which the abbot is admonished always to leave some seniors with the brethren for discipline when inviting brothers to eat at his table, he observes that the Rule would be more readily understood to mean that the abbot's table should be outside, were it not for those refectories which are so large and are so arranged that all the monks when seated cannot be seen by the abbot, as is the case at St. Gall. He shows, moreover, that were the abbot to eat outside the refectory other points of the Rule would be rendered difficult of execution if not wholly ineffective.[36] His arguments are ingenious but not too convincing. Other passages of the Rule might be cited to prove the contrary.[37]

In forming his conclusion on this point, Hildemar was probably influenced by contemporary and traditional practice.

35 *Commentary on the Rule of St. Benedict* (transl. by J. McCann, London, 1921), p. 358. The lengthy discussion by Hildemar (pp. 521-529) and several contemporary canons and statutes (*cf.* Albers, III, 83, 89, 122) corroborate this statement even for this early period.

36 Hildemar, pp. 521-529. Paul's treatment (pp. 432-433) begins much the same as Hildemar's but stops short before giving a conclusion to the dispute. This may well be an instance of foreshortening on the part of the scribe.

37 Delatte, *op. cit.,* p. 389.

From passing remarks in the commentary it is evident that he
was accustomed to the abbot's table being within the monastic
refectory.[38] Spreitzenhofer, in his study of the forerunners of
the Rule, observes that if St. Benedict intended the abbot's
table to be outside the refectory, his regulation would be contrary
to the general practice of the monastic world, to that prescribed
in contemporary monastic rules, and finally, to that contained in
subsequent rules.[39]

As we pass on to the monastic kitchen the glimpses we get
are broken but highly interesting. The kitchen was adjacent to
the refectory and there was access to each from the cloister.[40]
The utensils used in the kitchen were under the supervision of
the cellarer who consigned them to the brother who was to perform the kitchen service for the coming week.[41] Mention is
made of *scutellae,* open dishes or platters; it is possible that
these were used in the refectory and brought to the kitchen to
be washed.[42] Receptacles made of stone, *lapidea,*[43] probably
some kind of pitchers or jars, were also used; the commentator
speaks of them as kitchen vessels and says they were washed
by the cooks on Saturday. The *scamna* which were also washed
on Saturday were, doubtless, low tables or benches.[44] Besides
these culinary articles at the disposal of the weekly server in

---

38 Hildemar, pp. 419-420, 427, 462, 474. *Cf.* also Paul, pp. 347, 379.

39 *Die historischen Voraussetzungen der Regel des heil. Benedict von
Nursia,* pp. 58-59. Delatte thinks the intention of St. Benedict was to have
a separate room for the table of the abbot and guests, for he points out (*op.
cit.,* pp. 358-359) that " Bernard of Monte Cassino, Haeften, Perez, and
Calmet refuse to distort the plain meaning of the Rule, confirmed as it is
by other passages." However, for modern conditions he approves the current
practice of introducing guests into the common refectory (p. 360).

40 Hildemar, p. 397.

41 *Ibid.,* pp. 398-399. This is based on the Rule, chapter 35.

42 Such was the practice later at Cluny: cf. *Antiquiores consuetudines
monasterii Cluniacensis Udalrici, PL,* 149, cols. 727, 728, 729.

43 *Cf.* Meyer-Lübke, W., *Romanisches etymologisches Wörterbuch* (3d ed.,
1935), no. 4899.

44 *Cf.* Du Cange, *Glossarium, s. v.* " scamnum " (5).

the kitchen, mention is made of storage jars *(cuppae)* [45] which the cellarer is to wash every fifteen days " for the sake of cleanliness," and of *conchae,* basin-like vessels in which the servers are to wash the feet of all on Saturdays. The latter, together with the towels, are to be prepared by the cellarer.[46]

In the kitchen was heated the water for laundering the clothes, an event which took place every fifteen days.[47] Those brothers who prepared this water likewise placed the *conchae* in readiness and prepared the soap.[48] The actual washing according to previous observation,[49] took place in the cloister. Perhaps the clothes were dried there, too. At Hirschau they were hung to a rope in the cloister, and the footgear *(socci)* when washed was placed on the sand of the cloister to dry.[50] In order to facilitate the washing of the same, or at least a similar, covering for the feet, called *pedules,* our commenators explain that many monks divide them.[51] The linen towels used in the Saturday washing of the feet were washed immediately after this ceremony and in the same water which was heated for this purpose.[52]

45 Evidently this " cuppa " is not the same as that mentioned in connection with the refectory; *cf. supra,* p. 29; Du Cange *s. v.* " cupa " (1, 2).

46 Hildemar's account (pp. 204, 379, 397, 509) has been followed for these passages since it is more detailed than that of Paul (pp. 136-137, 332).

47 Paul, pp. 136, 430; Hildemar, pp. 203, 520.

48 Paul, p. 430; Hildemar, p. 520. At Cluny a special caldron was kept on an iron tripod so that anyone wishing to wash clothes could make soap in this vessel (*Antiq. consuet., PL,* 149, col. 729).

49 *Cf. supra,* p. 28.

50 *Consuetudines Hirsaugienses, PL,* 150, col. 1097.

51 Paul, p. 427; Hildemar, p. 513. For a fuller discussion of the articles of clothing, *cf. infra,* p. 41. Later at Farfa each monk was to wash his own *pedules* although the general laundry was supervised by the *horrearius* on Tuesdays (*Consuetudines Farfenses,* Albers, I, 181-182).

52 Paul, p. 332; Hildemar, p. 398. The text is somewhat ambiguous at this point but it seems only reasonable to suppose that the writer speaks of the unused water which remained after the *Mandatum* ceremony. The text in Paul reads: " Et isto modo debent abluere; idest, postquam laverint pedes et manus et terserint, statim de eadem aqua laventur "; in Hildemar: " . . . statim in eadem aqua lavamus, quae remanet post lotionem pedum."

From the frequent references to the dormitory it seems safe to say that at the period under study, the beds were in one large sleeping room as prescribed by the Rule (c. 22) rather than in private cells.[53] For the beds St. Benedict prescribes that there be a mattress, a blanket, a coverlet, and a pillow.[54] The comments made on these by Hildemar are brief and vague. He explains that the mattress is made of layers of rushes and hair.[55] In describing for Charlemagne the usages at Monte Cassino, Paul Warnefrid writes that the infirm are permitted to lie on a feather mattress (*culcita*);[56] this would seem to imply that to those in health a less comfortable type of bed was appointed at Monte Cassino. Nearly two centuries later at Farfa the *camerarius* renewed the straw or hay in the bed of each monk annually, and provided each with a cover inlaid with skins, a woolen blanket, and a pillow.[57]

Concerning the use of the bath and facilities for washing and personal care, the commentaries are much more explicit. They point out that the Rule distinguishes between the infirm and those in good health in granting the use of the bath. For the former, the phrase of the Rule, "as often as expedient," is understood to mean daily or even twice a day if necessary.[58] The meaning of the Rule as to the frequency of the bath for the others seems to have been less uniformly understood:

53 The one reference to *cubicula* (Paul, p. 396; Hildemar, p. 483) should be noted as an exception although this use of the word might signify rooms in general, for the term "dormitory" is used in the same phrase. It reads: "caeteri debent legere vero in Claustra, non per cubicula, aut singillatim, vel in dormitorio, sed sicut dixi in Claustra."

54 Chapter 55: "Stramenta autem lectorum sufficient matta, sagum, et lena et capitale."

55 Page 518.

56 Letter of Paul to Charlemagne, Albers, III, 63. The word "culcita" has been taken to mean "feather mattress" in this passage, although it may also signify "cushion" or "coverlet"; cf. *Thesaurus linguae Latinae, s.v.* "culcita" (col. 1285, l. 89), and Meyer-Lübke, *op. cit.,* no. 2372.

57 *Consuetudines Farfenses,* Albers, I, 180.

58 Paul, p. 341; Hildemar, p. 408.

Concerning [baths for] those in health, however, and the young, there are various opinions. Some speak generally, saying that the bath ought to be prepared for all in health but less frequently; there are others who think it should be prepared three times a year, namely, at the Nativity of the Lord, at Easter, and at Pentecost; others think only twice, i. e., at the Nativity and at Easter. Again there are some who understand that the words, *to those in health, however, and especially to the young,* which he [St. Benedict] used, were perhaps not spoken in general, but of those who through some work such as the building of a house or the like, become soiled; that for such as these the bath should be prepared, but not too freely; likewise should it be understood concerning the young, yet still less frequently.[59]

This much is found in both commentaries. In Hildemar's only, the following is added, " Nevertheless for them especially who become soiled through some work, the baths should be prepared more frequently than for those monks who do not engage in manual work." [60]

Apparently our commentators did not consider the frequent use of the bath essential to the maintenance of health and were satisfied with the partial substitutes which they mention elsewhere.[61] Perhaps they looked upon the bath as a sort of a luxury proper to the great of the world; more probably, they took objection to the public baths currently in use, seeing in promiscuous bathing an occasion of sin. They recommend that the bathing place be such that in it only one can bathe at a time as is the *tina* (a wooden tub) [62] in which one cannot be easily seen by others; the stone bath (*petrinum baleneum*) in which two, three, or four can bathe simultaneously is expressly condemned.[63]

---

59 Paul, *loc. cit.* Hildemar's account (p. 408) is much the same. The words italicized in this and other quoted passages throughout the present study are taken from the Rule. They are italicized likewise in the printed editions of the commentaries.

60 Hildemar, p. 408.   61 *Cf. infra,* p. 39.

62 *Cf.* Du Cange, *s. v.* "tina" (2).   63 Paul, p. 341; Hildemar, p. 408.

In prescribing the infrequent use of the bath, the commentators voice the general attitude contained in contemporary statutes and customs.[64] Among these, the twenty-first article of the Statutes of Murbach (ca. 816) is particularly descriptive. The Murbach Statutes are professedly a recapitulation of the canons of a former synod which have not been preserved elsewhere.[65] After stating the canon, the author frequently amends it with a view to its application in the monastery of Murbach. In the twenty-first article of the Statutes, after giving the canon which prohibits the bath except to the infirm, the following modification is made: permission is granted to use large vessels or measures intended for grain (*scaphae*) [66] for the bath until the beginning of Lent; in the meantime through the arrangement of the provost and the cellarer bathing vessels (*copae balneariae*) are to be made in such number that the brothers may wash singly when necessary; thus in turn will they offer themselves this comfort without the interference of outsiders. In this modification of the canon, the author hopes not to misinterpret the synod, but instead to prescribe a compromise during an interval in which the necessary may be procured in order the more carefully to remove the forbidden.[67]

At the appointed place in which the brothers wash their hands and faces, our commentators would have soap, towels,

64 O. Seebass has summarized these in " Ueber die Statuta Murbacensia," *Zeitschrift für Kirchengeschichte,* XII, 324.

65 It has been demonstrated that the canons on which the Statutes of Murbach were based were those of the Council of Aachen held in 816 instead of those of a council of the same name held in 802 as previously thought. They are believed to have been compiled by Haito, bishop of Basel and abbot of Reichenau, instead of by Abbot Simpertus. *Cf.* Seebass, *op. cit.,* p. 332; A. Hauck, *Kirchengeschichte Deutschlands,* II (3d and 4th ed., 1912), 595, n. 4; J. Narberhaus, *Benedict von Aniane,* Beiträge zur Geschichte des alten Mönchtums und des Benediktinerordens, Heft 16 (1930), 50.

66 *Cf.* Du Cange, *s. v.* " scapha," " scaphula," and " scapilus." According to Harper's dictionary (ed. 1889), *scaphium* is a concave vessel or basin in the form of a boat, and *scaphula* was used to signify bath tub, in a writing of the 5th century.

67 In Albers, III, 89.

and combs provided for common use.[68] The soap with which they were familiar was in liquid form and, no doubt, was different from that used in laundering the clothes; for, should this common soap have been stolen in the past, the abbot is to distribute to each monk a portion of soap in a small vessel such as he can keep near his bed, to be used only in washing his face and hands. The soap for washing the clothes, as given in an earlier passage, is to be prepared by those brothers whose turn it is to heat the water and place the *conchae* in readiness. Towels for common use, five or six in proportion to the number of brothers, are to be provided at this common wash place. It is expressly stated that no one, not even the abbot, should have an individual towel.[69] Combs, also in proportion to the number of monks, are to be supplied, and to avoid their being stolen they are to be attached to the place. Moreover, soap and towels are to be provided at other places: the sacristan should have soap available for the priest for washing his hands when he prepares to sing Mass, and each one in charge of any work in which it is necessary to wash the hands, as the cellarer or infirmarian, should provide soap for the purpose. In like manner, grease for dressing the shoes should be set out for common use; but if necessary to avoid its being stolen, it too should be portioned out to the individual monks.[70]

It was customary for the monks to shave every fifteen days, namely, on the Saturday preceding the washing of the clothes.[71] This practice was confirmed by the sixth article of the

68 Hildemar, pp. 519-520. There is an evident omission of several lines in Paul's version.

69 The term used in this passage for towel is *facitergulus* in Paul and *facitergius* in Hildemar. At Monte Cassino each monk was permitted to have towels called *manutergia* either for use in the tonsure or for folding around the books they received for reading (*cf.* letter of Paul to Charlemagne, Albers, III, 63).

70 Hildemar, *loc. cit.*

71 Hildemar, p. 203.

Monastic Capitulary of Aachen, 817, with the modification that they were not to shave during Lent.[72]

In legislating for the monastic dress, St. Benedict left details to the judgment of the local abbot, suggesting only that the norm for temperate climates be two tunics and two cowls to satisfy the needs for night wear and for washing, a scapular for work, and shoes and stockings as covering for the feet. When sent on a journey, however, the monks were to be fitted out with cowls and tunics somewhat better than those usually worn, and with breeches from the clothesroom, which, on their return, they would replace there, washed.[73]

The flexibility of the Rule in leaving matters of dress to the judgment of the abbot is doubtless the ultimate explanation of the variety of garments used and the confusion in the names applied to them. The commentators preface their discussion by emphasizing this feature of the Rule,[74] and Paul makes the same observation in his letter to Charlemagne.[75] Nevertheless, it appears that, despite this variety, the monastic garb was a distinctive costume. Thus Paul writes in the letter just mentioned: " That garment which the Gallic monks call the cowl (*cuculla*) and we call the *cappa,* which designates the characteristic habit of the monk, we ought to call the *melota,* as heretofore it has been named by some in this province." [76] The term *melota* was used by the Eastern monks to denote a piece of clothing made from the skin of goat or sheep.[77] Had Paul not included it in his chain of similar garments, there would be less confusion, for other references to the *melota*

---

72 *MGH, Cap. reg. Franc.,* I, 344. This corresponds closely to the fifteenth article of the Statutes of Murbach (Albers, III, 87) which deferred the mid-Lent shave till Holy Saturday.

73 *Regula,* c. 55.

74 Paul, p. 426; Hildemar, p. 512.

75 In Albers, III, 60-61.

76 *Ibid.,* III, 59.

77 *Cf.* Du Cange, *s. v.* " melote."

liken it to the scapular, and Hildemar states clearly that the *melota* is distinct from the cowl.[78]

The cowl must have been a hooded mantle or cloak, for the commentators say it is called a *casula*. This in turn is explained by Hildemar, quoting from Isidore's *Etymologiae* [79] in which the latter writes that the *casula* is a hooded garment and has received its name from the diminutive of *casa,* because it covers the whole man as if a little house.[80] This tallies with Paul's statement in his letter to Charlemagne that the Gallic cowl is looser and fuller than the short and closefitting garment worn by the Italian monks.[81] The latter, the *cappa,* is frequently mentioned in the commentaries.[82] It was to be made of coarse or hairy cloth to serve as a protection against the cold.[83] The tunic about which there was greater uniformity in its description, was the undergarment. It was to be made of wool although the commentators state that it may be made of linen or of silk, i. e., when used by others than monks. They also state that it was washable, implying that the cowl was not.[84]

The term *melota* appears to have been that currently used for the scapular, the garment specified in the Rule to be worn by the monks while at work (c. 55). Concerning it the commentaries read: " That garment is called the scapular—which the Greeks call *scima*—with which they cover the head and gird themselves, to the likeness of which seems to be that covering which we call the *melota.*" [85] Paul, some years later at Monte Cassino, writes much the same to Charlemagne, adding that

78 Hildemar, p. 513.

79 Lib. 19, c. 24, n. 17.

80 Hildemar, p. 513; The Monastic Capitulary of Aachen (817) rules that the *cuculla* should be two cubits long (*MGH, Cap. reg. Franc,* I, 345).

81 In Albers, III, 60.

82 Hildemar, pp. 390, 510, 513, 518; Paul, pp. 422, 429.

83 Hildemar, pp. 513, 515.

84 Paul, p. 426, 427; Hildemar, *loc. cit.* L. Gougaud (*Anciennes Coutumes claustrales,* pp. 25-26) notes that woolen garments were universally used, and that only the infirm were permitted to wear garments of linen.

85 Paul, p. 426; Hildemar, p. 513.

almost all the rustic people of his region wear this garment; and that the monks have a covering of rather coarse texture made like the *melota* except that it has long sleeves reaching to the hands.[86] Quoting from Isidore,[87] Hildemar explains that the *melota* is of goatskin, hangs from the neck, girds the loins, and is the costume worn particularly while performing manual work.[88] Elsewhere he speaks of a monk wearing the *melota* while cutting bread.[89] By way of contrast, the cowl *(cappa)* is frequently specified in the customs of Farfa and Cluny as a vestment to be worn in certain liturgical functions.[90] Thus Delatte's explanation that when the monk is at work his cowl is to be replaced by the less ample garment, the scapular, appears correct.[91] It cannot be deduced, however, that the scapular was a mere work apron, for such special work garments are mentioned in connection with the tools of the monastery.[92]

The commentators disapprove of the general use of the breeches (*femoralia*) mentioned in the Rule (c. 55) as a garment to be worn by those on a journey. They observe, however, that in some monasteries they are distributed to all but are not generally used, while in others they are generally distributed and worn.[93] At Monte Cassino, although all were permitted them, not all availed themselves of the permission.[94] The Capitulary of Aachen also permitted each monk to have two pairs.[95]

86 In Albers, III, 62-63.

87 *Etymologiae,* lib. 19, c. 24, n. 19.

88 Page 513.

89 Hildemar, p. 472.

90 In Albers, I, II, *passim.*

91 *Op. cit.,* p. 347.

92 Hildemar, p. 386.

93 *Ibid.,* pp. 515, 520-521. *Cf.* corresponding passage in Paul (p. 428) which is briefer.

94 Letter of Paul to Charlemagne, Albers, III, 62.

95 *MGH, Cap. reg. Franc.,* I, 345.

Concerning the footwear, the remarks made by our commentators are very brief. Besides the etymological notes, they tell that the stockings (*pedules*) were made in the manner of the *tribuci*;[96] and, as already noted, that many monks divided them to facilitate washing.[97] Hildemar quotes Isidore as saying that the shoe (*caliga*) consisted of a stiff sole bound to the foot and was therefore unlike the type of shoe called the *soccus* which was slipped into.[98] Whether or not Hildemar was familiar with the *soccus* as used by the monks, does not appear. He may have deliberately excluded from his discussion this article of clothing not recommended in the Rule. Certainly the *soccus* was in current use in some other monasteries. Adalard of Corbie, a personal friend of Warnefrid, provided both monks and clerics with felt *socci* as well as other footwear called *calcearii*.[99] The twenty-second article of the Monastic Capitulary of 817, if we may trust the authenticity of the passage, appoints to each monk four pairs of stockings, two pairs of shoes for day use, two pairs of sandals for night wear in summer and *socci* for night in winter.[100] The customs of Farfa, dating from a later period, prescribe that the *camerarius* distribute shoes and stockings for day and for night wear.[101] At Cluny the day shoes were exchanged for the night shoes after

96 According to Du Cange (*s. v.* "trabucus," "trebucus," "tubrucus "), a kind of footwear worn with shoes.

97 Paul, p. 427; Hildemar, p. 513.

98 Page 513. *Cf.* also Isidore's *Etymologiae*, lib. 19, c. 34, n. 12. Although the term *soccus* was applied to wooden shoes as well as to those made of felt, the latter is probably the type implied here. *Cf.* Du Cange, *s. v.* " soccus " (1), and Leclercq, H., " Chaussure," *Dictionnaire d'archéologie chrétienne et de liturgie*, III, 1232-1257, especially 1247.

99 Levillain, L., *Les Statuts d'Adalhard pour l'abbaye de Corbie*, pp. 21-22 (Reprint from *Le Moyen Age*, XIII [1900]).

100 *MGH, Cap. reg. Franc.*, I, 345. The authenticity of this article, along with a few others not found in all the early MSS. of the capitulary and which partially repeat or contradict other articles of the same document, is questioned by Albers (*Consuetudines monasticae*, III, xxi-xxiii); *cf.* also Narberhaus, *op. cit.*, p. 50.

101 In Albers, I, 180.

Vespers, and the latter were therefore worn for Compline and the Office of the Dead, on through the night, and for Prime and reading in the morning. Only those who had special work to perform wore their day shoes before Tierce.[102]

Had Hildemar disapproved of the use of special shoes at night, he would, doubtless, have expressed himself on this point in his customarily outspoken manner. Perhaps in his monastery the *pedules* were worn indoors and at night without the stiff-soled *caligae*. By way of concession he permits the monks to sleep without *pedules* if necessary because of extremely warm weather, and on condition that they rise promptly for Matins and put on the *pedules* before entering the church, " for at no time [i. e., during the day] are monks to go without them, nor should they wear gaiters." [103]

Hildemar restricts the use of gowns of pelt or fur to those to whom the abbot may grant them for necessity.[104] At Monte Cassino Paul wrote to Charlemagne that the pelisse was given to the old only.[105] Both gaiters and pelisse, however, were permitted to all in general by the Monastic Capitulary of 817.[106]

Regarding the number of garments, i. e., tunics and cowls, allowed, the commentaries are silent, whereas both Monte Cassino and Aachen availed themselves of the optional phrase of the Rule on this point: The Aachen Capitulary states that a third garment is given if necessary;[107] at Monte Cassino, Paul writes that " the tradition handed down by the elders and former abbots " was to permit three garments to each because of various kinds of work.[108]

Present-day religious might well interpret St. Benedict's admonition to his disciples not to be disturbed about the color

102 *Consuetudines Cluniacenses,* Albers, II, 2, 28.

103 Page 519.

104 Hildemar, p. 513.

105 Letter of Paul to Charlemagne, Albers, III, 63.

106 *MGH, Cap. reg. Franc.,* I, 345.

107 *Ibid., loc. cit.*

108 Letter of Paul to Charlemagne, Albers, III, 63.

of the garments given them (c. 55) to refer to the quality of
the dye. In the ninth century, however, the monks were told
they ought not complain if the tunic were of one color and
the cowl of another.[109]

St. Benedict's advice that the clothes should be such as can
be obtained locally and bought rather cheaply is commented
upon thus: " It should be observed that he does not say ' cheap '
or ' the cheapest,' but ' rather cheaply,' that is, of average
quality; for example, we may call that ' rather cheap,' which
is neither precious nor too abject." [110] There is nothing particularly striking about this explanation, yet what is worthy
of note is that it appears to have been taken over almost
verbally in subsequent statutes, offering evidence that the commentary of Paul Warnefrid was known at the imperial court
of Aachen; and it indicates also that a norm was necessary,
according to which tendencies to extremities in dress might
be moderated. The Monastic Capitulary of 817 stipulates that
clothing, not too cheap nor the most precious, but medium in
quality be given the monks;[111] the fourteenth article of the
Statutes of Murbach orders the giving of average quality clothing, and then adds that garments made of goatskin or trimmed
with silk are altogether forbidden to monks; that if anyone
should have a garment of either kind it is to be worn out quickly
or exchanged and he should take care not to acquire another
such.[112] Hildemar observes that there are some who wear better
clothing within the monastery than St. Benedict ordered to be
reserved in the wardrobe for the use of those who go on a
journey.[113]

In commenting upon the " somewhat better clothes to be
worn by those sent on a journey," [114] Hildemar explains that

109 Hildemar, p. 514.

110 Paul, p. 427.

111 *MGH, Cap. reg. Franc.*, I, 345, no. 20.

112 In Albers, III, 87. *Cf.* also the sixty-first canon of the Council of
Aachen (*MGH, Cap. reg. Franc.*, I, 347).

113 Hildemar, p. 516.   114 *Regula*, c. 55.

although St. Benedict intended that the monk be mortified, he did not wish his mortification to be displayed outside the monastery, for were he to wear a coarse shoddy garment beyond the enclosure, it would be a matter of reproach rather than a mortification; and, in the same strain, if a nobleman should come to the monastery, the brother who serves him should wear better clothes than usual because of the repulsiveness (*fastidium*) of the rustic monastic dress.[115]

Little information is given in the commentaries as to how the articles of clothing, stored in the clothesroom and given out at chapter as needed,[116] were to be procured. Indirect references are made to the brothers being occupied in sewing both cloth and leather,[117] and again they allude to the privilege of going beyond the enclosure to the master cobbler, which privilege that brother should have who is charged with making the shoes for the brethren.[118] Perhaps it was done as contemporaneously at Murbach, namely, those made their own clothes who were able to do so, and for those who could not this need was supplied by the provost and *camerarius* " so that there would be no necessity for anyone to seek help either from within or without the monastery." [119] Furthermore, provision was made at Murbach to train craftsmen for this work within the cloister;[120] until the cobblers be trained, leather was to be given the brothers as before.[121]

In winter the rooms were not heated except that one which corresponds to the *calefactorium* of later times. Our commentators point out that " the abbot ought to depute a place in which the brothers may warm themselves; the fire is to be

---

115 Hildemar, *loc. cit.*
116 Paul, p. 428; Hildemar, pp. 515, 516, 521.
117 Paul, pp. 126, 127, 373; Hildemar, pp. 191, 192, 454.
118 Paul, p. 498; Hildemar, p. 613.
119 " Statuta Murbacensia," Albers, III, 84.
120 *Ibid., loc. cit.*
121 *Ibid.,* p. 87.

made by those brothers who served in the kitchen the week previous ".[122]

The monastic infirmary spoken of by St. Benedict in the Rule as a "cell set apart for the sick brethren" was not to consist of only one room but rather of a cloister, a home in which there were different rooms, for, the commentators ask, " how could one room suffice should there be three brothers, one at the point of death, another suffering from nausea, and a third wishing to eat?" [123] It has already been noted that the infirmary should have an oratory for the convenience and spiritual benefit of the sick.[124] Furthermore, there should be a special room for the abbot to which at a time of illness he might retire, and at the same time, if there were necessity, speak with guests or others who came to him, without impediment to the other infirm.[125]

The guest-house was quite an extensive department. It is desirable, our commentators say, to have a cloister for the noble guests arranged like that of the monks; another for the poor arranged like that of the infirm; and still another, also like that of the infirm, for the guest monks, so that the needs of all classes be taken care of. If this cannot be, at least they should have separate rooms, for it would not be proper to assemble the rich and the poor, bishops, abbots, and monks together.[126] To what extent the ideal was realized we cannot know, but it is evident that these groups were given separate rooms in which to eat and sleep, except that guest monks and clerics were admitted to the monastic refectory.[127]

Accommodations for guests, such as the foregoing, appear to be elaborate and perhaps extreme. However, when it is considered that the monasteries were among the chief hospices

122 Paul, p. 136; Hildemar, p. 203.

123 Paul, p. 339-340; Hildemar, p. 406.

124 *Cf. supra*, p. 27.

125 Hildemar, pp. 406-407; *cf.* Paul, p. 340.

126 Hildemar, pp. 506-507. *Cf.* Paul (pp. 419, 420) in which there is an evident lapse on the part of the scribe.

127 Hildemar, pp. 507, 611-612; Paul, p. 420.

of the time, and were exhorted by the councils [128] to perform this service, the situation is seen in a different light. Nevertheless it was a function foreign to the primary monastic purpose and might easily contribute to a state of things similar to that expressed by the monks of Fulda, in their complaint to Charlemagne about 811 or 812. They ask his intervention that "immense and superfluous buildings and other useless works be omitted, because through these the brothers are exhausted beyond measure and the family destroyed from without." [129] It does not follow, of course, that the "superfluous buildings" of Fulda were used exclusively for guests, but it is quite possible that they were devoted in part to this service.

The only allusions to monastic possessions or interests beyond the enclosure are very brief and indirect. The garden, although not within the enclosure,[130] should be near the monastery so that the brothers who work there, or those to whom it is entrusted, may be ready for prayer when the time for the work of God is announced or be present for reading or whatever the Rule prescribes.[131]

A summary of the various forms of income received by the monastery is given in connection with the financing of the guest house of the poor: "From all the gold, silver, copper, iron, trees, wine, fruit, and livestock that come to the monastery and from whatever is acquired through labor in the monastery, a tenth part is to be devoted to the hospice of the poor."[132] It is possible that all these commodities were produced in the vicinity of the monastery, but the occasional mention of cells,[133]

---

128 To mention only two: The Council of Aachen (789), can. 74, and the Synod of Frankfort (794), can. 35. Cf. Hefele-Leclerq, *Histoire des conciles,* III, 1033, 1059.

129 In Albers, III, 75.

130 Cf. *supra,* p. 28.

131 Paul, pp. 117-118.

132 Paul, p. 418; Hildemar, p. 505.

133 Paul, p. 498; Hildemar, pp. 516, 612.

curtes,[134] and villas [135] points to outlying possessions as well. The cells, being dependent branch monasteries, may well have functioned in the economic interests of the larger monastery; the *curtes* and villas, however, were primarily economic units designed for the administration of the outlying lands of the lord.[136]

The extent to which these outlying lands were tilled or supervised by the monks themselves cannot be discerned from our commentaries. The Council of Aachen (817) permits abbots to have cells, provided they are so arranged that not less than six monks live in each.[137] This same council forbids the abbots to frequent the villas unnecessarily or to place monks in charge of them; if necessity demand that they go to the villas, when the business is transacted they are to return at once to their monasteries.[138] This same regulation is recorded in the Statutes or Murbach, having been taken over from the canons of a previous synod.[139] Abbot-bishop Haito, compiler of the Statutes, in complying with the canon, makes this arrangement:

The brothers who have been engaged in the cells and villas, the outside ministries, will return to the monastery in mid-August when the change is to be made. Sooner than this it could not be done because of the time needed to acquire the knowledge of the places which they supervise. By that time, however, good man-

---

134 Paul, p. 79; Hildemar, p. 123.

135 Paul, p. 79; Hildemar, p. 122. The terms *curtis* (or *cortis*) and villa were sometimes used synonymously, but the former was used more commonly in Italian documents. *Cf.* Luzzatto, *I servi nelle grandi proprietà ecclesiastiche italiane nei sec. IX e X*, p. 46.

136 *Ibid., op. cit.*, pp. 46-47. According to this study, the lands tributary to the villa were tilled by tenants having varying degrees of independence; the work on the villa itself was largely done by these tenants, and the supervision was exercised by one of the serfs designated by the name *scario* or *actor*. *Cf. ibid.*, pp. 36, 43, 47.

137 *MGH, Cap. reg. Franc.*, I, 346, can. 44.

138 *Ibid.*, 345, can. 26.

139 *Cf. supra*, p. 39.

agers will have been provided, who will supervise these places in the future.[140]

From the foregoing it appears that, in compliance with the synod, the work on the villas in so far as it was not done by the tributary tenants, was thereafter to be performed by laymen in the service of the monastery, and that it was undesirable that the supervision be exercised by the monks. As evidence that lay help was also employed in the domestic ministries of the monastery, several references to the same may be pointed out in our commentaries.

Along with the children, the guests, the sick, and the poor entrusted to the care of the cellarer by St. Benedict,[141] the commentators include serfs (*servi*), those assigned to work in the garden as well as those deputed to the kitchen.[142] The kitchen referred to is definitely that of the lay guests, for it is specified elsewhere that two monks are to be appointed with the laymen for the care of the kitchen of the lay guests; the latter were served apart from the clerical guests, " because a layman ought never be admitted into the monastic refectory." Since one of the monks deputed to the lay-guest kitchen was appointed for the poor and the other for the honorary guests, it is probable that each supervised the work in his particular division, and that the work itself was performed by serfs.[143] Another reference to lay help shows a brother in charge of serfs (*famuli*) who are digging, or again, caring for the grain or wine.[144] Finally, it is recommended that in building a mon-

140 Article 10 in Albers, III, 85-86. In his account of Carolingian monastic and ecclesiastic lands (*Feudal Germany*, pp. 1-125), J. W. Thompson has frequently translated the words *Hufen* and *Mansen* from his German sources, and *mansi* from the Latin, as "manors," giving results which are quite misleading. For an analysis of lands tributary to Italian monasteries during the period under study, cf. Luzzatto, *op. cit.*, especially pp. 14-19 for Bobbio, 34-35 for Farfa, 41-43 for Volturno, and 43-44 for Monte Cassino. *Cf.* also A. Doren, *Italienische Wirtschaftsgeschichte*, I (Jena, 1934), 55-67.

141 *Regula*, c. 33.

142 Paul, p. 313; Hildemar, p. 377.

143 Paul, pp. 419-420; Hildemar, p. 507.

144 Paul, p. 378; Hildemar, p. 459.

astery, the donor should consider the needs of the monks, the serfs, the guests, and the infirm.[145]

The foregoing allusions to *servi* seem to indicate that lay help was employed in the care of the guests and the poor, in the garden and in other outside work, but that in the monastery proper, the monks performed the services. It is specified clearly that a monk and not a layman is to serve as infirmarian.[146] It is likewise clear that the monks performed their own laundry, cleaning, and kitchen service.[147]

In the monastic polyptic of St. Julia of Brescia, serfs called *praebendarii* are listed as distinct from those who tilled the lands tributary to the monastery. The former received food, clothes, and lodging from the monastery and in turn labored in the various ministries such as the mill and the garden, and to a lesser extent, tilled the monastic fields.[148] A list of the names of serfs donated to the monastery of Saints Faustinus and Jovita by Bishop Rampertus of Brescia in 841 is contained in the same document which tells of Hildemar's contemporary mission to this monastery.[149] Evidently he was familiar with the employment of lay help and saw in it no occasion for comment.

To analyze the position which this type of laborer fills in the range between the earlier workman on the Roman *latifundia* and the later medieval serf, is not essential to this

145 Hildemar, p. 607.

146 Paul, p. 340; Hildemar, p. 407.

147 *Cf. infra*, p. 138.

148 Luzzatto, *op. cit.*, pp. 25-28, 79. Corresponding to the *praebendarii* of Brescia were the *provendarii* of Corbie. *Cf. ibid.*, pp. 79, 96-97; Levillain, *op. cit.*, 19-20.

149 *Historiae patriae monumenta (Codex diplomaticus Langobardiae)*, XIII, cols. 245-248. Longer lists of serfs dependent on the monasteries of Farfa and Volturno are contained in records said to date from Carolingian times; these accounts, however, were drawn up much later and cannot therefore be given full credence. *Cf. Chronicon Vulturnense* in Fonti per la storia d'Italia, LVIII (1925), 205-210, 333-337, and *Chronicon Farfense*, in *ibid.*, XXXIII (1903), 258-277.

study.[150] From the monastic viewpoint, however, we seem to have an intermediate stage between the original conditions in which all the brothers were to share equally in the manual work,[151] and the later institutions of the *fratres conversi*.[152]

150 *Cf.* Luzzatto, *op. cit.*, pp. 89-90.

151 *Regula*, c. 35, 48.

152 Dating from the eleventh century. *Cf.* G. De Valous, *Le Monachisme clunisien des origines au XVe siècle*, I, pp. 44-50.

CHAPTER III

THE MONASTIC HOUSEHOLD

THE ideally constituted monastery, according to the commentators, should number twelve or more monks. If it consists of less than twelve, it is considered a minor congregation; if of more, a major congregation. Twelve is a satisfactory number because that many monks, if learned and agreeable, can fulfill the law of the Rule.[1] Hildemar, however, qualifies the last statement thus: " The foregoing is true with reference to the desert;[2] but near a city it is not good that only twelve monks be under one abbot, for if all are sent to the several duties, none would be left to give proper attention to the various men who come to the monastery. Therefore a monastery near a city ought to have more than twelve members." [3] Through several allusions to a considerable number of monks assembled in the oratory or refectory, Hildemar gives the impression that he was accustomed to a rather numerous community.[4]

The government of the monastery is to be carried out in broad lines after the manner sketched in the Rule; the abbot, in whom the final authority is vested, is to be assisted by a

1 Paul, pp. 248, 263; Hildemar, pp. 309, 323.

2 By "desert" he probably means places removed from the highways of travel or the populated centers.

3 Hildemar, p. 309.

4 *Ibid.*, pp. 463, 468, 474. *Cf.* also Traube, *op. cit.*, p. 39. From the investigation made by Berlière (*Revue bènèdictine,* XLI, 230-261; XLII, 19-33) of the number of monks in the monasteries of Europe during the Middle Ages, we learn the enrollment of several monasteries related to this study: Inde (Cornelimünster), over which Benedict of Aniane ruled as abbot, numbered forty-four monks; Corbie, from which Hildemar is thought to have come to Italy, had three hundred fifty monks; Fulda, two hundred seventy. A century later than the period of this study, Reichenau numbered ninety-five monks, and St. Gall has a record in which are listed seventy-one monks in major orders and twenty boys.

provost or prior [5] and deans. In deciding matters of great importance, the abbot is to hold council with the whole community; in lesser matters, he is to consult the seniors only.[6]

In observing that the highest authority in the monastery rests in the abbot to whom matters of doubt on the part of the ministers are to be submitted,[7] and against whose will they are to do nothing,[8] the commentators do not fail to point out also that the authority of the abbot is not unlimited, for he is responsible to God to whom he must give an account on Judgment Day. This reminder of the final judgment is taken from the second chapter of the Rule, and, together with the simile of the shepherd's responsibility for his flock, is considered by the commentators to constitute a very real deterrent against arbitrary action on the part of the abbot. They develop the thought in a way somewhat like the following: because St. Benedict wished that the abbot should realize more fully and clearly the nature of the account he must give on Judgment Day, he likened him to a shepherd from whom the *paterfamilias* will demand an account of the sheep entrusted to him. If he cannot give a satisfactory account of both the spiritual and temporal state of his monks, he will be condemned; but each one, nevertheless, shall be judged according to his merit. The abbot, however, will receive a double punishment, one for his own negligence, the other for what his monks have done amiss through his neglect. If, however, he can show that the monks have been lost through no fault of his, he shall be freed.[9]

5 In the commentaries, as in the Rule, "provost" is used exclusively of the officer ranking next to the abbot, and "prior" is used interchangeably with "abbot" to signify the head of the monastery. For the first use of "prior" meaning "provost," i. e., second to the abbot, cf. Delatte, *op. cit.*, p. 456, n. 6.

6 *Regula*, c. 2, 21, 65 and *passim*.

7 Paul, pp. 313-314; Hildemar, pp. 377-378.

8 Paul, pp. 264, 313, 489; Hildemar, pp. 325, 377, 603.

9 Paul, p. 55; Hildemar, pp. 91-92.

In exercising his authority, the abbot is to follow the Rule as a constitutional guide. For example, in discussing his relations with the cellarer, the commentators point out that the Rule specifies what duties the cellarer is to perform, and it is most essential that the abbot commit to him neither more nor less power than is appointed by the Rule; for should the abbot's grant of authority disagree with that of the Rule, the cellarer, in obeying the one will offend against the other, the occasion being given by the abbot.[10] Thus it is stated clearly that the authority of the abbot is limited by that of the Rule; the presumption, however, that there can be a moral obligation to obey conflicting authorities is, of course, not sound. Even in matters which the Rule leaves expressly to the judgment of the abbot, " St. Benedict did not give to the abbot such power that he might dispose unjustly, but only because he [St. Benedict] could not fully define the procedure in doubtful things. Moreover, he gave this power to the abbot, not that he might do anything according to his own choice, but rather, that he might *discern justly, and temper and dispose* as St. Benedict bids him do [elsewhere]." [11] This principle is frequently repeated.[12]

The commenators did not consider the abbot's office an easy or enviable position. " It is well," they observe, " that the Rule speaks of his burden *(onera)* and not of his honors *(honores)* because to be placed over others is to bear the weight of a burden, not the decoration of an honor." [13] That which particularly makes the task onerous is the government of souls, for " it is not difficult to rule bodies, but to rule souls is difficult." [14] By souls is understood dispositions or minds, for the same passage continues, " the difficulty in ruling souls is

10 Paul, p. 313; Hildemar, pp. 376-377.

11 Paul, p. 422; Hildemar, p. 510.

12 Paul, pp. 362, 426, 461, 467, 478; Hildemar, pp. 439, 512, 568, 575, 586.

13 Paul, p. 264; Hildemar, p. 326.

14 Paul, p. 75; Hildemar, p. 118.

to adapt oneself to the dispositions *(mores)* of many," [15] and, further on, " at one moment, the abbot must be both sad and joyful, and again joyful and sad, corresponding to the different characters of his subjects." [16]

In his government of the monastery, very great discretion is called for on the part of the abbot especially in the meting out of penalties to offenders: " Not all manners of correction are equally adaptable to all characters, for the types of minds so differ that through the means whereby one is healed another is crushed. Wherefore the lash is to be used freely in constraining some but not at all in the case of others." [17] Likewise should the abbot use discretion as regards the physical welfare of his subjects upon whom he imposes penances. We shall quote the pertinent passage, replete as it is with current thought on medical science:

The abbot ought to use discretion with reference to the season of the year and the character of the person; i. e., he ought to consider the season, whether it is warm or cold, for both kinds are not equally suited to fasting; he ought also to consider the constitution of the brother whom he has excommunicated, whether he be weak or strong, subject to an infirmity or gifted with endurance. For it should be known that if anyone fasts overmuch his stomach becomes contracted by the heat of the liver, and when afterward he wishes to take food, that very food will injure him. Therefore it should be understood that he [the abbot] ought to have knowledge of medicines and if of himself he does not know them he should inquire, so that when he inflicts a fast on a brother, he may do so with moderation.[18]

The commentators recognize that it is not an essential requisite that the abbot be invested with the powers of the priesthood, for " the abbot offers the Sacrifice, not as abbot

15 *Ibid., loc. cit.*

16 Paul, p. 76; Hildemar, p. 119.

17 Hildemar, pp. 341-342. *Cf.* also *ibid.,* pp. 116-117, 371-372; Paul, p. 307.

18 Hildemar, p. 352. In the corresponding passage in Paul's commentary (p. 284), the scribe has evidently omitted the word, *stomachus.*

but as priest." [19] From this statement and from a few indirect
references to the abbot acting in the capacity of a priest,[20] it
is evident that the commentators were accustomed to think
of the abbot as being ordained. At the monastery of Inde
presided over by Benedict of Aniane, it was likewise customary
that the abbot be a priest.[21] Hildemar, relative to this subject,
cites the decree of Pope Eugenius II who orders that such men
should be elected abbots of monasteries as are able to rule
their subjects well and have attained to the sacerdotal
honor.[22] It must not yet have become universal that the abbot
was also a priest, for the contemporary canons of Aachen say
that the abbot, provost, or dean, although not a priest, should
give the blessing to the readers.[23]

According to the commentators, many monasteries were
ruled not by " regular " [24] but by " canonical " abbots, i. e.
by a bishop or by an ecclesiastic appointed by him. The favorable attitude of the commentators toward this state of things
is quite surprising—perhaps one of the most significant de-
partures from the Rule which meets with their approval. They
explain that although monasteries so ruled have no regular
abbot, they do have a provost, deans, and other regular ranking
ministers, and that many canonical abbots are no less solicitous
about the observance of the Rule than regular abbots would
have been.[25]

As an explanation of this favorable attitude, we offer, for
what it is worth, the conjecture that Paul Warnefrid and
Hildemar were each at one time in the service of canonical
abbots. We have already noted that Paul entered the clerical

19 Paul, p. 479; Hildemar, p. 588.

20 Hildemar, pp. 287, 508.

21 *Cf.* the report on the practices of Inde made by Tatto and Grimwald
about 817 in Albers, III, 105, no. 3.

22 Hildemar, p. 590; *MGH, LL,* III, *Concilia aevi Karolini,* I, ii, 578.

23 *MGH, Cap. reg. Franc.,* I, 347, no. 62.

24 In the sense of monastic, i. e., according to a Rule.

25 Paul, p. 36; Hildemar, p. 75.

state after having been educated at the Lombard court of
Pavia, and that the monastery at which he is thought to have
lived before the fall of the Lombard state is said to date from
King Desiderius as a founder and to have been dependent on
the church of Milan;[26] it seems quite possible that the learned
deacon and scholar might have been invited by the Metro-
politan of Milan at the suggestion of King Desiderius to join
this favorite monastery of his; perhaps, too, Paul was urged
by his royal friend to write the *Expositio* of the Rule, for, as
Traube suggests, it was likely while here that Paul wrote his
commentary.[27] We know that Hildemar, together with
Leutgar, was sent to assist in the administration of a monastery near Brescia at the request of Rampertus, bishop of
Brescia and founder of the monastery.[28] Contemporaneously
at St. Gall, the canonical Abbot Grimwald (841-872) was appointed by the Emperor. Being frequently occupied with royal
duties he was assisted by Hartmut of St. Gall who was made
pro-abbas with the right of succession.[29]

Although in these instances, the functioning of canonical
abbots may have proved beneficial, the institution in general met
with the disapproval of the reform at Aachen. Canonical abbots
were forbidden by the fifty-ninth canon of the Council of 817
to take monks with them on a journey except when going to a
general synod.[30] Benedict of Aniane used his influence to secure

---

26 *Cf. supra*, p. 22.   27 *Textgeschichte*, p. 43.

28 *Cf. supra*, p. 25.

29 I. Herwegen, *Geschichte der benediktinischen Professformel*, Beiträge
zur Geschichte des alten Mönchtums und des Benediktinerordens, Heft 3
(1912), 36, 37, n. 3. In *Die Klosterbischöfe des Frankenreiches*, published in
Beiträge zur Geschichte des alten Mönchtums, Heft 17 (1932), 171, n., H.
Frank points out that according to a recent study of the Reichenau confraternity book made by K. Beyerle (*Die Kultur der Abtei Reichenau*, I, 209,
n. 37) the Reichenau monk Grimwald (*cf. supra*, n. 21) is not to be identified
with the Grimwald who was chancellor to Emperor Louis the German and
later abbot of St. Gall.

30 *MGH, Cap. reg. Franc.*, I, 347. Since a canonical abbot, especially if a
bishop, would be likely to travel more than a regular abbot, the purpose of
this restriction was, doubtless, to minimize the travels made by the monks.

for each monastery the right of election;[31] however, where canonical abbots were already in possession, a compromise was made by imperial decree in order to make the monastic property secure. The estates of the monastery were to be divided; one portion was to be set aside for the support of the monks; the other, for the canonical abbot who was to draw therefrom the tribute *(servitia)* to the crown.[32]

Relative to the "major matters" concerning which the Rule (c. 3.) calls for the abbot's taking counsel with the entire congregation, our expositors tell us that the major matters *(praecipua)* are those "which pertain to the whole community and which are of doubtful issue, i. e., which cannot be discerned as beneficial or harmful by mere argumentation." [33] The argumentation, doubtless, refers to the method of evaluation along the lines given in the commentary preceding this passage; it is explained in a somewhat curious discussion concerned with the balancing of the "congruencies" and "contrarieties" of the question.[34]

The major matters, therefore, are to be brought before the entire community so that what cannot be decided by human arguments may be referred to God by prayer.[35] In this we have a striking yet typical illustration of the medieval procedure relative to the settlement of disputes and court procedure. Greater reliance is placed in God's action through human means than in human reason alone.

As examples of what should be considered major matters, both commentators cite the following: the admission of a

31 Narberhaus, *Benedict von Aniane*, pp. 42-43.

32 *Ibid.*, pp. 66-67.

33 Paul, p. 87; Hildemar, p. 130.

34 Paul, pp. 86-87; Hildemar, pp. 129-130.

35 Paul, p. 87: "necesse est super hoc ut interrogetur omnis Congregatio quatenus placabiles sint exinde fratres, ut eorum precibus quod non potest humanis rationibus discerni, Dei iudicio discernatur." Hildemar's version (p 131) is somewhat different: "ut Deo hoc placabile sit, necesse est super hoc ut interrogetur omnis congregatio, ut quod non potest humanis rationibus discerni, Dei judicio discernatur."

novice into the community, the expulsion of a brother because of some vice, the length of time an excommunicated
brother is to do penance, the hour at which he is to eat, and
the quantity of his food.[36] Hildemar gives in addition: " It
is likewise a major matter if the abbot wishes to make a
donation of importance, such as the giving of twenty *amphorae*
of wine, or more or less, in proportion to the wealth of the
congregation, or the exchanging of a large tract of land." [37]

Minor matters, according to both commentators, are those
which pertain to the duty of an individual, such as the purchase
of vessels by the cellarer, of clothes by the *vestiarius,* or the
exchange of a small tract of land. Questions such as these may
be decided by the advice of the seniors only.[38]

Regarding those ministers with whom the abbot is to share
the burden of his office, the provost and the deans, we find
little in the commentaries over and above what is contained in
the Rule (c. 21, 65). The only duty which they ascribe to these
assistants is to preserve discipline; it is nicely summarized in
the following excerpt from Warnefrid's commentary:

It should be understood that the sole duty of the deans is to
exercise custody over their subjects. And if through their admonition the latter are not corrected, then the deans are to report to the
abbot; should the abbot not be present, to him who has been appointed in his place. And the abbot or the one in his place ought
to rebuke the offender publicly or excommunicate him. What is
understood with regard to the deans is applicable likewise to the
circatores.[39] Thus when the abbot is not present there ought to
be a prior in his place with equal authority; and if the prior is
absent a dean should fill the position.[40]

36 Paul, p. 87; Hildemar, pp. 130-131.

37 Page 131.

38 Paul, p. 91; Hildemar, p. 136.

39 The *circatores* were, doubtless, minor disciplinarians corresponding to
the " one or two seniors," mentioned in the Rule (c. 48), who were to go
about while the brothers read so that no one be given to idleness or useless
talk, or disturb others.

40 Paul, p. 268. *Cf.* also Hildemar, pp. 329, 604.

It appears that in this passage the commentators are more concerned with the duty of the deans than with that of the provost; elsewhere, however, they tell us nothing more about the latter. Quite unlike this disciplinary service, the duty of the monastic provost in the early ninth century, according to a recent study, was the direction of external and secular affairs, leaving the inner guidance of the monastery to the abbot.[41] Another work asserts that although the abbot was the nominal administrator of the abbey's patrimony, the actual work was carried out largely by the provost; that the latter, being in charge of the raw materials, was supervisor of the gardener and similar ministers, and was custodian of the vineyards, whereas the cellarer supervised the immediate supplies for the kitchen and refectory, and the *camerarius,* the weaving and sewing of textiles and the metal ware.[42]

This assertion is in general agreement with the commentaries with reference to the official duties of the cellarer and *camerarius.* If it implies however, that these ministers were under the immediate supervision of the provost, in this respect it does not correspond, for the commentators make it clear that the cellarer received his instructions from and was directly responsible to the abbot; they observe that if the cellarer is such as the Rule recommends,[43] the abbot can rely on his judgment in everything as if his own. If, however, such a one cannot be found for the office of the cellarer, the abbot should specify to the one who fills the position what shall be under his care, and should he wish to do other things, he is to advise with the abbot.[44]

The Rule prescribes in general that the sick, the children, the guests, and the poor are to be entrusted to the care of the

41 J. Narberhaus, *op. cit.,* p. 55. This arrangement seems to have prevailed throughout the Middle Ages.

42 G. Volpe, "Per la storia giuridica ed economica del medio evo," *Studi storici,* XIV (1905), 165-166.

43 *Cf.* chapter 31.

44 Paul, p. 314; Hildemar, p. 378.

cellarer. The commentators add to these charges and give details as to the extent of the care in each case. With reference to the children, the abbot should instruct the cellarer regarding the choice and measure of food to be given them and also the hour at which it is to be served. In the case of the guests, the service is to be in keeping with their rank and station. It was a custom among the " ancients," the commentators explain, that the cellarer should perform the services of guestmaster; but now, due to the multitude of guests who come to the monastery, others have been appointed to receive the guests. It is to be understood of the cellarer, therefore, that he is to care for those guests only who are taken into the refectory to eat. The abbot will likewise admonish the cellarer that he warn his helpers *(manipuli)* lest they neglect the services proper to the sick, and the cellarer in person will frequently visit the infirmary and zealously correct any negligences. The serfs of the monastery, the weak as well as the strong, will likewise be cared for by the cellarer. Finally, in setting the daily fare before the community, the cellarer is to follow the precepts of the Rule; exceptions may be made only with the permission of the abbot.[45]

The key position of the cellarer and his influence for good or for evil in the monasticism of the eighth century is thus expressed: " Through the cellarer many vices may be nourished or cut off in the monastery. It is well that he [St. Benedict] stipulated what kind of man he ought to be, for he realized the great good which would follow if the cellarer of the monastery were wise, and the great danger which would threaten were he unwise." [46]

The remaining officials mentioned in the commentaries are few and of minor importance. Reference has already been made to the *camerarius,* whose duty it was to provide the textile, leather, and metal supplies for the monks.[47] Closely related to his service, if not identical with it, was that referred to the

---

45 Paul, pp. 313-315; Hildemar, pp. 377-379.

46 Paul, p. 310; Hildemar, p. 373.

47 *Cf.* Du Cange, *s. v.* " camerarius (officium monasticum)."

keeper of the wardrobe called the *vestiarius*. The latter is spoken of as the one who dispenses clothes in the chapter, [48] and again as responsible for the purchasing of the clothes.[49] Since it is the duty of the *camerarius* to sweep the chapter house and the dormitory in front of the wardrobe, and since the various ministers are expected to clean their respective departments,[50] the service ascribed to the *camerarius* at one time and to the *vestiarius* at another appears to be one and the same service.[51]

The infirmarian, according to the Rule (c. 36), should be God-fearing, diligent, and solicitous. In explaining the last requisite, the commentators take occasion to add three more qualities: " In that *solicitude* three things are to be sought, i. e., wisdom, in order that he may understand how to serve the infirm wisely and prudently . . .; strength, to be able to lift the infirm from the bed and to carry him where he may wish to go; zeal, i. e., love for one's neighbor, so that by loving him he may serve him zealously for the love of God." It is at this point, too, that the commentators observe that this service is to be rendered, not by a cleric or a layman, but by a monk. If necessary, however, a canonical person or layman may wash the soiled clothes of the sick and bring meat as food for him.[52]

Although the commentaries tell us much about the reception of guests, they tell us little about the duty of the guestmaster. We have already noted that certain monks are appointed for the care of the many guests who come to the monastery, as against the custom of the " ancients " whereby the cellarer per-

48 Hildemar, p. 516. *Cf.* also *ibid.*, pp. 515, 613; Paul, pp. 428, 498-499.

49 Paul, p. 91; Hildemar, p. 136.

50 Hildemar, p. 397. Paul's account (p. 332) prescribes that all the porticos of the cloister except the refectory be swept by the brothers who served in the kitchen the previous week.

51 According to the customs of Farfa the *camerarius* was charged with the procurement, distribution, and mending of the clothes and shoes, as also with the providing of bedding, towels, and table covers. There is no mention of the *vestiarius* (Albers, I, 180).

52 Hildemar, p. 407; the corresponding passage in Warnefrid's commentary (p. 340) is not so complete.

formed this duty.[53] Elsewhere the senior *hospitalarius* is bidden to petition the abbot for help when the guests are particularly numerous.[54]

In regard to the doorkeeper of the monastery, the commentators likewise tell of a development in the ministry due to the increased number of guests as compared with earlier times: the two brothers who served in the abbot's kitchen formerly were the doorkeepers as well; but now since so many guests come, there should be two porters who do nothing else but announce the guests to the abbot or prior. Two are required so that when one goes to recite the Office, to meals, or is detained with a guest, the other may remain to answer the call of arriving guests.[55]

The *magistri,* those charged with the care of the small boys, did not devote themselves exclusively to this work, but shared in the daily tasks of the monastic life. To make sure that at no time the boys be left without custody, the commentators recommend that for the supervision of ten boys, three or four *magistri* be appointed so that when one or two of the masters are otherwise engaged, e. g., in the kitchen service, another may be with the boys to prevent their playing, idle talking, straying about, or mingling with others.[56] In his relations with the boys, the *magister* should be guided by moderation; "he ought not whip them too severely nor treat them badly, but should exercise great care and custody over them, for the rod and excommunication will avail nothing unless there shall have been custody." [57]

---

53 *Cf. supra*, p. 63.　　　　54 Paul, p. 420; Hildemar, p. 509.

55 Paul, p. 492-3; Hildemar, p. 605. The accuracy of these allusions to ancient customs, particularly the one regarding the monastic porters, is open to question; St. Benedict provided that "a wise old man be placed at the door of the monastery" and that his cell should be near the gate so that those who come may always find him present (*Regula,* c. 66). It does not seem plausible that this same porter was also the abbot's cook. Perhaps by "*antiquitus*" the commentators refer to pre-Benedictine monasticism.

56 Paul, pp. 271, 345; Hildemar, pp. 331-332, 418.

57 Paul, p. 346; Hildemar, pp. 418-419. We shall have more to say about the subject of custody from time to time.

Having outlined the chief agents through which the monastery was ruled, we shall now turn to the subjects, and survey the regulations relative to their admission into the community and subsequent discipline. New members were received according to the Rule (c. 58, 59) either as adult novices or as child oblates.[58] Besides the lay adult, the Rule also provides for the admission of priests and of monks from other monasteries, upon the satisfaction of certain requirements.[59]

In interpreting the chapter of the Rule concerned with the admission of a layman, the commentators make some notable errors. The " few days " specified in the Rule during which the candidate is to remain in the cell of the guests are lengthened to two months; this extension is erroneously based on a subsequent phrase of the Rule which prescribes that after the lapse of two months the Rule is to be read to the novice for his consideration as to future acceptance.[60] Now it is clear from the wording of the Rule that these two months are to be spent in the department of the novices where the newcomer is to " meditate, sleep, and eat." [61] The misinterpretation is not merely a question of the department in which the novice will spend the first two months of the novitiate, but of the significant decision which the commentators would have him make at the close of this brief period—whether or not he will assume the clerical state. At this early stage the decision is final; if he decides in the affirmative he will no longer be free to return to the world. Although not bound to the monastic state until he makes profession at the close of the year, he is, nevertheless, subject to canon law whereby the bishop may not permit him to return to the world.[62] This interpretation, contradictory in itself, and quite contrary to the Rule which calls for three readings of

58 Cf. infra, p. 76.

59 Chapters 60 and 61.

60 Paul, p. 440; Hildemar, p. 534.

61 ". . . et sit in cella hospitum paucis diebus. Postea autem sit in cella novitiorum, ubi meditetur et manducet et dormiat " (c. 58).

62 Paul, p. 442; Hildemar, p. 537.

the Rule during the year of probation which precedes any obligation on the part of the novice, is traceable to a misunderstanding of the canons of Nicaea (325) to which the commentators themselves allude. The twelfth canon of this council ruled that those Christians who apostatized for the sake of a military position, and later wished to return, were subject to a long penance.[63]

This misinterpretation was not universally accepted, for Hildemar adds: " there are some who understand that only when the novice promises [to observe] the Rule, i. e., after a year, he is to be tonsured and his arms laid aside. These do not understand correctly for the canons of the Nicene Council speaking on the subject, require him who returns to the world to do penance for ten years." [64]

It does not appear, however, that the commentators, in making this error, were insincere or deliberately desired to restrict the novice's liberty of choice; on the contrary, they would have the candidate exhorted at the end of the two months to consider well whether or not he is able to fulfill the Rule, and they suggest that an interval of time be appointed during which he may deliberate with himself.[65] Hildemar, in warning against the dread state of the unfaithful religious for whom it would have been better had he remained in the world,[66] appears to be offering these considerations for the wavering novice to prevent his entering rashly. In the same chapter, too, he condemns those " who, poorly understanding, persuade others to come to the monastery out of zeal for God. . . . If we do this we act contrary to the Rule, for it says that he [who asks admission]

---

63 Mansi, II, 681, c. 12: " Quicumque vocati per gratiam, primum quidem impetum monstraverunt, deponentes militiae cingulum; postmodum vero ad proprium vomitum sunt relapsi, ita ut quidam et pecunias tribuerent, et beneficiis militiam repeterent; hi decem annis, post triennii tempus quo inter audientes erunt, in afflictione permaneant." On this canon, see Hefele-Leclercq, *Histoire des conciles,* I, 591-593.

64 Page 537.

65 Paul, p. 441; Hildemar, p. 535.

66 Pages 541, 542.

should be proved and all but rejected." [67] He then cites various passages which indicate that not all are called to the extraordinary way of life. This idea, he tells us, is not original with him but he thinks it well to repeat it in his book lest anyone might "solicit by gifts or deter by threats those about to believe; rather let him speak only what is holy and let him lead to the faith those about to believe or to religion those who are to enter, voluntarily." [68]

In view of the frequent canonical and imperial regulations between the years 789 and 817 concerning the admission of novices, we are led to conclude that abuses in this connection were not lacking. Most of these references demand that the Rule of St. Benedict be observed in the reception of novices, especially that easy admission be not granted them. Some add a clause against forcing or enticing the novice; others forbid the taking of a premium from those who enter. [69]

In keeping with the last prohibition and, doubtless, in an effort to forestall unworthy motives on the part of the novice or the monastery, the commentaries make the following recommendation. If, at the end of the year of probation, the novice desires to assume the monastic obligations and he has been found acceptable to the community, he should be urged to bestow his property on the poor, or on his relatives, or on other monasteries who perhaps need it more than the monastery he is about to enter. If the novice, however, prefer to give it to the latter for the benefit of his soul, then it may be bestowed on the poor or on the monastery. [70]

Having disposed of his property, the novice then proceeds to the solemn act of profession, the essential parts of which are the oral promise to observe the Benedictine vows of stability, conversion of morals, and obedience, and the written petition,

---

67 Pages 545-546.

68 Hildemar, *loc. cit.*

69 *MGH, Cap. reg. Franc.*, I, 60 (no. 73), 76 (no. 16), 122 (no. 13), 228 (no. 19), 346 (no. 34), 348 (no. 75); Albers, III, 74 (no. 8), 88 (no. 20).

70 Paul, pp. 442-443; Hildemar, pp. 538-539.

drawn up, or at least signed and placed on the altar, by the novice. The latter " was at once a request for admission, a promise, and the schedule, or written and signed instrument, testifying forever to the obligations contracted." [71]

In their description of the profession ceremony the commentaries of Warnefrid and Hildemar differ but slightly, and in general, both conform to the Rule.[72] The following outline is based on the earlier account. On entering the oratory the novice is divested of his garments and clothed with the monastic habit, the written promise having already been drawn up. Approaching the altar, he pronounces the three-fold promise mentioned above and then places the petition on the altar. After the triple chanting of the " Suscipe," he prostrates himself while the other brothers on bended knees chant several appropriate psalms. The newly professed then rises, and the rite is concluded with the recitation of versicles and a prayer proper for the occasion.[73]

The interesting ceremony of the monk's head being covered with the *melota* from the time of his promise until the octave day, did not originate with the Rule. Paul Warnefrid explains it as equivalent to Baptism, according to the tradition of the Holy Fathers.[74] He meant to say, doubtless, that this ceremony

71 Delatte, *op. cit.*, p. 385. Our commentators illustrate only the *promissio* (Paul, p. 443; Hildemar, p. 539). For examples of the petition and the promise, cf. *MGH, LL*, V, *Formulae Merowingici et Karolini aevi*, pp. 568-571.

72 Hildemar (p. 539) takes over Warnefrid's account (p. 443) almost verbatim in chapter 58. At the end of the chapter, however, he adds, as if a formula, the " Order to be followed by a novice in promising the Rule " (pp. 546-547). It is in this latter account that occur whatever variations there are.

73 Paul, p. 443.

74 Paul, *loc. cit.*: ". . . ut caput eius promissione veletur, et in die octavo develetur, quia vice baptismi est Melota"; *ibid.*, p. 446: " Ideo vero dicit Monachum caput coopertum usque ad octavum diem habere, quia secundum sanctorum Patrum Catholicorum dicta, vice Baptismi est hoc." In his first passage relative to profession (p. 539) Hildemar gives seven days, and in the second passage (p. 547), three days, as the time during which

is in imitation of the newly baptized catechumen's wearing a special garment from Easter Sunday until its octave, an act which symbolized the transformation effected in the soul by Baptism. The pious belief, though of course not a doctrine, that the act of religious profession is equivalent in its effects to a second Baptism, is traceable through the Middle Ages and prevails currently among many writers and religious.[75]

The various extant formulas containing the *promissio* and the *petitio* made in European monasteries from the seventh to the ninth centuries show notable variations. Abbot Herwegen has made a careful legal study of these formulas with results important in themselves, and important likewise in their bearing on the work of the Carolingian commentators of the Rule—on that of Warnefrid in particular.[76] We shall briefly sketch the results of Herwegen's study.

Within the years intervening between the time of St. Benedict and that of the Carolingian commentators, the second of the three vows disappeared from the currently used formulas, leaving stability and obedience as the expressed obligations of the monk. Herwegen sees the peculiar expression used to indicate this vow in the vulgar tongue at the time of St. Benedict, " *conversatio morum,*" as a contributing factor in the evolution of the two-part formula. When once the traditional meaning attached to this expression disappeared at Monte Cassino (the monastery was plundered by the Lombards in 581 and restored only about 717), the term " *conversatio,*" so generally understood to connote the life of the monk, appeared complete in itself; the addition of " *morum* " became unintelligible and was, therefore, omitted. Furthermore, since " stabil-

the monk's head is to be covered after profession. In prescribing the three-day interval he coincides with, and was doubtless influenced by, canon 35 of the Council of Aachen, 817.

75 U. Berlière, *L'Ascèse bénédictine des origines à la fin du XII⁰ siècle,* p. 120; B. Poschmann, *Die abendländische Kirchenbusse im Ausgang des christlichen Altertums,* p. 129.

76 I. Herwegen, *Professformel,* especially pp. 52-57.

ity " implied the idea of constancy in the monk's life, there appeared no reason to retain *conversatio morum* as a distinct vow. Either implicitly as in the promise instituted by Warnefrid's predecessors at Monte Cassino, or expressly as in the petition of Flavigny, the two terms "*stabilitas*" and "*conversatio*" were combined in the expression *stabilitas conversationis in congregatione*.[77]

Herwegen finds this two-part formula to have originated in the first monasteries founded on Gallo-Frankish soil which followed the Rule of St. Benedict. Thus the Rule composed for nuns by Bishop Donatus of Besançon, about the middle of the seventh century, and the Gallic Rule of the Master, also of the seventh century,[78] call for the two-fold promise. Whether this fact is traceable to difficulties in interpreting the Rule relative to the phrase, "*conversatio morum*," or to Gallic monastic traditions, Herwegen hesitates to decide. He does hold as certain, however, that the two-part formula originated in Gaul, and that from the practice there, influence was brought to bear on the Frankish cloisters such as that of Flavigny in the late seventh century, and on Monte Cassino in the eighth century; from these the custom was extended to the monasteries of Italy and Germany.[79] Flavigny was in Burgundy near Annegray and

77 *Ibid.*, pp. 48-49. A recent discussion covering the literature concerning the phrase "conversatio morum" is given by Justin McCann in *St. Benedict* (New York, 1937), pp. 147-167.

78 Thus Herwegen ascribes to the Rule of the Master a seventh-century Gallic origin. Traube (*op. cit.*, p. 36) also dates it from the seventh century. Recently, however, some writers would trace it to a Spanish origin, and one writer would have it antedate the Benedictine Rule. *Cf.* J. Pérez de Urbel, "La Règle du Maître," *Revue d'histoire ecclésiastique*, XXXIV (1938), 707-739; *ibid.*, "Le Maître et Saint Benoît," *ibid.*, 756-764; M. Alamo, "La Règle de Saint Benoît éclairée par sa source, la Règle du Maître," *ibid.*, 740-755.

79 *Professformel*, p. 50. Thus the "*petitio*" contained in the profession book of Reichenau and written about 950 (not about 826 as Zeumer incorrectly thought: *cf. MGH, Formulae Merowingici et Karolini aevi*, 568) appears to be a later recension of the Formula of Flavigny: *cf.* Herwegen, *op. cit.*, pp. 14 (n. 3), 17.

Luxeuil, monasteries founded by Columban; the extant formula of Flavigny, the oldest Frank-Benedictine formula known, dates from the time of the transition from the Columban to the Benedictine Rule.[80]

Along with the omission of the vow of conversion of morals in the formula of Flavigny, Herwegen points out other items of interest. He sees in the *petitio* and its supplement, the *promissio,* a resemblance to the Frankish personal tradition: in its terminology the *petitio* corresponds to the act of commendation; the *promissio,* to the oath of fidelity.[81] Furthermore, in place of the local stability of the Rule, there is substituted perseverance in the monastic calling.[82] Finally, there are inserted in the formula certain Frankish reservations which contrast notably with the more absolute obedience of the Benedictine Rule.[83]

After the adoption of the two-part formula, the consciousness of departing from the Rule in its clearly distinguished three vows must have been the more strongly felt, the more the text of the Rule was studied. It is therefore intelligible that the commentators of the Rule were the first to offer again the three-part formula. In doing so, however, they gave, not the original phrase, *conversatio morum,* but in its place *conversio morum.* We find the latter used not only in the commentaries and profession formulas but in the text of the Rule currently used. Thus the authentic reading, *conversatio morum,* fell into complete oblivion until recent times.[84] In tracing this change in terminology, according to Herwegen, we need be concerned only with the work of Paul Warnefrid, for although Smaragdus and Hildemar used " *conversio,*" the originality lies with Paul. He distinguishes between *conversio* and *conversatio,* thereby showing his acquaintance with the other manuscripts

80 *Ibid.,* pp. 14, 17.
81 *Ibid.,* p. 25.
82 *Ibid.,* pp. 21-22, 31.
83 *Ibid.,* p. 29.
84 *Ibid.,* pp. 51-52.

and, at the same time, establishing his reading to be *conversio*.[85]
Herwegen's conclusion is, then, that the three-part profession
formula was reestablished by Warnefrid, and that its general
acceptance in the monasteries of the Frankish Empire was
effected by the efforts of Benedict of Aniane in behalf of
uniformity of practice.[86]

Besides the adult novice, as already mentioned, priests and
monks from other monasteries might also be admitted to the
community according to the Rule (c. 60, 61). Warnefrid points
out that a priest is to be put to the same tests as a layman
seeking admission: the four or five days at the gate of the
monastery, the two months in the guesthouse, and the ten
months in the department of the novices.[87] Hildemar states
that a priest is to be proved even more than a layman, and then
vaguely indicates that he refers to those provisions of the Rule
whereby a priest may be promoted in the monastic rank if his
life be deserving and he may be permitted to celebrate Mass and
to bless if the abbot so order him.[88]

A monk from another monastery, having received his
monastic training elsewhere, is not required by the Rule (c. 61)
to repeat his novitiate, for " during his stay as a guest his life
could be known." Should he desire admission he is requested
only to declare his stability; but should he have come from a
known monastery, he may not be admitted without the consent
of his abbot or commendatory letters. These precepts of the
Rule are taken over by the commentators with no substantial
changes. They quote the formula used by the newcomer in

85 Paul, p. 439; Herwegen, *op. cit.,* pp. 52-53.

86 *Op. cit.,* p. 63. Dom Butler's account in *Benedictine Monachism* (pp.
134-139) relative to the disuse and restoration of the vow of conversion of
morals in the profession formula, and the substitution of " *conversio* " for
the unintelligible " *conversatio*," conforms largely with that of Herwegen
without, however, ascribing the change to any individual.

87 Paul, p. 452.

88 Hildemar, pp. 553-554.

confirmation of his stability,[89] and give, moreover, the following information regarding the commendatory letters.

Both expositors cite three ways in which a monk may be given permission to reside in another monastery. The first is by consent, i. e., one abbot asks and receives the consent of another abbot to admit to residence a monk from his monastery; the second is by a commendatory letter, i. e., one in which an abbot certifies to a known abbot that he has given permission to the bearer to live in the monastery of the second abbot, and therefore recommends the monk to the latter to be dealt with and accounted for to God in the same manner as the first abbot was under obligation to do; the third is by a letter to all in general, the clergy and the faithful, stating that the bearer has the permission of his abbot to take up residence in any monastery of regular observance in which it shall be found mutually beneficial for him to be.[90]

Hildemar makes some notable additions to the foregoing. A monk fleeing persecution, he writes, should not be dealt with in the same manner as he who lightly leaves his monastery and goes to another. The latter, as the canons declare, may not be accepted without the permission of the bishop;[91] the former, also according to the canons, deserves kind consideration, and should be permitted to remain in the place to which he has come for refuge until he can return safely or his injury shall have been removed.[92]

89 Paul, p. 459: " Ego talis, veniens de longinquis Provinciis in hoc Monasterio, quia placuit mihi conversatio Fratrum, istius loci, et illis mea placuit conversatio; ideo stabilitatem meam in hoc Monasterio, per hanc scripturam manu mea scriptam, in perpetuum confirmo." In Hildemar, p. 561.

90 Hildemar, p. 560; *cf.* also Paul, pp. 458-459. The accounts are quite similar, but where they differ, Hildemar's reading, because it is less obscure, has been followed.

91 Charlemagne's capitulary of 789 recalls that the Council of Nicaea (can. 16), that of Antioch (can. 3), and that of Chalcedon (can. 13) forbad fugitive clerics or pilgrim monks to be received or ordained without commendatory letters and the permission of their bishop or abbot (*MGH, Cap. reg. Franc.*, I, 54).

92 Hildemar (pp. 560-561), cities the twentieth canon of the Council of

In his discussion of the letters of commendation, Hildemar distinguishes three types:

It should be known that some letters are "*commendatitiae*," others are "*formatae*," and still others are "*absolutae*." The *commendatitiae* are those which are sent to someone known, either an abbot or a bishop, without the Greek letters; these are given to commoners. The *formatae* are sent to a known person also, but are sent identified with the Greek letters. The *absolutae* are sent not only to known persons but to abbots, bishops, and all the people generally.[93]

The distinction between the *commendatitiae* and the *formatae* was not always adhered to closely, even by Hildemar, for in the three illustrative letters which he gives, one is introduced under both names.[94] The Greek letters referred to formed a sort of code device designed to safeguard against forgery. In explanation of the code, Hildemar lifts bodily into his work a passage contained in many early collections of the canons. [95] It states that the three hundred eighteen Fathers assembled at Nicaea instituted the device for use in canonical letters to prevent fraud. The authenticity of this document itself, however, cannot be clearly established. In his study on the sources of canon law, F. Maassen finds this document in twelve collections of canons compiled before the middle of the ninth cen-

Neocaesarea as the basis of this passage, and then quotes Bishop Hosius in support of the same. The Council of Neocaesarea, however, drew up only fourteen canons; the quotation from Hosius constitutes the twenty-first canon of Sardica as given in the Pseudo-Isidore version (Hinschius ed., p. 269), and in that of Dionysius Exiguus (Mansi, III, 30). The text quoted by Hildemar conforms more closely to the latter. It is to be noted that this and all the other canons of Sardica refer to the clerical order. Hildemar has, therefore, made adaptation of a canon designed for the ecclesiastical rank, to the monastic order.

93 Hildemar, p. 561.

94 *Ibid.*, p. 564: "Incipit epistola, quae formata dicitur sive commendatitia." *Cf.* also E. Loening, *Geschichte des deutschen Kirchenrechts*, I, 143, n. 2.

95 Hildemar, p. 562.

tury. In many of them it is related to the version of Nicene
canons made by Bishop Atticus of Constantinople who died in
the year 425. In some it is related only by position; in others,
by a fabricated title. It is ascribed to him directly in only one,
the *Hispana,* which was compiled in the early seventh century.[96]
The earliest collection in which it is found, that of Freising,
is thought by Maassen to have been compiled in the early sixth
century; however, in this collection the document concerning
the *formatae* is given after the Council of Constantinople, a
fact for which Maassen has no explanation.[97] Hefele considers
it to possess no more historicity than the ninth-century " False
Decretals," since it was unknown in the earlier centuries.[98]
This view is substantiated by the fact that the extant *formatae*
employing the Greek letters date only from the eighth century
or later.[99]

The regulations of the Rule (c. 58) concerning the child oblate are now obsolete.[100] In the Carolingian period, however,
that institution functioned much the same as in the time of St.
Benedict. If the child's father were living he promised in the
name of his son the three vows of stability, conversion of
morals, and obedience. If the father were dead, the mother
might make the promise; no other relative, however, was permitted to do this. The ceremony in which the child was offered
to the monastery is described in the following manner:

After the reading of the Gospel [at Mass] and before the
Offertory is begun, the father will place in the right hand of his

96 For the date and authorship of the *Hispana,* see C. H. Lynch, *Saint
Braulio, Bishop of Saragossa,* pp. 147-148.

97 *Geschichte der Quellen und Literatur des canonischen Rechts,* I, 399-
403, 479.

98 *Histoire des conciles* (transl. by H. Leclercq), I, 527.

99 Zeumer has edited a number of *formatae* in *MGH, LL,* V, *Formulae
Merowingici et Karolini aevi,* 218-219, 383, 409, 557-568.

100 Canon law forbids the making of perpetual vows before the age of
twenty-one and until the religious has spent at least three years in temporary
vows (Delatte, *op. cit.,* p. 388).

son the oblation with the altar cloth, and in his left, the container of wine (*amula*).[101] Holding before him the child, he will wrap its hand in that cloth with which he makes the offering, for it is of this cloth the Rule speaks, not of the sacred covering of the altar. Then he will hold in his hand, the hand of his son wrapped in the cloth and the *petitio* whereby he will confirm his son in the monastery. In the presence of witnesses, the abbot will ask what he seeks; to this the father will respond: " I wish to offer my son to Almighty God to serve Him in this monastery; since thus in the Law the Lord hath ordered the sons of Israel to offer their sons to God. I desire in like manner to offer this my son." . . . Then he will lead his son to the place where men are accustomed to make their offerings. The priest will take from the child's hand held by the hand of the father the bread *(oblata)* and the wine (*amula*), and the abbot will receive the child and the *petitio*. [102]

The symbolism involved in this rite is explained by the commentators thus: " St. Benedict ordered the child to be offered with the oblation [of the Mass], so that through what is manifested exteriorly, there might be signified what is effected within, i. e., as the oblation is made a holocaust to the Lord, so also the child may become a holocaust to the Lord." [103]

It is evident from the general tenor of the account and from the references to the boy's future that the promise made by his parent was regarded as valid and final. His parents are to promise on oath that never by them or any other person will any property or any occasion be given him which will give rise to his leaving the monastery. Measures are to be taken that he shall never fall heir to his inheritance. If the parents so desire they may bestow it upon the monastery, reserving the usufruct to themselves.[104] Hildemar adds, moreover, that the father

101 The word " amula " had the same signification as " ampula," meaning " cruet "; *cf.* Du Cange, *s. v.* " ama, amula."

102 Paul, pp. 448-449; Hildemar, pp. 548-549.

103 *Loc. cit.*

104 Paul, pp. 449-450; Hildemar, p. 550. These prescriptions are based directly on the Rule, c. 58.

promises in the name of his child the three vows, just as those promise who come to the monastery at a legitimate age. With reference to the foreswearing of the child's future inheritance, he explains that, in itself, swearing is not to be sought for as something good, but, when done for the salvation of the boy's soul, which is something entirely good, it is permissible;[105] thus the parents, fearing for the boy's salvation, permit him no occasion of sin that he may not perish forever.[106]

Evidently the commentators regard the boy monk as the chief recipient of a benefaction, and take no cognizance of the fact that this arrangement deprives him of future liberty of choice. Herwegen opines that the child oblate, upon reaching his majority, was given an option in the matter of assuming the obligation of the monastic state.[107] This seems to have been true with reference to the monasticism of the East, particularly that of St. Basil.[108] In the West some councils made a like provision for boys vowed to the clerical state.[109] The monasticism of the West, however, appears not to have been so minded.[110] The Monastic Capitulary of 817 ambiguously states that when the oblate has reached the legitimate age he will confirm the *petitio* made by his parents at the altar in the presence of witnesses.[111]

---

105 The occasion of this remark was, doubtless, to reconcile the precept of taking an oath as contained in this the fifty-eighth chapter of the Rule, with the passage in the fourth chapter which forbids swearing. *Cf.* Hildemar, pp. 154-158.

106 Hildemar, pp. 551-552.

107 *St. Benedict, a Character Study,* pp. 77-78.

108 De Valous, *op. cit.,* p. 40; Delatte, *op. cit.,* p. 407.

109 Second Council of Toledo (527), can. 1 (Mansi, VIII, 785); Third Council of Vaison (529), can. 1 (Mansi, VIII, 726).

110 De Valous, *op. cit.,* pp. 41-44; Delatte, *op. cit.,* pp. 407, 410. For an extended account of the institution of the oblates, *cf.* U. Berlière, *La Familia dans les monastères bénédictins du moyen âge* (Brussels, 1931), in which the author notes (p. 65, n. 1) that his earlier article, "Les Oblats de Saint Benoît au moyen âge," *Revue bénédictine,* III (1886-87), 55-61, 107-111, 156-160, 209-220, 249-255, should be read with caution; and M. P. Deroux, *Les Origines d'oblature bénédictine* (Vienne, 1927).

111 *MGH, Cap. reg. Franc.* I, 346, no. 36.

Whether this provided the boy freedom to accept or reject the monastic state, or whether it signified a strengthening of his obligation—a renewal of vows, as it were—writers are not agreed. In general, other pertinent conciliar legislation seems to favor the latter view, although this evidence is not uniform in tenor.[112]

On the other hand, by a careful reading of the Statutes of Murbach (816), we obtain information which seems to justify the conclusion that the oblates were permitted to choose at some later date whether or not they would remain in the monastic state: " We who almost from our very cradles have been trained by our seniors have lived in this same arrangement . . .," and " Since it was left to our option to assume the discipline of the more religious life, . . ." [113] The test case of Gottschalk, oblate at Fulda, indicates a lack of defined and uniform thought in the ninth century regarding the binding power of the oblate's promise made by proxy.[114] In our commentaries, however, the institution of the child oblate, whether a carry-over from Biblical times, an application of the *patria potestas* of the Romans, or an instance of the medieval preference given the spiritual over things material, was accepted literally as outlined in the Rule.

From the general remark made by the commentators regarding the age at which the oblate may be accepted, it appears that the parents might offer a son at any age until he attains to majority: " He [St. Benedict] does not speak of him only who is beginning his eighth year, as a boy, but he calls him also a boy who cannot of himself profess the law under which his parents live." [115] The frequent use of the term " *infans* " leads

112 Council of Macon (583), can. 12 (Mansi, IX, 934); Fourth Council of Toledo (633), can. 49 (Mansi, X, 631); Tenth Council of Toledo (656) can. 6 (Mansi, XI, 36-37); Council of Worms (868), can. 22, 23 (Mansi, XV, 873). *Cf.* also Leclercq, " Oblat," *Dictionnaire d'archéologie chrétienne et de liturgie*, XII, 1857 ff., especially 1861-1862.

113 Albers, III, 82, 85.

114 Deroux, *op. cit.*, pp. 26-27.

115 Paul, p. 448; Hildemar, p. 548.

us to conclude that the commentators have in mind the offering of boys under the age of seven; elsewhere they specify that the Rule legislates not only for those boys who are under seven, but also for those above seven.[116] As to the conventional age periods they tell us that childhood extends to the seventh year, boyhood to the fourteenth year, adolescence to the twenty-eighth, youth to the fifty-sixth, old age to the seventy-sixth, and after that is decrepitude.[117]

Unlike the practice at Cluny,[118] the oblates about whom our commentators write passed through no formal novitiate. "If at the age of fifteen years his life accords with his age, the boy is to stand in choir and keep his rank among the rest." [119] One further caution is recommended, however, before the boy is removed from general oversight. If the youth is seen to be good and staid at fifteen so that it is no longer necessary for him to be under the *magistri,* he may leave their discipline and instead will be commended by the abbot to a particular brother of a good and holy life who will exercise supervision over him inasmuch as he will accompany the youth while engaged in reading, when he leaves the oratory, and on like occasions. If, after observing the conduct of the youth during the year following his release from general custody, the senior brother knows him to be solicitous and disinclined to vice, he is to report to the abbot who will then constitute this young member in the same status as that of the elders *(maiores).*[120] If at fifteen, however, his life has not been such that he may leave the general custody, he is not to take his rank in choir or in other places; even if he is twenty years of age, he shall remain under supervision until the abbot can have faith in him as in the other good brothers.[121]

116 Paul, p. 347; Hildemar, p. 420.
117 *Loc., cit.*
118 De Valous, *op. cit.,* pp. 29, 32.
119 Paul, p. 471; Hildemar, p. 581.
120 Paul, pp. 471, 472; Hildemar, pp. 581, 582.
121 Paul, p. 471; Hildemar, p. 581.

Thus we see that when the young monk transfers from the oblateship to that of competent membership in the community, no further ceremony or act of profession is customary. In saying that the youth is now entitled to his rank in choir or in other places, the commentators, doubtless, refer to that rank in the monastery which is his by reason of the time of his entry, as prescribed in the Rule (c. 63).

CHAPTER IV

DISCIPLINE WITHIN THE MONASTERY

IN discussing the subject of rank, the commentators offer some interesting explanations of the pertinent passages of the Rule. Commenting on the basic principle of equality contained in the Rule (c. 2), " We are all one in Christ, and we all bear an equal burden of servitude under one Lord," our glossators write that " God is equally the creator of us all, wherefore we ought equally to serve Him; for men have invented the condition of the slave." [1] Hildemar adds: " Likewise in accordance with the precept which commands us to love God with our whole heart and mind, we ought equally to love Him. As to the other service which is performed by works, we do not all render it equally, for some serve Him more, other less." [2]

In the passage of the Rule which reads, " Let not a freeborn be preferred to a freedman except there be some other reasonable cause," according to the commentators, the " reasonable cause " can be explained in two ways: the first, and that which is the more applicable here, is to understand that he who has been found to excel in good works and obedience—the only condition for which the Rule permits discernment of persons—may receive a preference; the second way, and one which is in accordance with the human way of thinking, is to consider him who possesses a talent or skill useful in the monastic functions, worthy of promotion—e. g., he who can sing, may be promoted in choir. In applying these two criteria, however, the following distinction should be made: the elevation for good works and obedience is to obtain in all places such as the refectory and the chapter; on the other hand, advancement for talent in singing, reading, language, or an art, should be granted only in those places where necessity compels. [3]

1 Paul, p. 65; Hildemar, p. 104.
2 *Loc. cit.*
3 Paul, p. 63; Hildemar, pp. 101-102.

Finally, to the words of the Rule (c. 2), " otherwise let them keep their own places," which follow the excepted cases, the commentators add: " For if the abbot shall have made a promotion for the sake of worldly honor or privilege, he is not of God, but of the world or the devil." [4]

According to Hildemar, the provost and major dean should have a place of preference; the minor deans and *circatores,* however, should not, " for it would not be reasonable that in the one year of their ministry they should be elevated, and in the following year when they are no longer in office, they should again sit in the lower place corresponding to the time of their entrance." [5]

In commenting on those passages of the Rule (c. 60, 61) wherein power is granted to the abbot to advance priests, clerics, or monks from other monasteries above the rank due to the time of their entrance, if he sees fit, both commentators give as the basis of the promotion, the merit of their lives, the degree of merit determining the position in the rank. [6] In this connection, Hildemar remarks that the number of priests in the monastery at the time of St. Benedict was few as compared with the number in his own time. [7] Additional evidence that the proportionate number of priests in the monasteries was steadily increasing is offered in the references to the various parts of the Divine Office which were sung by them. [8]

In his comments on the sixty-second chapter of the Rule which concerns the elevation of a monk to the priesthood, Hildemar exceeds the functions of a glossator. In describing who is worthy to fulfill the priestly office he employs the negative method of pointing out the obstacles which would wholly

4 Paul, p. 64; Hildemar, p. 103.

5 Page 576.

6 Paul, pp. 453, 454, 458; Hildemar, pp. 555-556, 559-560.

7 Pages 555-556.

8 Paul, pp. 260-261, 352, 355; Hildemar, pp. 321-323, 424, 428. There were over thirty priests in the monasteries of St. Riquier and of St. Denis in the early ninth century (Berlière, *L'Ascèse bénédictine,* p. 40).

debar a candidate, and also those blemishes of character which would render him less desirable. He enumerates violations of the Commandments, the fifth to the eighth inclusive. He who at any time of his life has been guilty of homicide, even though his life and doctrine have been exemplary since, may never be elevated to the priesthood. He who has sinned against chastity with a married or consecrated person, or who has been guilty of sodomy, is likewise ineligible. Sins of youth, if repented of and replaced by a life worthy of imitation, do not absolutely exclude one from Holy Orders; but only if there is a dearth of clerics, should such a one be promoted.[9] He who has been guilty of major theft, especially of things consecrated, is excluded from the altar, whereas one who has stolen only small things, and particularly if he has done so out of necessity, may be promoted (cum pavore). He who has violated his sworn word given at a responsible age, and especially if his motive was cupidity, is never to be ordained; likewise is he excluded who has borne false witness in a case in which another has thereby been punished or proscribed. On the other hand, if one has violated his sworn word given lightly and at a less responsible age, he may be promoted (cum pavore); likewise one who has borne false witness which did not result in another's being punished or proscribed, may be ordained, if in every way his subsequent life has been unspotted and exemplary.[10]

After this long list, Hildemar observes that if a monk has been trained under that custody which he has described earlier, there can be no doubt about his being worthy to be made a priest

9 Hildemar adds for this and other cases where those guilty of less grievous sins may be ordained, that they are to be raised to orders cum pavore. Just what he means is not clear. Perhaps it is merely to emphasize the need of great prudence in the matter.

10 Hildemar, p. 569; cf. also ibid., p. 350, and Paul, pp. 282-283. The above passage is introduced with the words: "Moreover the same master Hildemar has written also this concerning the subject"; the editor (n. 2) infers that the insertion was made by Hildemar's hearers, his scribe, or by him who has arranged his writings. The passage is not to be found in Paul's Expositio.

or deacon. If, however, the abbot should wish to ordain a brother who has not been reared under this custody, he is advised to consult the brother's confessor. The latter, in order to evade answering directly, will propose to speak to the candidate to learn whether or not he desires to be ordained. If the confessor knows him to be unworthy, he will try to dissuade him from the step. Should the candidate express his unwillingness to be ordained, the matter is closed by announcing the same to the abbot. If, however, he will not be persuaded in this way, the confessor will tell the abbot that he neither encourages nor discourages the promotion. Having received this non-committal report, the abbot will not proceed with the ordination, nor will he manifest the source of the information which has led to this decision. Instead, he will call the brethren for consultation, requesting that anyone who knows any reason why the brother under discussion should not be ordained will make it known within a given time. If, at the expiration of that time, no report has been made, he will solemnly " adjure and conjure " the brethren to manifest any cause which would prohibit the candidate from offering the Holy Sacrifice. If, even now, no one vouchsafes information, the abbot will confer with each brother individually regarding the demeanor of the candidate, and will be guided by the opinion of the majority, presuming that they are spiritually minded.[11]

In recommending that the advice of the confessor be sought, the commentator, through his zeal for the sanctity of the priesthood, has been led to infringe somewhat on the secrecy of the confessional, at least as it is now understood.[12] Although the ecclesiastical law requiring the inviolability of the seal was only gradually taking form in the period in which our commen-

11 Hildemar, pp. 570-571. Paul's treatment of this question (pp. 461-462) is much more brief, but as far as it goes, it agrees with Hildemar's.

12 Cf. Bertrand Kurtscheid, A History of the Seal of Confession (transl. by F. A. Marks, St. Louis, 1927), pp. 115-118, 192-243; P. Bernard, " Confession (Du concile de Latran au concile de Trente)," Dictionnaire de théologie catholique, III, 894-926, especially 923; B. Dolhagaray, " Confession (science acquise en)," ibid., 960-974.

taries were written,[13] theologians point out that the natural law as well as the divine law demands that the sins confessed by a penitent to a priest may not be betrayed.[14]

The commentator, in this case, has taken precautions that there be no specific revelation of a sin committed nor a public manifestation that recourse was had to the confessor; in his naïveté he felt, doubtless, that his suggestions were above criticism. It is quite possible that the case in point does not refer to sacramental confession and to what would be private penance; in the Carolingian period, public and private penances coexisted.[15] As we shall see, the space devoted to public penance by our commentators indicates that the earlier discipline was the prevailing and perhaps the only method visualized by them in the reconcilation of a sinner.

Their comments on confession, in the majority of cases, arise as glosses to passages in the Rule which allude to the subject. These passages refer not to sacramental confession, but are intended to supply a means of securing spiritual direction from the " abbot or senior brothers " or a means of penance and self-humiliation.[16] Our commentators seem to have the same viewpoint when they elaborate on these points of the Rule. They do not appear to have sacramental confession in mind. Thus in speaking of the satisfaction which the murmurer should make, Hildemar writes:

So, as I have said, it is uncertain whether he ought to make satisfaction, i. e., confess the fault, to God or to man; although it is uncertain, nevertheless it seems to me that he should make satisfaction by confession to man—to a spiritual brother, who, as

13 Kurtscheid, *op. cit.*, pp. 76 ff.

14 *Ibid.*, p. 2.

15 *Cf.* Amann, " Pénitence, la réforme carolingienne," *Dictionnaire de théologie catholique,* XII, 862-879.

16 B. Poschmann, *Die abendländische Kirchenbusse im Ausgang des christlichen Altertums,* pp. 230-233. Even here, as Kurtscheid points out (*op. cit.*, p. 77), St. Benedict provided for secrecy on the part of the one receiving the confidence.

the Rule says in the forty-sixth chapter, knows how to cure his own and others' wounds, not to expose and publish them.[17]

It is true that this and similar passages do not preclude the possibility of private penance. It may be significant to note that the only allusion to confession in which the confessor is specifically referred to as a priest is the one mentioned above in connection with the promotion of a candidate to the priesthood.

In general, no lines can be accurately drawn which will distinguish the teaching of the commentaries concerning external discipline, public penance, and the penal code.[18] For that reason it seems best to treat of these subjects conjointly. The few exceptions, i. e., disciplinary regulations not directly connected with penalties, will be noted first; most of these have to do with the monastic enclosure.

A monk may leave his monastery whenever sent on a mission or to lead a better life in another monastery or in the desert. Whether he leaves a place of bad observance to enter one of good observance, or whether he exchanges one of good observance for one of more zealous observance, he is in either case subjecting himself the more to the Rule.[19]

As for the unfaithful monk who has not profited by monastic discipline and who wishes to depart, he should not be held against his will; moreover, if he does not make amends for his infidelities through the various steps of correction, even though

---

17 Hildemar, p. 198. Other instances might be cited: Paul, pp. 110, 124-125, 172-174; Hildemar, pp. 171, 189, 244-245. The references in Paul (p. 388) and in Hildemar (pp. 472, 473) concern the public acknowledgment of external faults as prescribed in the Rule, c. 46.

18 Perhaps a word of explanation is necessary to distinguish between public penance and the penal code as here used. By the former is understood the penances imposed by canonical authority and performed by the penitent preliminary to receiving the forgiveness of grave sin. By the latter, is understood the various penalties which were imposed on transgressors of monastic customs and regulations. Thus we shall see that expulsion is the final penalty inflicted on him who, even for lesser faults, fails to amend in the earlier steps of correction.

19 Hildemar, pp. 543-544. Paul's account (pp. 445-446) is more brief.

he be unwilling to depart, he should be expelled.[20] If, however, he has been reared in the monastery and later wishes to enter a less worthy manner of life, and the abbot has learned that such is the case, he is not to be expelled so that he can live a worse life; instead he should be put in prison, to be kept there until such time as he shall wish to remain in the monastery and accept its discipline—even till death.[21] To vindicate this view, the following explanation is given:

That one of such evil intent should be cast in prison, St. Benedict has manifested in the twenty-seventh chapter of his Rule wherein he says: " The abbot must exert the utmost care, and strive with all prudence and zeal that none of the flock entrusted to him perish." Is it not better that he who has been reared according to what is right and good from his infancy, be put in prison for the salvation of his soul, than that, after his good rearing, he be lost (as the Rule forbids) by being dismissed to enter upon an evil life in the world? [22]

This explanation is not wholly satisfactory, for there is no evidence that St. Benedict did not intend this same principle to be equally applicable to him who entered the monastery as an adult. Perhaps we are to infer that in the thought of Hildemar, the monastery, and the abbot in particular, has assumed a greater responsibility in accepting the child oblate than in admitting the adult layman. However this may be, the underlying idea cannot fail of observation, namely, that the spiritual welfare of the monk supersedes all else that may be desired— certainly the liberty to choose evil or a lesser good. Viewing the situation from our present perspective, we might not agree with the commentator that a forced subjection to a way of life, even though this way of life is good in itself, will always be conducive to one's spiritual welfare.

It is customary, the commentators tell us, that the monks sent on a journey return, if possible, in time for the last

20 Paul, p. 300; Hildemar, p. 364.

21 Paul, pp. 69, 299, 513-514; Hildemar, pp. 109, 363, 627-628.

22 Hildemar, p. 628.

canonical hour, Compline, at the latest. Should they arrive after this hour, they were excluded from the monastic enclosure for the night, and were expected to go to a lodging which the monastery had in another place if possible. If this, too, could not be, then they were to remain at the gate of the monastery where food and beds would be prepared for them as for guests.[23]

If sent on a short trip from which they were expected to return on the same day, the monks were not permitted, according to the Rule (c. 51), to eat outside unless commanded by the abbot to do so. Hildemar enumerates three conditions, for any one of which the abbot should permit his monk to eat outside: if the friend who invites him is of a religious character, such that they will eat in a becoming manner, with reading, and in the fear of God; if there is danger of offending a man of power, who, through indignation at his invitation being declined, might bring injury or severe loss on the monastery; finally, if there is necessity in that the monk would otherwise be without food or a place in which to eat.[24] The second of these conditions, especially if unaccompanied by the first, appears to be a concession somewhat out of harmony with the general tone of the Rule. It is one of several indications that the monks of the eighth century entertained a spirit of subserviency toward the powerful nobles for fear of injury or loss.[25]

It was considered by our commentators wholly improper for a monk to go to a court of justice *(placitum)* in order to plead a case there.[26] Several contemporary councils and capitularies likewise forbade monks to enter or dispute in secular courts.[27]

In discussing the Rule relative to the penal code, the commentators begin with a classification of transgressions. To dis-

23 Paul, p. 497; Hildemar, p. 611.

24 Hildemar, p. 497. Paul's account (p. 409) is less extended.

25 *Cf. infra,* p. 149.

26 Paul, p. 105; Hildemar, p. 152.

27 *MGH, LL,* III, *Concilia aevi Karolini,* I, i, 256 (no. 29), 276 (no. 11); *Cap. reg. Franc.,* I, 60 (no. 73), 75 (no. 11).

tinguish further the faults designated in the Rule (c. 24) as
lighter from those designated as graver (c. 25), they explain
that the lighter faults are those which refer primarily to the
mind or spirit, such as contumacy, disobedience, and pride, and
are called, therefore, spiritual sins; the grave faults are those
which refer chiefly to the body or things material, such as
theft, adultery, and intoxication, and are called carnal sins.[28]

At this point, Hildemar introduces, without indicating his
source, a passage in which a four-fold classification is twice
enumerated, special emphasis being placed on different classes
each time.[29] Of the four classes of faults, the second and fourth
correspond to the two-fold division of spiritual and corporal
sins—the latter being denominated as " criminal sins." The first
class consists of minor breaches of discipline for which the
degree of atonement is left to the judgment of the abbot by
the Rule *(passim)*; the third consists of external failings for
which the Rule (c. 46) prescribes public acknowledgment. As
a separate survey of the various penances prescribed throughout the Rule, this summary serves a useful purpose; when inserted at this point of the commentary, however, its worth is
greatly diminished. Not only is it repetitious, but it may tend
to confuse the reader who is not familiar with the Rule.

Beyond this passage, the commentators adhere generally to
the two-fold classification, occasionally designating the graver
sins as " mortal " or "criminal." They realize, however, that
such a hard and fast distinction cannot be wholly satisfactory

28 Paul, pp. 276-277, 279-280; Hildemar, pp. 338-339, 348. This classification is, of course, basically unsatisfactory. Objectively considered, an offense
is mortal or venial depending on its degree of gravity.

29 Hildemar, pp. 339-343. This account has been published under the title,
" Excerptus diversarum modus poenitentiarum a Benedicto Abbate [Ani-
anensis] distinctus de Regula S. Benedicti abbatis," by Baluze (*Capitulum
Regum Francorum,* II, 1385-1387, from which it is reprinted in *PL,* 103,
col. 1417-1418) and by Albers, III, 145-149; Seebass (*Realencyklopädie,*
3d ed., II, 575) and Traube (*Textgeschichte,* pp. 49, 69) have accepted it as
authentic. In embodying this tract in his work, Hildemar made slight changes
and additions, just as he did generally, in revising Paul Warnefrid's
Expositio.

since motives, dispositions, and circumstances are involved; thus they recommend that the character of the offender be considered, his motives weighed, and the gravity of the offense investigated by him who metes out the penalties.[30]

It is the abbot's duty, they observe, to discern whether a fault be light or grave; it is not in his jurisdiction, however, to decide what the respective penalties for these faults shall be, for that has already been specified in the Rule.[31] Nevertheless, within each class, all sins are not to be rated equally; the abbot should prudently weigh their gravity, for, " although the more serious faults are called ' grave,' when balanced one with another, all are not found to be equally grave ";[32] likewise " the spiritual sins which are also called ' light,' are not all to be weighed by the same balance, because some among them are light, others are grave, and still others are graver." [33] The degree of gravity of the lighter faults should condition the manner in which the offending brother is to pass through the various steps *(gradus)* of correction.[34]

The " steps of correction " constitute, according to the commentaries, the " discipline of the Rule " *(disciplina regularis),* or the " regular discipline." [35] This consists of a graduated series of seven stages of correction through which the transgressor of monastic discipline is to pass, i. e., if he does not amend through the first means, the second will be applied,

30 Paul, pp. 223-224, 282-283, 285; Hildemar, pp. 288-289, 342, 343-344.

31 Paul, p. 279; Hildemar, p. 347. Evidently the lists of lesser and grave faults given by Hildemar (pp. 345, 346-347) were not considered definitive, but were compiled by him more or less arbitrarily. The resemblance they bear to the lists given in Isidore's monastic Rule *(PL,* 83, cols. 885-886) leaves no room for doubt that he had the latter before him in making the compilation. Poschmann observes *(op. cit.,* pp. 9, 82-83) that in the earlier practices the boundary between some of the lesser and greater sins was ' *fliessend*," and that the classification given to some sins then, would not be accepted today.

32 Hildemar, p. 345.

33 *Ibid.,* p. 344.

34 *Ibid., loc. cit.; cf.* also *infra,* p. 95.

35 Paul, pp. 90, 320, 499; Hildemar, pp. 136, 328, 387, 613, 622.

and so on to the end of the series. As enumerated by Paul Warnefrid, the several steps are: secret admonition, public correction, excommunication, severe fasts, corporal punishment, prayer, and expulsion.[36]

These seven methods of discipline have been culled from four several chapters of the Rule (23, 24, 28, 30), and in the passage just cited, have been expressed in ten words. The series is frequently repeated in the course of the commentaries, and is more frequently alluded to as the " seven steps," or, as it often occurs that the reference is to the penalties this side of expulsion, as the " six steps." It forms, as it were, a code of penal discipline—a convenient summary of penal procedure extracted from the Rule. It is contained in Benedict of Aniane's " Excerpted Methods of Penance," [37] and a similar series is introduced in an eighth-century " Ordo regularis " as the " seven methods of penance which they call regular." [38] Thus it appears that this penal code, although originating in the Rule, enjoyed a tradition distinct from that of the Rule.[39]

In the practical application of the code, the commentators offer some noteworthy information. The secret admonition is in order only if the fault has been secret; if the fault was public, the admonition should likewise be public. Admonition is secret even if delivered in the presence of as many as four' or five brothers; for a correction to be public, it must be administered before the whole brotherhood or such number as is accustomed

36 Paul, p. 296; the corresponding passage in Hildemar (p. 361) is expanded with elaborations which will be discussed later.

37 Cf. supra, p. 90.

38 Albers, III, 17. This document, according to the date ascribed to it by Albers, antedates Warnefrid's commentary by a decade or two. In the series of penances given in the former, the lesser and greater excommunication each constitute a " step " and corporal punishment forms but one; in the latter, excommunication constitutes but one " step " and corporal punishment is divided into two: severe fasts and flagellation.

39 In this connection it is interesting to note that Herwegen would ascribe to the penal code a tradition anterior to the Rule itself (St. Benedict: A Character Study, p. 87).

to assemble in chapter, the refectory, or oratory.[40] In general, it is expressed or implied that the secret admonition be given twice,[41] although the principle is stated that an offender should remain in one stage of correction so long as it proves profitable to him.[42] Public correction seems always to have been delivered but once to an individual for one fault.

The excommunication for lighter faults as prescribed in the Rule (c. 24) deprives the offender of participation at the common table and of taking a leading part in the Divine Office. Hildemar points out that the latter stipulation implies that the excommunicate is not to sing Mass if a priest, nor to make an offering if a monk.[43] Both commentators observe that, unlike the major excommunication, this separation does not deprive the penitent of his rank nor diminish his allowance of food; and that the "due satisfaction" which the Rule calls for should be the same as that which it specifies elsewhere, namely, "when the brothers kneel at the litany, the excommunicated brother will go to the place which the abbot has appointed and there lie prostrate until the Office is completed." [44]

The severe fasts can be executed in two ways: either a diminished portion of food and drink is received at the times at which others eat, or the same quantity of food which others eat is received at intervals prolonged to the second or third day.[45] In diminishing the quantity, there is a difference of opinion as to the proportions to which the food should be reduced: "Many understand a severe fast to consist in eating only one-half *libra* of bread with one measure of water in winter; in summer, the same quantity of bread with two measures of water. There are others, again, who understand

40 Paul, pp. 90-91, 267; Hildemar, pp. 136, 329, 338.

41 Paul, p. 267; Hildemar, p. 329, *et passim.* The Rule (c. 2, 23) calls for two secret admonitions.

42 Paul, pp. 296, 298; Hildemar, pp. 342, 361, 362.

43 Hildemar, p. 348. *Cf.* also Paul, p. 280.

44 Paul, p. 280; Hildemar, *loc. cit.*

45 Hildemar, p. 370.

that only a fourth *libra* of bread, and water as above, are permitted. These latter, however, do not discern well."[46]

No details concerning the administering of corporal punishment are given, but it is frequently observed by the commentators that the chastisement of the rod is not beneficial to all characters, nay, rather, some are made the worse for it; since even St. Benedict made this distinction, saying that the offender should be coerced either with severe fasts or sharp blows, those characters whom the abbot knows will not profit by the rod are to endure fasts instead.[47] In support of this principle it is noted furthermore that the corporal chastisement prescribed in the Rule (c. 23, 44) consists in either severe fasts or flagellation.[48]

The final and seventh step in the correction of lighter faults is expulsion. The brother who has passed through the six preceding stages of correction without amendment is considered " incorrigible," and as such, is subject to expulsion.[49] This step was not looked upon as final, however, in the sense that there was no possibility for the offender to return. On the contrary, expulsion seemed to be merely another way of bringing him to repentance; his return was not only expected but encouraged. The stipulation of the Rule (c. 29) that a brother who has been received again must take the last place, still obtained.[50]

If, after his return, he shall have fallen into the same fault for which he was expelled or another lesser fault, he shall again be admonished in secret, as if he had newly come to the monastery.[51] The fact that the offender has submitted to the

---

46 Paul, p. 307; Hildemar, p. 372.

47 Paul, pp. 280, 306-307; Hildemar, pp. 117, 341-342, 349, 361, 371-372.

48 Paul, pp. 267-277, 306; Hildemar, pp. 330, 339, 371.

49 Paul, pp. 73-74; Hildemar, pp. 115-116, 341.

50 Paul, pp. 74, 87; Hildemar, pp. 115, 130. That an expelled member may return accords neither with the original text of the Rule (see *infra*, pp. 103-106) nor with current legislation.

51 Paul, p. 74; Hildemar, pp. 116, 341.

humiliation of expulsion and of occupying the last place upon readmission is taken as evidence of his repentance; his stigma of " incorrigibility " is thereby removed. Likewise will he who has relapsed into a fault, for which he had amended at any of the six stages, be returned to the first step, if there has been a considerable interval—a year or even six months—between the two offenses.[52] Otherwise, as stated earlier, a repeated fall into the same fault would lead the offender into the successive stage of correction. Although only lesser sins are concerned, the degree of their gravity should determine the length of time during which an offender is to be detained in each step:

The lighter the fault appears to be, the longer is he to delay in each step; the graver the fault, the more quickly is he to pass to the next step, noting the custom of physicians who, although they give out various medicines and potions to the infirm, do not quickly prescribe a second medicine so long as they have not learned that the first cannot help, or that the illness itself has not become dangerous.[53]

The question is raised as to whether or not a monk who has been ordained should be submitted to the " steps of correction," particularly that of flagellation. From the various opinions cited, it is evident that the procedure was not clearly defined in practice. Hildemar notes, too, that the wording of the Rule (c. 62) on this point admits of various interpretations.[54] Those who understand that a priest ought not to be punished corporally or excommunicated are thought to be influenced by reverence for the canons and by that precept of the Rule which orders that appeal be made to the bishop if frequent admonitions are of no avail; then, according to this group of thinkers, if the offender be deposed, he should be punished with the rod or excommunicated.[55] Numerous conciliar and papal de-

---

52 *Ibid., loc. cit.*

53 Paul, p. 296; Hildemar, pp. 344-345, 362.

54 Hildemar, pp. 572-573.

55 *Ibid.*, p. 572.

crees had declared that the clergy were not subject to public penances, but to deposition instead;[56] that is, of course, with reference to grave offenses. The commentators, however, are speaking of the "regular discipline" which they relate to the lesser faults only. The question, therefore, is not so much one of canonical authority as of monastic discipline.

The conclusion arrived at by the commentators is that the monk in Orders should be corrected by the same methods as are applied to the other monks, with the additional "appeal to the bishop" before expulsion. Regarding flagellation in particular, the same principle, which was enunciated for the others should likewise be followed: the character of each person should determine whether or not corporal punishment should be administered, "for the abbot should apply a remedy, not inflict a wound on his monks." [57]

Unlike the several degrees of correction through which the monk who commits lesser faults must pass, there is but "one step" for him who is guilty of grave fault.[58] Such a one "is not to be first admonished either secretly or publicly, but is to be excommunicated at once." [59] If he does not atone by sub-

56 Amann, *loc. cit.*, cols. 803, 832; Poschmann, *op. cit.*, pp. 172-203. In place of the many pertinent canons from which he might have selected, Hildemar (p. 553) cites a decree ascribed to Pope Sylvester, who died in the year 335, which rules that forty-four witnesses are necessary to condemn a priest. Although he does not consider it practical for his time, he gives it as an illustration of the canons for reverence of which some would not subject a priest to corporal punishment. This particular canon is ill-chosen because it concerns not the penalty but the accusation; furthermore it is taken either from the "Excerpted acts of St. Sylvester" as given in the Pseudo-Isidorian Decretals (Hinschius ed., p. 449) or from the spurious document from which these *gesta* were compiled, namely, the *Constitutio Sylvestri,* which gives the canons of the pretended Second Council of Rome in the year 324 (Mansi, II, 615). This document was probably forged in the sixth century; in any case it is found in almost all the collections of councils, and scholars are unanimous in considering it spurious: *Cf.* Hefele-Leclercq, *Histoire des conciles,* I, 407 (n. 2), 627-628.

57 Paul, pp. 453, 462-463; Hildemar, pp. 553-555; 571-574.

58 Hildemar, p. 353.

59 Paul, p. 285; Hildemar, p. 352.

mitting to the penalty, he is subject to expulsion.[60] The penalty according to the Rule (c. 25, 44), is exclusion from the oratory and the common table. When the brothers assemble to recite the Hours of the Divine Office, the excommunicated brother will remain prostrate at the entrance until the abbot receives him back into the choir. There he will occupy the place appointed to him, and at the end of each of the Hours he will prostrate himself until bidden by the abbot to cease from this penance. In the meantime he will take his meals alone, and at the hour and in the measure appointed by the abbot.

To these regulations the commentators add that the penitent should be required to make satisfaction in the oratory only a few days if he has been held in custody for many days; and if he has been held in custody only a few days, he should do penance in the oratory for a longer time.[61] The words " held in custody " indicate that he was held under some kind of surveillance during the period of expulsion from the oratory. In another passage it is recommended that a character under excommunication whom the abbot cannot trust should be imprisoned and secured with chains lest he flee. This measure is justified by the words of the Rule (c. 27), " the abbot should exert the utmost prudence and zeal lest any of the flock entrusted to him perish "; according to the commentators, this precept is equivalent to saying that the abbot should hasten with all speed, and use any device which can be thought out, to save each soul entrusted to him.[62]

That it was customary in the monasteries of the period to set aside a place in which to confine the unruly is evident from the Monastic Capitulary of 817. It requires that such place be provided with heat in the winter time and that an atrium be near in which the occupants may work when so ordered.[63]

60 Hildemar, p. 360.

61 Paul, p. 384; Hildemar, p. 467.

62 Paul, p. 293; Hildemar, p. 358.

63 *MGH, Cap. reg. Franc.*, I, 346, can. 40. *Cf.* also the eighteenth article of the Statutes of Murbach (Albers, III, 88).

The commentators staunchly defend that precept of the Rule which forbids the brothers to speak with the excommunicated. They explain that although many would not have an evil intention in speaking with him, St. Benedict did not act harshly in making the command absolute; only, it requires a discreet " doctor " to apply the rule. Thus if one did not know that the brother to whom he spoke was excommunicated, he is free from fault, and consequently, from all penance. If he did not know that the Rule forbade such conversation, he is likewise free, but the master who should have taught him this as a novice will assume the penance. If his purpose were to exhort the erring to satisfaction by humility, he must undergo excommunication, but, due to his good zeal, the term of his penalty should be reduced to two or three days. Finally, if his motive were evil—either to encourage the offender to remain steadfast in his error, or even to flee, and he offered the means— such a one should undergo the same penalty of excommunication as the brother to whom he spoke.[64]

Hildemar offers two reasons why no one should speak with the excommunicated. The first is to inculcate fear lest another should dare to sin in like manner; the second, lest those of evil intent who are wont more to pervert sinners than to lead them to humility, should take the occasion granted to the good to speak with the offender.[65]

Notwithstanding the prohibition against speaking with the excommunicated, the Rule (c. 27) prescribes that the abbot, in his concern for the offending brother, send in secretly, as it were, wise consolers to mitigate his sorrow and to lead him to make satisfaction. The commentators suggest that, if he be capable, the cellarer, who also gives the excommunicate his meals, perform this service with the abbot's knowledge and sanction.[66]

---

64 Paul, pp. 287-288 ; Hildemar, pp. 354-355.
65 Page 355.
66 Paul, pp. 285, 292 ; Hildemar, pp. 352, 357.

A still further and final solicitude for the separated brother is manifested in the following quotation which is not given by way of a gloss to the Rule:

The abbot should have great concern lest it happen that a brother under excommunication die before he be reconciled; because if he should die first, which God forbid, according to canonical authority the Sacrifice [of the Mass] should not be offered for him . . . Therefore, as I have said, if the abbot knows the brother is about to die, he should be very eager to have him reconciled first and receive the Body and Blood of our Lord Jesus Christ, because no sinner ought to depart this life without the Viaticum.[67]

This passage indicates that the monastic greater excommunication was considered equal to the ecclesiastical excommunication. Twice in his chapter on grave faults Hildemar relates the two disciplines. He states that the chapter of the Rule (c. 25) entitled "On Graver Faults" has a common origin with "the sacred canons which separate a man from the Church";[68] and again: "It should be understood that this chapter is derived from the canonical authority." He then compares the leprosy which in the Old Testament excluded one from the camps, with the grave sins which now exclude one from the Church.[69]

Writers are not agreed as to the power of the monastic excommunication. Spreitzenhofer thinks it was certainly an imitation of ecclesiastical discipline without being wholly identical with it in weight or importance. He notes that Martène and Calmet take the contrary view in their commentaries, but he considers them unsuccessful in overcoming the objections of their opponents.[70] Delatte, however, agrees with these

---

67 Hildemar, p. 360.

68 *Ibid.*, p. 350.

69 *Ibid.*, p. 352.

70 *Die historischen Voraussetzungen der Regel des heil. Benedikt von Nursia*, p. 39.

commentators that the abbot had sufficient authority to pronounce a sentence of excommunication; he sees it as an exercise of the power of jurisdiction, not of Orders. He concludes
that the effects of the monastic excommunication were identical
with those of the Church's excommunication.[71] Viewing this
controversial question in the light thrown on it by our commentaries, we must accept the second opinion for the Carolingian
period.[72]

Hildemar evidences particular interest in the canonical
aspects of excommunication with relation to the individual.
Thus he offers the following instructions to the official who
administers the penalty of excommunication:

It is necessary to weigh carefully the character of the person
and his fault. Although the Rule seems to order him who has
been guilty of grave fault to do penance by being excluded from
the oratory, the refectory, and the fellowship of the brethren,
nevertheless a discreet and prudent " doctor " ought to distinguish between the person whom public penance will hinder from
attaining to Holy Orders and whom it will not. If the grave fault
is such that, according to canonical authority, one may not ap-
proach to the clerical rank, then anyone whether lettered or unlet-
tered, learned or unlearned, who is held guilty of a fault of this
kind, should be sentenced accordingly; if, however, a person commit a grave fault such that the canons do not prohibit him from
entering the clerical order, . . . he ought not, for this sin, perform a public penance which pertains to the aforementioned
canonical authority. Now it is of canonical authority that he who
has performed public penance may not become a priest or a
deacon; and if after his elevation to such rank, he performs public
penance, he is to be deposed.[73] That penance which a monk

71 Delatte, op. cit., p. 212.

72 For the abbatial authority as currently understood, see the legal explanation given by Heinrich Suso Mayer in Benediktinisches Ordensrecht, II, i,
164 ff.

73 E. Loening (Geschichte des deutschen Kirchenrechts, I, 132 ff.) cites
a number of councils beginning with the Synod of Elvira in 306, and a
number of papal decrees beginning with that of Pope Siricius in 385, which
either implicitly or expressly forbid one who has done public penance to
perform the office of a priest or deacon.

endures alone in sorrow, excluded from the oratory, refectory, and the comradeship of all the brothers is a public penance.[74]

Here we have, in no ambiguous terms, the commentator's opinion regarding the gravity of monastic excommunication and its relation to the public penances still in vogue. In order to distinguish between him who sins lightly and him whose sin is classified as grave, but is such as would not be an impediment to ordination, the commentator creates a sort of borderline state and corresponding penance. Such an offender is to be held under judgment of lesser fault, yet more gravely than if he had committed a light fault, " lest one who is eligible to promotion be impeded from elevation in the holy Church through an ill-considered judgment." [75]

The need for this arrangement seems to have arisen out of the situation which was created by the criteria used in classifying sins, namely, the spiritual or corporal nature of the fault. It is probable, too, that a fault committed by a monk was considered grave more readily than the same offense committed by a layman, due to the greater obligations which the former had assumed in "promising the Rule"; for example, the commentators observe that the bald transgression of the precept not to eat before the appointed hour, [76] or the abuse of monastic property is, *prima facie,* a criminal sin.[77] Modifying circumcumstances must therefore be reckoned in determining what the proper penance shall be.

From the general presentation of these views as expressed by the commentators, the relation between monastic and canonical penances is made to stand out in clearer form, at least for the period under consideration. Whether or not the commentators are justified in making the "regular discipline" consist in the penalties inflicted for light faults, to the exclusion of those for grave faults, is a question. The fact is that such is

74 Hildemar, pp. 346, 352-353; *cf.* also Paul, p. 285.
75 Hildemar, p. 346.
76 Paul, p. 282; Hildemar, p. 350; *Regula,* c. 43.
77 Hildemar, p. 353; *Regula,* c. 31.

their disposition of the matter. Thus the correction of lesser faults is proper to monastic jurisdiction; when it is a question of grave faults, however, the proper penance is that dictated by canonical authority. In this way only can we understand Hildemar's comment relative to that chapter (44) of the Rule which explains how satisfaction is made for grave faults. He remarks that " it was not necessary for him [St. Benedict] to describe how satisfaction is made for grave faults, but because he was about to speak of satisfaction for light faults, he discussed also the satisfaction for grave faults." [78] Furthermore, in the summary of penances compiled by Benedict of Aniane and incorporated by Hildemar in his commentary,[79] it is stated that capital crimes can be purged in no other way than by corporal penance according to the canonical authority.[80] Thus Poschmann's theory, that the penances contained in Cassian's *Institutes* for monks and in Isidore's monastic *Rule* were merely monastic penances distinct from the truly canonical penances, seems applicable only to those penalties which our commentators regard as constituting the " regular discipline." In fine, the conclusion seems to be that in the monasticism depicted in our commentaries, the ecclesiastical penances obtained for grave faults; and, over and above these, quasi-public penances even for lesser faults were performed as an integral part of the monastic observance.

The foregoing analysis of the penal discipline presents the main currents of the system as contained in the commentaries. There are further minutiae scattered throughout the *Expositio* which concern such minor breaches of discipline as tardiness in coming to prayer or to meals, misuse of monastic tools, and errors made in reciting the Office;[81] and again penances are adjudged on the basis of the intention and degree of volition

78 Page 467.

79 *Cf. supra.*, p. 29.

80 Hildemar, p. 343.

81 Paul, pp. 265-266, 320, 326, 377, 379, 386, 388, 490; Hildemar, pp. 327-328, 387, 393, 458, 462, 469, 470-471, 472, 474, 603.

which modify the gravity of the fault committed.[82] All of these and like details might well find a place in a specialized treatise on monastic penance, but they seem superfluous for the present study.

A final point which has considerable bearing on the constitutional aspect of Carolingian monasticism is the readmission of a monk who has been expelled or who has left the monastery on his own initiative. The subject has been touched on as the " seventh step " in the correction of lighter faults.[83]

Before presenting the commentator's interpretation, it is necessary not only to state the provision of the Rule (c. 29) on this subject, but particularly to point out the interpolation which had entered the text of the Rule in general use when our commentaries were written.[84]

The original text of the Rule provides that if a monk who has left the monastery through his own fault wishes to return, he may be received in the last place, if he promises to make full amendment for the cause for which he left; should he leave again, he may be readmitted even to a third time, " knowing that after this every means of return will be denied him." [85] Delatte sees in the phrase " through his own fault," a distinction between the departure of a monk for a cause such as

---

82 Paul, pp. 223-224, 274, 382, 388; Hildemar, pp. 288-289, 336, 349, 465, 473.

83 Cf. supra, p. 94.

84 After much research and writing, scholars are reaching accord on the history of the text of the Rule. The standard history is that by Traube frequently cited in this study. Dom Butler offers an excellent summary of the manuscript tradition as the Prolegomena to his edition of the Rule. Brief accounts in English may be read in his article, " The Cassinese Manuscripts of the Rule," Casinensia, I, 124-127, and in his Benedictine Monachism, pp. 170-177. The most recent account of the subject is given by Justin McCann, in St. Benedict (New York, 1937), pp. 117-129.

85 Regula, c. 29: "Frater qui proprio vitio egreditur de monasterio, si reverti voluerit, spondeat prius omnem emendationem, pro quo egressus est, et sic in ultimo gradu recipiatur, ut ex hoc eius humilitas conprobetur. Quod si denuo exierit, usque tertio ita recipiatur iam postea sciens omnem sibi reversionis aditum denegari" (ed. B. Linderbauer in Florilegium patristicum, 1928).

instability and a departure which is sanctioned by his abbot or the Church.[86] From this reading of the text, it seems to follow, by implication, that the way is not open to an expelled monk to be received again; such is Herwegen's view of the question, and it accords with the present canonical legislation on the subject.[87]

The version of the text used by the commentators, called the "*textus receptus*," contains an interpolation which extends the privilege of return also to an expelled monk—"a brother who has left through his own fault or has been expelled . . ."[88] Perhaps this phrase was inserted when the expulsion for light faults came to be looked upon, not as final, but as one of a series of corrections after which the offender was expected to return.[89] However this may be, the interpolated version created a need for some means whereby a character wholly undesirable could be refused readmission on grounds other than what might appear arbitrary to the one being rejected. To satisfy this need, the commentators build up an interpretation, far-fetched, it is true, yet more in keeping with the spirit of the original text than the interpolated version. In the phrase, "if one leave because of his own fault," they place special emphasis on the words, "his own," thereby inferring that one whose sin is such that others are involved, whether it be a lesser fault such as detraction, or grave, such as sodomy, is to be denied readmission, lest, as the Rule states elsewhere, "one diseased sheep contaminate the whole flock."[90] On the other hand, one who commits sin alone, such as pride, among the lesser faults, and theft, among the graver, is not for this to be refused readmission.[91]

86 Delatte, *op. cit.,* p. 228.

87 Herwegen, *St. Benedict,* pp. 94-96. *Cf.* also J. McCann, *The Rule of St. Benedict,* p. 123.

88 "Frater, qui proprio vitio egreditur aut projicitur de monasterio . . ." (*cf.* Hildemar, p. 364).

89 *Cf. supra,* p. 94.

90 This quotation occurs in the twenty-eighth chapter of the Rule where it is used to justify expulsion in general for the incorrigible.

91 Paul, p. 302; Hildemar, pp. 365-366, 368-369.

Hildemar permits one exception to the rule just outlined. Should the abbot, through mercy, desire to readmit one whose sin was not restricted to himself, he may make the following proposal to the monk petitioning entrance. If the monk will agree to remain in an isolated place from which he cannot influence others to sin, he will be readmitted. Should the monk accept these terms, the abbot may receive him and keep him in seclusion until he can have perfect faith in him.[92]

The clause of the Rule which provides that the departing monk may be received even to the third time, is addressed, the commentators explain, not to the abbot nor to one asking information, but to the fleeing monk;[93] they would reproduce the intention of St. Benedict in the following manner:

I restrict and I place a limit on the fleeing brother so that he may know how many times he may be received. The abbot, however, I bind by no such law nor do I set up a limit for him; I leave him free in mercy because he ought to take the place of Christ. I limit the one who leaves so that when not received after the third time he may not complain against the abbot for not receiving him even after the third time. Therefore, I give this command that he may know that every means of return will be denied him, lest he disturb the monastery by his frequent coming and going. But the abbot I constitute free in mercy so that as often as a brother may wish to come, the abbot may receive him; for God, whose place he takes, does not judge according to the past nor the future, but according as each one is.[94]

In permitting the abbot to receive a monk even more than three times, and in extending the privilege of return to an ex-

92 Pages 368-369.

93 In this passage the monk is described as "fleeing"; several other passages in the same chapter refer to him "who has left or has been expelled"; on page 304, Paul speaks of him who has been expelled. Evidently there was no intention to distinguish.

94 Hildemar, pp. 367-368. By mistaking "*praescientia*" for "*praesentia*," the scribe who copied Paul's account (p. 304) gives "the present" for "the [fore-knowledge of the] future."

pelled monk, the commentators were influenced, doubtless, by traditional practice; in the second case, certainly, the custom had become so well established that it had found its way into the text of the Rule as noted above.

As to the stipulation of the Rule that the readmitted monk must make full reparation for the fault for which he left, and then take the last place, it is explained that the returning monk must first perform the penance to which he was subject when he left or was expelled, and then occupy the last place in rank. The objection that the penance is not necessary because it suffices to take the lowest place, is declared to be highly ridiculous *(valde stultus)*; for if the monk is readmitted without the penance, it is as if the flight itself were the penance, whereas he has entered the world and perchance committed another sin there. Therefore, the returning monk must first perform the the penance which he was obliged to undergo before he departed, and then occupy the lowest rank; thus by the penance he will make satisfaction to God, and by taking the last place, he will give evidence of his humility to the brothers.[95]

In concluding the discussion, Hildemar observes that all do not so keenly understand and discern between the fault which is common to several or limited to one; thus they readmit to the third time all who return, without discrimination. Furthermore, those received a second or third time are not held responsible for the penance which they deserved on leaving. He notes that this is particularly true of many monasteries among the Franks; as for himself, he disposes, and exhorts others to dispose, according to the better way which he has just described.[96]

[95] Hildemar, pp. 366-367. Paul (p. 304) specifies that the monk who has left for a lesser fault, need not, upon readmission, perform the penance, for the demotion is sufficient; thus he bears out consistently the principle that expulsion for a lesser fault is merely a means of correction, not the final separation from the monastery.

[96] Page 369.

CHAPTER V

THE MONK'S DAY: DEVOTIONAL AND INTELLECTUAL

IN order to understand the daily life and occupation of the monk as described in the commentaries, it is necessary first to outline briefly some prescriptions of the Rule on these points. The horarium varies with the time of the year, both the liturgical and the annual season.

In defining the hour at which Matins, the night Office,[1] should begin, the Rule (c. 8) divides the year into two seasons: from the Calends of November until Easter, Matins should begin at the eighth hour of the night; from Easter until November, the hour for Matins should be so arranged that shortly after the completion of the night Office, Laudes, the morning Office, may be begun at the break of day. In appointing the hours for manual work and for reading, the Rule (c. 48) distinguishes three seasons: summer, winter, and the liturgical period of Lent. Finally, in arranging the hours at which the monks are to eat, the Rule (c. 41) outlines four seasons: summer, winter, Lent, and the Paschal time.

Furthermore, within these seasons, the precise time at which a canonical hour is to be recited varies with the relative length of the day and the night hours. Thus a few words are needed to indicate the method of computing time used by St. Benedict and by the Carolingian commentators. Recent writers are agreed that the Roman method was still current at the time of St. Benedict.[2] According to it, the day—the interval from

1 With reference to the canonical hours, differences of nomenclature have given rise to some confusion. Thus in J. Evans' *Life at Cluny*, Matins is consistently denoted as the "nocturnes," and Laudes is referred to as Matins. In the present study, the current monastic and ecclesiastical usage will be followed. The early medieval *"vigilae"* or *"nocturnale officium"* is now called Matins, and the early *"matutini"* or *"matutinum officium"* is now called Laudes.

2 Butler, *Benedictine Monachism*, pp. 275-276; Berlière, *L'Ascèse bénédictine*, p. 52; Delatte, *op. cit.*, 139-140.

sunrise to sunset—was divided into twelve equal parts; like-wise the night—the interval from sunset to sunrise—was divided into twelve equal parts. Only at the equinoxes, there-fore, would these subdivisions of the day and the night be of equal duration, i. e., sixty minutes each. Thus in summer a day hour was longer than a night hour, and in winter a night hour was longer than a day hour.[3]

Our commentators, recognizing the difficulty involved in computing the hours of the day or the night, raise the question:

Why should Blessed Benedict assign the eighth hour of the night as the time for rising, when in November the nights con-tain fourteen hours and in December, sixteen hours? This appears difficult [to understand] and even contradictory in itself, espe-cially if one considers the number, for the eighth hour of the night sometimes occurs before midnight and sometimes at mid-night.[4]

Apparently, the Carolingians reckoned the hours at sixty minutes each, but like the Romans they reckoned the length of the day from sunrise to sunset.[5]

The commentators offer a solution, but unfortunately do not carry it out to completion: " Nevertheless, what he [St. Benedict] said is neither difficult nor contradictory because in saying this he regarded the equinox which contains the same

3 Taking into consideration the latitude of Monte Cassino, Butler (*op. cit.*, pp. 275-283) has calculated the horarium for several points of the year. Berlière (*op. cit.*, pp. 51-52) gives a briefer account without reference to any special region. Butler finds the longest day of the year to have fifteen of our equinoctial hours, or twelve hours of seventy-five minutes each; the shortest day he finds to have nine of our equinoctial hours, or twelve hours of forty-five minutes each. For the night these figures are reversed.

4 Paul, p. 211; Hildemar, p. 278.

5 According to G. Bilfinger (*Die mittelalterlichen Horen und die modernen Stunden*, p. 141), hours of fixed length were known in the Middle Ages but their use was restricted to technical purposes; hours of varying length were used generally in the daily social life until about the end of the four-teenth century (*ibid.*, pp. 143, 149). It appears that this opinion needs modification in view of the pertinent references in the commentaries.

number of hours in the day as in the night—twelve in each." [6]
There is no mention of hours of unequal length. Perhaps the
commentators imply that, disregarding the seasonal changes,
the eighth hour should be fixed as at the equinox. The diagram
which Hildemar gives, accompanying his discussion,[7] seems to
support this explanation; so also does the remark that, in determining whether the signal for rising should be given at the beginning, middle, or end of the eighth hour, discretion can be
used since the longer the nights, the nearer to the beginning of
the hour should the signal be given, and the shorter the nights,
the nearer the end of the hour should the signal be given.[8]

This last suggestion, however, is offered by way of exception, for both commentators state as a general principle that
any canonical Office which has received its name from the hour
at which it is to be chanted, should be celebrated at the termination of that hour.[9]

Evidently it was quite difficult to announce the community
exercises, particularly the night Office, with absolute precision.
Hildemar observes that to do this it would be necessary to have
a water clock, implying that the device was not commonly available.[10] In explaining how it might occur that the signal for
Matins be given tardily, he mentions, among other causes, the
cloudiness of the night; "for although he [the signal giver]
rose before the hour, he could not see the stars because of the
clouds, and through fear of sounding the signal before the
proper time he gave it tardily." [11]

The number of signals given for the different Offices varied,
the least being given for those hours preceding which the monks

6 Paul, p. 211; Hildemar, p. 278. On p. 193, Hildemar states that the
motion of the sun is the basis of time computation, the elements of which
are: *momentum, minutum, punctum, hora, quadrans, dies,* and *septimana.*

7 Page 278.

8 Hildemar, pp. 279-280.

9 Paul, pp. 395-396; Hildemar, p. 480. *Cf.* also Butler, *op. cit.,* pp. 277-278.

10 Page 278.

11 Page 289.

were already assembled for reading or prayer: three signals
were given for Matins and for Vespers; two for Tierce, Sext,
and None; and only one for Laudes, Prime, and Compline.[12]
The Rule (c. 48) contains but one indirect reference to the
giving of more than one signal for an exercise;[13] it is sufficient, however, to indicate that there was, doubtless, an un-
written tradition which is the source of the system just outlined[14]

The manner of giving the signal was perhaps little unlike
that found in institutions today in which an electric device is
not used. The terms employed by the commentators—" *tangere*
signum " and " *pulsato signo* "—indicate that the signal consisted in striking a gong or cymbal-like instrument. A contemporary document cites a *tintinabulum* as the device used to
signal the time for assembling in the refectory;[15] another
speaks of a *cymbalum;*[16] still another, of a *schilla.*[17]

Having introduced the terminology and the variables involved in the horarium as intended by St. Benedict, we shall
note the changes or additions reflected in the commentaries.
However, since these notes will be more or less fragmentary,
it seems best to superimpose them on the framework of the
horarium as dictated in the Rule. Two Benedictine scholars
have reconstructed this order of the day approximately, and
perhaps as accurately as the data will permit. The winter and
summer schedules as given below are taken from Berlière's

12 Paul, p. 261; Hildemar, p. 322.

13 *Regula,* c. 48: " When, however, the first signal for the hour of None
hath been given, let each one cease from work and be ready when the
second signal shall strike."

14 The Council of Aachen calls for two signals for Tierce, Sext, and
None (*MGH, Cap. reg. Franc.*, I, 347, can. 60). For other contemporary
regulations concerning the giving of signals, *cf.* Albers, I, 15, 16, 100 (no. 21),
106 (no. 5), 109 (no. 8).

15 *Cf.* Albers, I, 100 (no. 21), 106 (no. 5), 109 (no. 8).

16 *Cf.* Albers, III, 44.

17 *Cf. Vita Benedicti abbatis Anianensis et Indensis auctore Ardone,*
MGH, SS, XV, i, 216.

L'Ascèse bénédictine,[18] and the Lenten schedule, from Butlers' *Benedictine Monachism*.[19]

WINTER

Rise	2– 2:15 A. M.
Matins	2:25– 4
Prayers, chant	4– 5:30
Laudes	5:30– 6
Interval	
Prime	6:30– 7
Reading	7:30– 9:30
Tierce-Sext	9:30
Work	9:45– 2:30 P. M.
None	2:30
Repast	3
Vespers	4
Reading-Compline	6
Retire	6:30

SUMMER

Rise	1:45– 2 A. M.
Matins	2:15– 3:15
Laudes	3:30– 4
Prime	4:30– 5
Work	5– 8:30
Tierce	8:30– 8:45
Reading	9–11:30
Repast	12
Siesta	
None	2:30 P. M.
Work	3– 5:15
Vespers	5:15
Repast	6
Reading-Compline	6:30
Retire	7– 7:30

18 Page 52.
19 Page 281.

LENT

2	A. M.	Rise
2–3:30		Vigils
3:30–4:30		' Meditatio '
4:30		Aurora
4:30–5		Matin Office (Lauds)
5–9		Reading (Prime at 6, sunrise)
9		Tierce
9:15–4	P. M.	Work (Sext at 12)
4		None
4:40		Vespers
5		Meal
5:45		Collation
6 (Sunset)		Compline
6:30		Retire

One of the first things the reader will observe in scanning these horariums is that the amount of time devoted to Matins in summer is one-half hour shorter than that devoted to the same Office in winter including Lent. The commentators explain that in his dispensing with the lessons at the summer Office, St. Benedict acted out of discretion—nay even condescension toward the faint-hearted; that this is so is evident in his explanation, " because of the brevity of the nights." [20] They point out that the nights would be too short to permit sufficient sleep, particularly for those who do extraordinary work during the day.[21] The question is then raised as to why this arrangement should continue through the months of September and October since the nights in these months are equal in length to those of March and April. The answer given is that during September and October the work is more strenuous because it is the time of harvest.[22] This discussion brings into clear relief

20 Paul, p. 218; Hildemar, p. 284.

21 *Ibid., loc. cit.* This interpretation of the text requires a very free translation; however, it seems to express the mind of the commentator. The passage reads: " In hoc quippe loco, cum dixit *brevitatem noctium,* intelligitur quia maxime illis efficitur *brevitas noctium* in dormiendo, qui in die laborant."

22 *Ibid., loc. cit.*

the fact that the Rule provides the longest hours of sleep for the harvest season. By retiring early (at sunset) and by rising comparatively late (at such time as to be able to complete the shorter summer Office by dawn), they enjoyed a long unbroken sleep. Apparently the Cluniacs rose at an early hour to say Matins during this season, for an interval followed the night Office in which they retired to sleep until daybreak, the time of Laudes.[23]

Only on condition that, by some error, the monks have risen so early that it is not yet dawn when they have completed the night Office, will Hildemar permit them to return to sleep.[24] This concession was granted in connection with his comments on the Sunday Matins in summer, for which, because of its length, the Rule prescribes that the monks rise earlier than on week days.[25] Furthermore, it is stated clearly in the Rule and duly emphasized in the commentaries that Laudes may not be chanted before dawn.[26] Under these conditions, therefore, the hardship of awaiting the time for Laudes will not be imposed on the monks; they may return to sleep.

In winter the situation is different. The order of the day calls for an interval after Matins to be devoted to meditation or the study of the psalms.[27] Moreover, they have retired earlier the previous evening; there is no thought of returning to bed between the Offices of Matins and Laudes. On the contrary Warnefrid offers the following instruction—somewhat amusing, yet probably true to life, at least true to human nature:

In this passage [of the Rule] it is ordered that the time which remains after Matins until daybreak should be devoted to reading, i. e., employed by those brothers who are lacking in the

23 *Consuetudines Cluniacenses*, Albers, II, 1.

24 Pages 287-288.

25 *Regula*, c. 11; Paul, p. 222; Hildemar, pp. 286-287.

26 *Regula*, c. 8; Paul, pp. 212, 223; Hildemar, pp. 279, 288.

27 This passage of the Rule (c. 8) has been variously interpreted; it reads: " Quod vero restat post vigilias, a fratribus, qui psalterii vel lectionum aliquid indigent, meditationi inserviatur " (Linderbauer, ed.).

[knowledge of the] Psalter or lessons. Perchance some monk will object: "I do not wish to keep vigil till morning, but to sleep, for with God's help I am not lacking in this knowledge." To him the abbot should put such a [difficult] proposition that the brother cannot solve it, and will thereby be humbled. For this reason the abbot ought to be wise and learned in order that he be fully competent to instruct his monks.[28]

Contemporary customs and regulations are of a like tenor regarding this point. The Monastic Capitulary of Aachen reads: "They should never return to bed to sleep in the interval after Matins unless it happen that they have risen before the appointed hour." [29]

According to Berlière's schedule, there would be an interval of about one-half hour between Laudes and Prime for which no duty is assigned by the Rule. In his observations for the more southerly latitude of Monte Cassino, Butler finds a longer period—from one to one and one-half hours unaccounted for; he suggests that it was presumably devoted to "meditatio." [30] A document thought to be a report on the discipline of Inde, the model monaster ruled by Benedict of Aniane,[31] prescribes that the interval between Laudes and Prime should be of such length that the brothers may conveniently pray before each of the altars, and prepare themselves so that when they depart from Prime they may be in readiness for reading or the work enjoined on them.[32] In the biography of Benedict of Aniane, written by a contemporary, it is related that he introduced like practices among his monks.[33] As a consequence he has been generally accredited with the origin of the custom of making miniature pilgrimages, as it were, from altar to altar as stated times.

28 Paul, p. 211; Hildemar, p. 279.

29 MGH, Cap. reg. Franc., I, 344 (no. 5). Cf. also Albers, III, 14.

30 Op. cit., pp. 282, 284-285.

31 Albers, I, Prooemium, xix.

32 Ibid., III, 103.

33 Vita Benedicti abbatis Anianensis et Indensis auctore Ardone, MGH, SS, XV, i, 216-217.

Warnefrid's commentary, which antedates the abbatial rule of Benedict of Aniane by three or four decades, makes mention of the custom, apparently already in vogue, of chanting psalms while going from altar to altar after Laudes. The commentator points out that this custom is not authorized by the Rule and therefore he will neither encourage nor condemn it.[34] Thus the origin of the practice appears to be more remote than has generally been thought.[35] Beyond this vague reference, the commentaries make no provision as to the manner of passing the interval between Laudes and Prime; but from what has been said it would seem that the time was left to the disposal of the individual monk to be used for his private devotions.

The morning chapter, a daily assembly of the brotherhood, took place immediately after Prime. It is not formally mentioned in the Rule, but its chief functions are either expressed or implied in the Rule. The universal establishment of the chapter in the monastic life of the Carolingian age is evident from contemporary consuetudinaries.[36] Assuming that the recitation of Prime required twenty to thirty minutes, we are led to infer from a remark of Hildemar that the chapter assembly consumed about one-half hour daily: " By the time Prime has been chanted and chapter has been held, the first hour will be nearly spent." [37]

References to the chapter, scattered throughout the commentaries and contemporary accounts, indicate the main purposes which it served. A public reading, of which a chapter of the Rule formed a part, was held;[38] this was probably followed by a few words of instruction by the abbot;[39] matters for con-

---

34 Paul, pp. 232-233; Hildemar, p. 296.

35 L. Gougaud, *Dévotions et pratiques ascétiques du moyen âge,* pp. 58-59; cf. infra., p. 158.

36 Cf. Albers, III, 14, 30-32, 71, 91, 97, 141.

37 Page 488.

38 Albers, III, 71 (no. 1); MGH, Cap. reg. Franc., I, 347 (no. 70).

39 Albers, III, 79 (no. 1), 103 (no. 30); MGH, Cap. reg. Franc., I, 344 (no. 1).

sultation were discussed;[40] transgressions of discipline were acknowledged and public corrections were administered;[41] the duties of the day were assigned;[42] and articles of clothing were distributed as needed.[43] In fine, it was a sort of clearing house for the family affairs of the community—spiritual and temporal, instructional and remedial.

In general, the time for manual work and for reading, as also the arrangement for the canonical hours and meals, as prescribed in the Rule (c. 48) and outlined by Berlière and Butler appear to have prevailed at the time of our commentators. A modification was necessitated, however, by an addition to the order of the day as planned by St. Benedict, and one which the commentators point out as a new development, namely, the daily celebration of the Sacrifice of the Mass.[44] In commenting on the Lenten order, Hildemar, remarks:

He [St. Benedict] gave that precept to work until the completion of the tenth hour because at that time in his monastery [daily] Mass was not sung; now that Mass is sung [daily], the brothers cannot work until the end of the tenth hour and then sing Mass and still finish everything while it is yet daylight. Instead, the abbot should arrange that they work until such hour as will permit them to attend Mass, chant Vespers, partake of the daily repast, and yet do all things by the light of day. Therefore, None ought to be sung not at the termination of the tenth hour but at its beginning.[45]

40 Paul, pp. 266-267, 461-462; Hildemar, pp. 328-329, 570-571.

41 Paul, pp. 91, 266, 386; Hildemar, pp. 136, 328, 470, 472, 473.

42 Paul, p. 103; Hildemar, p. 150; Albers, III, 31. In other accounts this connection between the chapter and the daily duties seems to be implied by position; cf. Albers, III, 14 (no. 2), 99 (no. 14).

43 Paul, p. 428; Hildemar, p. 515.

44 As may be gleaned from the Rule, it was customary to have Mass only on Sundays and on the major solemnities; cf. Butler, op. cit., 283-284, 294.

45 Hildemar, p. 481; Paul's account (p. 396) is similar but shorter. This passage of the commentary may well be the source of the thirty-ninth article of the Capitulary of Aachen, 817: "Ut in quadragesimo usque ad nonam operentur fratres, quatenus missa celebrata tempore congruo reficiant" (MGH, Cap. reg. Franc., I, 346).

Thus we see that in Lent the week-day Mass was celebrated late in the afternoon before Vespers; this is with reference to what was then called the " public " Mass and what would now be called the conventual Mass. Preceding it, private Masses were offered.[46] The one meal of the day, a short reading from the Fathers, and Compline completed the exercises of the day.

During the winter season when the daily refection took place at the ninth hour, Mass was sung at the eighth; in summer, Mass followed the recitation of Tierce.[47] All this and even the exact hour at which the *mixtus* should be received is worked out with the precision of modern punctilio. Thus it is explained that during the season in which the brothers eat at the ninth hour, Mass is sung at the eighth; after this all those who are to receive the *mixtus,* the weekly cooks, the reader, and those who wait on the guests and the sick, go into the refectory and there receive the allotted portion of bread and wine while the priests are unvesting and putting away what pertains to the Sacrifice. In the meantime the signal-giver awaits until all are in readiness and then gives the signal for None.[48]

In summer a special signal is given for the *mixtus* a very short time before the signal for Sext. When the psalm *Miserere* is begun at the close of this Office, the weekly cooks and the cellarer go into the refectory and place the wine and the cooked food on the tables.[49]

The importance of precision in announcing the time for the canonical hours is well recognized and emphasized. Again, in the tone of a modern regulation, Hildemar, writes:

Beautifully has he composed that chapter concerning the signals for the Office, for without promptitude in sounding the signal, great confusion would result because the same Father Benedict ordains that [the Offices such as] Tierce and None be chanted

---

46 Hildemar, pp. 399-400.

47 Paul, pp. 333-334; Hildemar, pp. 399-400.

48 Paul, p. 333; Hildemar, p. 399.

49 Paul, pp. 333-334; Hildemar, p. 400.

not at the same hour during all seasons. And he has entrusted
this duty to no one except to the abbot or a solicitous brother
the abbot should commit it to a zealous brother who will perform
it diligently. Wherefore the abbot should instruct this solicitous
brother that in case he [the abbot] should be prevented from re-
pairing promptly to the Office at the appointed hour through some
cause such as the entertaining of a guest, the fulfillment of the
Office, whether an Hour of the day or the night, should not be
delayed because of his absence. Occasion would thereby be given
to the great evil of murmuring, if through awaiting the abbot,
there should be a negligent attitude toward the time of the Office
and it should not be performed at the appointed hours.[50]

Leaving the detailed account of the Divine Office and the
more religious aspects of the monk's life to a later discussion,
we shall turn now to an examination of the other occupations
of the day.

Besides the public reading at the night Office, during meals,
at the morning chapter, and at the evening collation, several
hours each day were set aside for private reading or study. The
early morning interval between Matins and Laudes was devoted to the study of the psalms and the *lectiones* required for
the Divine Office and was spent, presumably, in the oratory.[51]
During the hours of the day assigned to reading, the monks
were to assemble in the cloister, not to read singly in the rooms
or in the dormitory. They were not to group together, however,
but to sit apart while reading in the cloister so that if one were so
disposed, he might give himself up to contemplation or to
tears.[52] Thus it is evident that those who would ascribe to Benedict of Aniane the origin of this regulation that the monks read
in the cloister and not in the cells, have not consulted Warnefrid's commentary.[53] Silence was to be observed in a particular

50 Hildemar, p. 476. *Cf.* also *ibid.*, pp. 322, 460; Paul, pp. 261, 379.

51 *Cf. supra*, pp. 113.

52 Paul, p. 396; Hildemar, p. 483. *Cf.* also Albers, III, 14.

53 *Cf.* G. Morin, "La Journée du moine," *Revue bénédictine*, VI (1889),
p. 400.

manner during the time of reading, i. e., with greater emphasis
than during the time of manual work; if necessity demanded,
however, the abbot, was to arrange for those who needed as-
sistance to read aloud before a learned brother in a place in
which others would not be disturbed.[54]

In these precepts we discern several aspects of the so-called
reading: for some it meant learning to read; for others, the in-
spiration to affective prayer and centemplation. The latter group
we will consider in a subsequent chapter, noting here that they
did not form a large proportion of the total. As to the former, it
is to be observed first that ability to read meant the ability to
read and understand Latin from the written page—the manuscripts then in use. Several remarks of our commentators
indicate that not all could do this equally well, not even sufficiently well to fulfill the service of public reader in the Office of
Matins or in the refectory.

In order that only those shall read in the refectory who can
fulfill the office in a manner edifying to their hearers, as the
Rule (c. 38) ordains, the commentators suggest that the abbot
select those who qualify, whether there be twenty or a lesser
number even to four; those, then, will read in turn.[55] They also
recommend that if the reader perform his service poorly, the
abbot should appoint a capable brother to prompt the reader;
this the brother will do by sitting near enough to him that he
can see the book and thus correct him in a low voice.[56]

In regard to the reading of the *lectiones* at Matins, it was
desired that there be a different reader for each lesson; thus
when the longer Office occurred, such as that of a Sunday or a
feast day, there would be twelve lessons and, consequently,
twelve readers. The commentators tell us, however, that it
would be preferable for one brother who reads in an edifying
manner to read three or four or even six lessons than that

54 Paul, p. 396; Hildemar, p. 483. This same provision is given in two
contemporary documents; *cf.* Albers, III, 14-15, 42.

55 Paul, p. 354; Hildemar, p. 427.

56 Paul, p. 354; Hildemar, p. 426.

many read who do not edify.[57] Provision is also made that a brother be appointed before whom the prospective lector may read his portion of the lessons, and who will correct the book if necessary.[58] Hildemar notes that should the book be defective at the places where the reader errs, he is not obliged to do penance for such errors.[59]

With reference to the private reading, it appears that the majority of the monks were expected to read independently and intelligently. The commentators state that " the brothers ought to understand what they read," and therefore they prescribe that the one who gives out and receives the books question the brother who returns a book about its content. If he can give a satisfactory report he is eligible to receive another; if he cannot, he must retain the book he has had.[60]

The distribution of books at the beginning of Lent is described by Hildemar with a penchant for details which makes the account highly interesting and perhaps unique in the intellectual history of this period. The following lines reproduce the passage in substance.

With the help of the brethren, the librarian of the monastery ought to bring all the books into the chapter at the beginning of Lent. A carpet is spread out and the books placed on it. When the chapter meeting is over, the librarian reads the name of each brother who has a book. As his name is called, the brother places the book which he has been reading on the carpet. Then the prior, or one ordered by him, takes up that book and wisely questions the brother, to prove whether or not he has read the book studiously. If he can answer, then he will be asked to suggest what book would be useful to him; whatever book he asks for will be given him unless the abbot knows it to be unsuited to his needs, and substitutes another, explaining his reason for so doing. If the brother cannot report on the

---

57 Paul, p. 355; Hildemar, p. 428.
58 Paul, p. 386; Hildemar, pp. 469-470.
59 *Loc. cit.*
60 Paul, p. 396; Hildemar, p. 481.

ook and the abbot sees that he was negligent in his reading, it
s to be returned to him. But if the abbot knows that, despite
he brother's diligence, he cannot understand the book, another
hall be given him. When the brothers have left the chapter,
he abbot will inspect whether all the books on the list are
resent; if any are missing, he will search until they are
ound.[61]

This passage from Hildemar's commentary implies that a
urplus of books remained after each of the monks was supplied
vith a book suitable for reading during Lent. Since the com-
nentator was accustomed to a rather numerous community,[62]
t follows, too, that the library consisted of no mean collection
f books.

There is implication, also, that the bulk of these books was
f a religious nature, such as would instruct and exhort the
nonk in the ways of God. Both commentators approve the
ursuit of secular studies, not for their own sake but as a means
o understand better the things of God.[63] This is, of course,
1 keeping with the patristic and early medieval attitude in gen-
ral.[64] In substantiation of this view, Hildemar cites the then
ecent decree of Pope Eugenius II in which it is ordered that
 in episcopal and parish centers and other opportune places
here be appointed *magistri* and *doctores* who are versed in let-
ers and the liberal arts, because it is chiefly in these that the
ivine commands are declared and made known." [65]

---

61 Hildemar, p. 487. A list of books and the readers to whom they were
istributed at Farfa in the beginning of Lent has been preserved but, since
  dates from the eleventh century, it has little significance here (Albers,
  185-186).

62 *Cf. supra*, p. 54.

63 Paul, p. 111; Hildemar, p. 172.

64 *Cf.* M. L. W. Laistner, "The Christian Attitude to Pagan Literature,"
istory, XX (1936), 49-54; P. de Labriolle, *Histoire de la littérature latine
rétienne*, pp. 15-45.

65 Canon 34 of the Roman Synod of 826 (*MGH, LL*, III, *Concilia aevi
arolini*, I, ii, 581).

Hildemar takes another occasion to give expression to hi
interest in the art of grammar, and in what was then considere
one of its branches, the art of effective oral reading:

Since the Rule [c. 38] orders [only] those to read [in th
refectory] who will edify their hearers, it is necessary that w
subjoin here the instructions of the various holy Fathers wh
teach how one should read—instructions gathered from the say
ings of Augustine and Ambrose, of Bede and Isidore, or eve
of Victorinus and Servius and other grammarians who teac
how to distinguish accurately the obscure meanings and to rea
properly according to the accents.[66]

Then follows an interesting discourse on the divisions o
grammar, of which, according to Victorinus, reading is th
first. Reading is then subdivided, also according to Victorinus
into four parts.[67] After defining each of these elements, an
after quoting at length from Isidore concerning the reader,[68]
a letter is introduced (evidently by the scribe) in which Hilde
mar prepared for Urso, the Bishop-elect of Benevento,
treatise on artistic reading. The discussion becomes quite tech
nical, explaining, as it does, how structure and euphony shoul
control the manner of public reading.[69] In the course of the ex
position, attention is drawn to the " manner of the ancients

66 Hildemar, p. 428. The poor structure of this sentence so obscures it
meaning that the reader cannot know whether Hildemar compiled the ex
cerpts himself or whether he merely incorporated into his work a collectio
already made. In the original it reads: ". . . quia regula dicit, illos leger
qui aedificent audientes, ideo necesse est, ut auctoritates diversorum san
torum patrum, quae docent, qualiter legendum est, hic subjungamus, videlice
ex dictis Augustini et Ambrosii, Bedae necnon et Isidori, sive etiam Vi
torini et Servii et aliorum grammaticorum collectae existunt, quae doce
recte et distincte obscurorum sensuum secundum accentuum sonos lege
atque distinguere." Unfortunately, the editor omitted the excerpts, givin
only the names of the writers quoted: cf. Hildemar, p. 433, n. 2.

67 Ibid., pp. 428-429. The four divisions of grammar are said to be: lecti
enarratio, emendatio, and judicium. The divisions of reading as given ar
accentus, discretio, pronuntiatio, and modulatio.

68 De ecclesiasticis officiis, lib. II, c. 11, n. 2-5.

69 Hildemar, pp. 431-432.

or to the "custom of the modern masters," or to both, thus
making the commentator, in phraseology at least, a forerunner,
long in advance, of the Scholastic, post-Scholastic, and the post-
Renaissance "moderns." The most "modern" writer whom he
cites is Alcuin.[70]

Paul Warnefrid likewise was attracted by the art of grammar. Besides the frequent references to points of syntax
throughout his commentary, he compiled an abridgment of
Festus' *De significatione verborum* and he wrote, presumably,
a treatise on the *Ars* of Donatus.[71] It is not surprising, however, to find Lombard scholars interested in the late Roman
grammarians. In his study of the monastic and clerical education in early medieval Italy, G. Hörle finds that under the Lombard regime, particularly in the cities, profane education main-
tained itself more easily than in other parts of the peninsula;
that if and when the clergy were educated, it was through a
free combination of theological studies and the traditional
Roman arts.[72]

In attempting to form an estimate of the literary level of the
time and region represented by our commentaries, too much
weight cannot be placed in the fact that Hildemar quotes from
more than thirty authors. To begin with, he was a native Frank
who came to North Italy only after his monastic profession.
Although he probably had access to many of the works cited in
his commentary, the authors less frequently quoted, particularly
the classical writers such as Terence, Cicero, and Ovid, may
well have been known only through excerpts in medieval texts

70 *Ibid.,* pp. 428, 430, 432, 433 (n. 2).

71 *Cf. supra,* p. 20, for Paul's epitome of Festus' work; A. M. Amelli
edited the second work, *Ars Donati quam Paulus Diaconus exposuit,* at
Monte Cassino in 1899. It has not been proved beyond all doubt, however,
that it is a genuine work of Warnefrid: *cf.* C. Cipolla, "Note bibliografiche
circa l'odierna condizione degli studi critici sul testo delle opere di Paolo
Diacono," *Miscellanea di storia Venetia,* ser. 2, VIII (1902), 29.

72 *Frühmittelalterliche Monchs- und Klerikerbildung in Italien,* published
in Freiburger theologische Studien, Heft XIII (1914), 36-47.

and compilations.[73] It is possible that the collection of excerpt on the art of reading given (and apparently compiled) b Hildemar was used thereafter for scholastic purposes. His oc casional quotations from Vergil and from the Servian com mentaries on Vergil raise the question as to whether he knew and used the poet's works in the original or only throug Servius.[74] He appears also to have had at his disposal the gram matical works of Priscian and Victorinus. Donatus and Festu are less freely used. The various citations from papal and con ciliar decrees may likewise have been taken from one of th many canonical collections current at the time. His frequen and long quotations from some of the Fathers, however, in dicate intimate knowledge of their major works. The leadin writers in the order of their importance through use in h commentary are: Gregory, Isidore, Augustine, Cassiodoru Cassian, Bede, Ambrose, and Jerome. All of these except Bed are also cited, though much less frequently, in Paul Warn frid's commentary.

In the transmission of these and other works, whether i the original or abridged form, it is evident that a considerab amount of literary labor went into transcription and compila tion. In this connection Paul Warnefrid relates an inciden

73 Hörle (*op. cit.*, p. 43) writes of a Lombard *florilegium* which appear about the year 800 at Reichenau where it was revised and enlarged. Th Reichenau version served as the basis of the collection of literary excerp made by Mico of St. Riquier in 825 and for the *Exempla diversorum au torum* originating in Laon about the same time. *Cf.* also M. Maniti Geschichte der lateinischen Literatur des Mittelalters, I, 469-470, 472.

74 The quotations from Servius in his *Expositio* indicate personal use the Servian commentaries on Vergil. An important manuscript of the larg version of Servius, known as Servius Danielis, is Bern, bibl. publ. 172. bears a dedication by a monk Ildemarus to St. Benedict (J. Savage, " T Manuscripts of the Commentary of Servius Danielis on Vergil," *Harva Studies in Classical Philology*, XLIII [1932], 98, n. 3). Since there seen to be no record of a Hildemar at this time other than the author of t commentary on the Rule, and since the script of Bern 172 appears to be th of Fleury of the ninth or tenth century, it is quite possible that Hildem (of Civate) was instrumental in securing this copy of Servius for t monastery of St. Benedict at Fleury.

slight in itself, but noteworthy in its implications. The occasion is given in that passage of the Rule (c. 41) which orders that the abbot " should so arrange and dispose all things that souls may be saved and that what the brothers do, may be done without a just cause for murmuring." Paul states that some copies of the Rule at this point are worded " *absque murmuratione,*" and others, " *absque justa murmuratione.*" He explains that some think the proper text cannot be *justa murmuratio* because murmuring can never be just. Others, however, through studious search have found parallel cases in which this phrase occurs in the writings of Cassiodorus and Gregory. Therefore, the commentator decides that this reading should be retained, " especially [since] it is found in [the copy of] the Rule which St. Benedict himself wrote."[75]

In this account we see how individual opinion could be responsible for the alteration of a text. It is evident also that varying texts of the Rule were collated by Paul's contemporaries who were so much exercised by the discrepancies that they inaugurated a search to establish the correct text. Having found that the passage in question was used by eminent contemporaries of St. Benedict, the matter is solved; it is confirmed, at least for Paul, by the external evidence of the autograph copy of the Rule.

The several brief allusions to the generality of the monks being engaged in writing implies that it was a common occupation, but further information on the subject is lacking in our commentaries.[76]

Formal education is not discussed directly in our commentaries, doubtless because it is not mentioned in the Rule. That it was the normal procedure to provide at least the rudiments

75 Paul, p. 368; Hildemar, pp. 450-451. According to Traube (*Textgeschichte*, p. 39), the text of the Rule referred to is the autographed copy which was at Monte Cassino at the time Paul wrote, and from which a copy was made for Charlemagne on request. There are other instances in which mention is made of textual differences: Paul, pp. 167, 199, 307, 358; Hildemar, pp. 228, 263, 372, 434.

76 Paul, pp. 377, 397; Hildemar, pp. 458, 484.

for the *pueri* is evident from some indirect remarks. If a boy is to be punished for habitual mistakes in chanting the Office, the chastisement is to be administered by his master in the school.[77] Elsewhere the commentators indicate roughly what subjects were taught in the *schola magistri*. When learned guests come to the monastery, the abbot should call one of the boys and, by way of a test, tell him to go and speak with the guest about the chant, the *computus,* grammar, or some art. In the meantime the abbot, unobserved by the boy, should note the manner in which he speaks and acts in the guest's presence. After the departure of the guest, the boy should be admonished if he was careless in his speech, or too timid or too forward.[78]

It is very probable that these boy monks were trained in the elementary arts during the time devoted to reading by the adults. The commentaries prescribe that those who are under supervision read together with their master while the rest assemble in the cloister.[79]

The second article of the Murbach Statutes gives an idea of the intellectual pursuits outlined for the monks of Murbach. The occasion is the canon of a recent council calling for the memorization of the Rule by the monks. According to the statute, this memory work is to be adjusted to the capacity of the individual. Those whose names are listed in the monastic catalogue, the number of which exceeds thirty-six, are required to commit to memory the entire Rule; certain others whose names are also indicated by list are expected to memorize the ten chapters designated, unless prevented by old age or poor vision. Those who can learn neither the whole nor a part of the Rule, are to prove by their works that they have grasped the teaching of the Rule through hearing it read. In the time appointed for reading, the *scholastici* are to memorize the psalms, the canticles, and the hymns, and after these have been learned, the text of the Rule. In the meantime they will read aloud before their masters

77 Hildemar, pp. 470-471; *Cf.* also Paul, p. 386.

78 Paul, p. 346; Hildemar, p. 418.

79 Paul, p. 396; Hildemar, p. 483.

the history and exposition of the Scriptures as also the *Lives* and the *Collations* of the Fathers. After adequate training along these lines, they will then turn to the literary art and the flowers of devotion. Those, however, who have newly come from the way of the world and are lacking in the knowledge of letters will learn the Lord's Prayer and the Creed and then the penitential psalms; after this they will continue with the rest of the psalms as long as they are able.[80]

Evidently the "*schalastici*" mentioned in this account were the *pueri oblati;* the educational advantages which the oblate system offered are easily recognized.

In the additions appended to the Murbach Statutes, some practices of the monastery of Inde are recorded.[81] Among these practices it is related that at the time of reading no one ever dares to sit down without his reading frame *(lectorinum)*, a device with which each one is supplied.[82] Those among the brothers who are called "*scholastici*" pursue the use of Latin rather than the rustic speech, for in such *colloquia* the knowledge of the Scriptures is sometimes better understood than by reading, the *ars dictandi* is acquired, and the senses are sharpened for learning.[83]

80 Albers, III, 80-81.

81 *Ibid.*, III, 90, and the corresponding note of the editor.

82 It is not clear whether the *lectorinum* was used in copying material read or perhaps dictated by another, or whether it was used in the memory work referred to above (p. 126). The passage reads: " Cum tempus legendi est, numquam sine lectorino suo residere audent, sed singuli singulos habentes, lectionem suam in eis memores commendant, qui quoquomodo a nobis etiam facti fiant, a nobis ordinandum est " (Albers, III, 92).

83 *Ibid.*, III, 92-93. This distinction between the use of Latin and the rustic speech seems to indicate the use of a vernacular tongue along with the Latin in the monastery at this period. The passage in the original reads: " Usum Latinitatis potius quam rusticitatis, qui inter eos scholastici sunt, sequuntur. In tali etiam confabulatione notitia scripturarum aliquotiens magis quam lectione penetratur, et dictandi usus discitur, et ad discendum sensus acuitur." An allusion to the "rustic speech" made by the commentator associates it with the unlearned and appears, therefore, to refer to vulgar Latin rather than to a vernacular (*cf. infra*, p. 131). The question might be raised as to whether these references to rusticity of speech

This glimpse of Inde, over which Benedict of Aniane ruled as abbot, seems not to accord with Hauck's opinion that Benedict disapproved of learning and refrained from open opposition to Charlemagne's cultural policy in order not to lose the emperor's support in the spread of his reform.[84] Furthermore, Ardo, Benedict's contemporary and biographer, writes that he instituted cantors, taught the readers, had grammarians and those skilled in the Scriptures, and collected a multitude of books.[85] Hauck seems to have formed his judgment chiefly from Benedict's emphasis on manual work, and from the forty-fifth canon of Aachen, 817, which forbids that a school other than that for the oblates be held in the monastery;[86] neither of these features, however, offers adequate grounds for his opinion. Certainly a regulation which had for its purpose the exclusion of lay students from the monastic precincts, cannot justly be interpreted to arise from opposition to learning as such.

Our commentators do not allude, even indirectly, to schools for others than the oblates. In view of the fact that important schools for the so-called " externs " existed about this time in the neighboring monasteries of St. Gall and Reichenau,[87] this silence is noteworthy. Probably no such schools had come within the immediate experience of the commenators. The chaotic political situation in Lombardy at the time Paul wrote may have been responsible in part for their absence in his time;

together with an occasional allusion to rusticity of dress (cf. supra, p. 47) and of food (Hildemar, p. 502) are indicative of a conscious distinction between things rustic and urbane, i.e., whether the towns were sufficiently numerous and populous to make the distinction felt, or whether the reference to things rustic was merely a linguistic carry-over from Roman times.

84 Kirchengeschichte Deutschlands, II, 590-597.

85 Vita Benedicti abbatis Anianensis et Indensis auctore Ardone, MGH, SS, XV, i, 206-207.

86 MGH, Cap. reg. Franc., I, 346.

87 Cf. J. M. Clark, The Abbey of St. Gall as a Center of Literature and Art (Cambridge, 1926), pp. 93-95; Hefele-Leclercq, Histoire des conciles, IV, 27; Wattenbach, Deutschlands Geschichtsquellen im Mittelalter, I, 267-280.

and the Capitulary of 817, doubtless, retarded the establishment of such schools in the newer monastic foundations.

For the time and place represented by our commentaries, perhaps our most important monuments of the instruction given, as also of the intellectual level of the recipients of this instruction, are none other than the commentaries of Warnefrid and Hildemar.[88] Interspersed as they are with numerous grammatical, historical, and literary notes, to say nothing of the instructions in courtesy and virtue, all of which are but by-products of the central study—the elucidation of the Rule—our commentaries indicate that those for whom they were designed possessed at least a modicum of literary training.

Furthermore, if in the extant commentary of Hildemar we have a sample of the work done by his oblate pupils at his dictation, as the manuscript inscription would seem to indicate,[89] then the pupils of ninth-century Civate performed a literary feat, in size as well as in manner of execution, which would do credit to pupils of a like age in any period of history.

Besides the more or less formal training given the boy oblate, courteous conduct was instilled in his daily life. We have already noted that he was expected to speak in a becoming manner with learned guests. Hildemar observes that before the oblates enter the refectory they should be taught carefully to do so in silence and to incline properly to those opposite on enter-

88 It is thus that Traube regards them. He sees in Paul's commentary "an animated picture of medieval instruction" (*Textgeschichte,* p. 39), and in Hildemar's work, "a *buntes Gemenge* which, together with the *Expositio* of Paul and similar accounts and commentaries, offers for the history of instruction material which to the present has been wholly unexplored" (*ibid.,* p. 41).

89 The best extant manuscript of Hildemar's commentary was written in the eleventh century; it came from Dijon to Paris where it now is to be found in the Bibliothèque Nationale as *Lat. 12637.* The inscription it bears reads: "Incipit traditio super regulam sancti Benedicti, quam magister Hildemarus monachus tradidit et docuit discipulis suis, quocirco obsecro, cum aliquid incompositum sive inhonestum ibi inventum fuerit, non magistro sed discipulis imputetur" (Traube, *op. cit.,* p. 40).

ing or leaving; nor should they leave until all have praised the Lord in prayer.[90]

Warnefrid considers that precept of the Rule (c. 37) in which St. Benedict groups the old with the children most fitting, for " it is proper that the old sit while eating and that the boys stand and serve." [91] In this remark the commentators refer to the special consideration which is to be shown the old and the children by way of some nourishment in anticipation of the community meal. That it was customary for the boys to stand also during the common meal is evident from the following directions of Hildemar.

If there are as many boys as tables, then at each table one boy should eat, standing; however he should stand before such a brother as may exercise custody over him lest he eat with levity or any misconduct. If there are more boys than tables, then two boys should stand at each table while eating. Likewise one of the boys should always eat at the abbot's table, but he should be one who knows how to eat with proper etiquette, lest, because of the guest who eats with the abbot, there be some disgrace.[92]

Commenting on a precept of the Rule (c. 38) concerning some points of monastic courtesy, Hildemar remarks that "although these are little things they are not to be considered insignificant, but are to be carefully observed, since charity is thereby nourished, and peace and harmony preserved." [93] Besides being zealous in living well, the ministers of the monastery are to be affable and kind in their manners, thus rendering themselves agreeable to others.[94] On the other hand, if they are such as possess a sanctity which is severe and uncondescending, they cannot be of help to others.[95]

90 Page 418.

91 Paul, p. 345; Hildemar, *loc. cit.*

92 Page 427.

93 Page 578. As an illustration of these courtesy rules, see Paul, pp. 469-470; Hildemar, pp. 580-581.

94 Hildemar, p. 386; *cf.* also Paul, p. 320.

95 Paul, pp. 263, 311; Hildemar, pp. 326, 374.

After the brothers have expressed their opinion when assembled in council, the abbot will neither spurn nor confound
those who have spoken unwisely or in a rustic manner; instead,
he will thank them saying, " We thank you and may the Lord
bless you, for what you knew you have spoken." [96]

The commentators describe the manner of saluting person-
ages of noble or ecclesiastical rank. In greeting a king, bishop,
or abbot, a monk should prostrate himself; upon meeting a
queen, he will only bend his knee or bow his head profoundly;
others, such as counts, priests, or monks are greeted by simply
inclining the head.[97]

96 Hildemar, p. 132; cf. also Paul, p. 88.

97 Hildemar, p. 505. The manner of saluting a queen is not given in Paul's
account (p. 418). Perhaps his early training in the royal court of Pavia
is responsible for the introduction of this gloss, although the Rule (c. 53)
prescribes that guests be greeted " with head inclined or whole body prostrate." For a discussion of Paul's courtesy poems, see Filippo Ermini, " La
poesia enigmistica e faceta di Paolo Diacono," *Memorie storiche Forogiuliesi*,
XXV (1929), 97-110.

CHAPTER VI
SOCIAL CHARACTERISTICS OF THE COMMUNITY LIFE

THE second major occupation of the monk's day, other than the Divine Office, was manual work. In brief and comparatively infrequent remarks scattered throughout the commentaries, mention is made of the monks being engaged in outdoor work such as gathering the harvest,[1] working in the garden,[2] cutting wood,[3] constructing a mill,[4] or building a house.[5] References to such crafts as that of the tailor or cobbler are likewise comparatively scant and few.[6] Domestic work, such as the service in the kitchen and the care of the infirm and the guests, receives greater space in the commentaries.

The kitchen service evidently entailed considerable fatigue and, consequently, there was a tendency to shun it on the part of the monks. " It is well," the commentators remark, " that he [St. Benedict] referred to the reward, for the kitchen duty is laborious. There are some who would prefer to perform another duty than that of the kitchen because of the [drudgery of the] work." Then enlarging on the words of the Rule, they continue: " The greater the labor, the greater the reward, and in this service also is fulfilled the duty of charity."[7] Not satisfied with this, Hildemar repeats the admonition with even greater emphasis and in his characteristically repetitious manner:

That sentence [which, in a preceding part of the Rule, forbids murmuring] has inspired this chapter even though there was

1 Paul, p. 218; Hildemar, p. 284.

2 Paul, pp. 117-118; Hildemar, p. 613.

3 Hildemar, p. 479.

4 *Ibid., loc. cit.*

5 *Ibid., loc. cit.,* and p. 408.

6 Paul, pp. 117, 126, 127, 373; Hildemar, pp. 183, 191, 192, 454.

7 Paul, p. 330; Hildemar, pp. 394-395.

an opportunity to refer to the evil of murmuring in an earlier passage; thus it gave rise to this chapter, for it is as if St. Benedict had said in other words: "I forbid the evil of murmuring, but seeing that it might arise from the shirking of this duty, I order therefore that no one be excused from the kitchen service. There are wont to be many who excuse themselves in shunning the work, and through this an occasion is given to murmuring." Therefore to avoid this evil, let no one be excused from the service in the kitchen.[8]

In order that help be given to the weak as the Rule (c. 35) prescribes, two ways are suggested: either several brothers are to assist this weaker brother for the week, or one stronger brother will help him one day, another on the following day, and so on. The caution which follows betrays the abiding continuity of certain traits in human nature: " Nevertheless, because of this, that stronger one may not excuse himself from his weekly turn in the kitchen saying, ' I have already served in the kitchen.' "[9]

Thus far we have considered the monastic kitchen. With respect to the abbot's kitchen wherein the food was prepared for the clerical guests who were permitted to eat in the refectory, and the kitchen for the lay guests—both the poor and the high-born guests, the commentaries make some detailed provisions, as follows: The kitchen of the abbot and guests ought to be near that of the monks, yet so that it may not be entered from the cloister, but, when necessary, from the outside. Between the two kitchens there is to be a window through which the prepared food may be passed for serving in the refectory. A canonical cleric will prepare the food in this kitchen. When there are guests to be served, the monk who is assistant cellarer will supply the food to be cooked in this kitchen; when it is prepared he will receive it through the window and serve it in the refectory. If, however, the cleric needs help, he will be assisted by this subcellarer and the senior cel-

8 Hildemar, p. 397.
9 Paul, p. 331; Hildemar, p. 396.

larer will serve the food. Finally, the abbot should appoint two monks with the laymen in the kitchen of the lay guests; one will serve the poor and the other, the honored guests.[10]

Thus it appears that laymen assisted the brothers in the kitchen in which the food was prepared for the lay guests; that a cleric served in the abbot's kitchen; and that the monks themselves served in the monastic kitchen. The last point is verified by another statement of the commentators in speaking of the monastic kitchen—the Rule orders that only monks perform the work in the kitchen, not canons.[11]

Hildemar concedes that a canon may fetch meat for the infirm or launder his clothes, but the immediate nursing should be done by a monk; for, he asks, how can a canonical or a lay person who is not a member of the monastery, serve the sick monk, any more than an eye or a foot can serve the body if not of it?[12] This comment was occasioned by the use of the word "*servitor*" in the rule (c. 36) in referring to the infirmarian. It is clear from the general context of this chapter of the Rule that St. Benedict had in mind only a monk infirmarian. The same term "*servitor*" is, however, used in another chapter in which it is not so plainly evident that the reference is not to lay servants.

The passage in question alludes to the weekly reader; it orders that after having read during the meal, he should take

10 Paul, pp. 419-420; Hildemar, pp. 506-507.

11 Paul, p. 332; Hildemar, p. 397. Apparently the commentators use the term "cleric" to refer only to one in ecclesiastical orders; in several instances it is used in the same sense as "canonical cleric" or "canon," and in contradistinction to "monk." Cf. Paul, pp. 332, 340, 419; Hildemar, pp. 397, 407, 507. The presence of canonical clerics in the monasteries of this period seems not to have been unusual. In his statutes, Adalard of Corbie speaks of services rendered by clerics (cf. Levillain, Les Statuts d'Adalhard pour l'abbaye de Corbie, p. 20). The Monastic Capitulary of 817, however, restricts the admission of secular clerics for residence in the monasteries to those who wish to become monks (MGH, Cap. reg. Franc., I, 346, no. 42).

12 Page 407; Paul's account, at least as it reads in the extant version (p. 340), would not even permit the food or clothes to be cared for by anyone but a monk.

his refection with the weekly cooks and the servers.[13] Since other passages refer only to those who serve for the week in the kitchen, some historians are inclined to conclude that laymen served in the monastery as early as the time of St. Benedict.[14] Delatte points out that the two-fold duty of preparing and serving the food was fulfilled by the same persons. He questions any real intention on the part of St. Benedict to distinguish between those who worked in the kitchen and those who served at table. His solution of the difficulty is that the servers *(servitores)* were brethren given as assistants to the officials of the week.[15]

The following explanation, however, seems equally satisfactory. Since, in the Rule, St. Benedict speaks of the infirmarian as a *servitor,* he may well have had in mind those who care for the infirm and the guests, in using the word in this particular passage. In an early ninth-century document an almost identical usage occurs which has reference only to ministers who are monks. The phrase in its context is: " At the proper time, let the prior or the one appointed in his place, i. e., the senior dean, sound the signal for the weekly [cooks] and other servers *(ebdomadari et caeteri servitores)* to receive, according to the Rule, the *mixtus* over and above the appointed allowance." [16] Paul Warnefrid and Hildemar indicate specifically that those who are to receive the *mixtus* are the weekly cooks, the reader, the guest waiters, and those who care for the sick.[17]

For the Carolingian, and for the preceding period, in so far as the strength of tradition may lend value, the question may well be disposed of by evidence contained in our commentaries and contemporary literature. We have already noted the direct

13 *Regula,* c. 38: " Postea autem cum coquinae hebdomadariis et servitoribus reficiat " (Linderbauer, ed.).

14 De Valous, *op. cit.,* p. 50; Delatte, *op. cit.,* pp. 364-365.

15 *Op. cit.,* p. 254. Cf. *supra,* p. 133.

16 Albers, III, 106, no. 5.

17 Paul, p. 333; Hildemar, p. 399.

comments of both Paul and Hildemar, namely, that the work of caring for the sick and the kitchen service should be performed by monks, and not laymen. But lest these remarks be regarded as the statement of the ideal which may or may not have been carried out, it may be significant to note that there are a number of indirect allusions to the servers *(servitores, ministri)*, sometimes in connection with the reader, the context of which indicates clearly that the commentators have in mind not lay servants, but monks serving in the kitchen or in the infirmary.[18] We shall quote from two of these:

It should be known that it is not in keeping with the Rule that the abbot give the reader or the other servers *(ministri)*, by way of a favor, any bread, or drink, or [any other] food, because that is the custom of laymen; for the Rule prescribes that they receive their " justice," [19] i. e., the *mixtus*, before [their service].[20]

That " *servitores* " was used with the same signification as " *ministri* " follows from the passage in which the commentators explain that the interval between the evening meal and the collation should extend " until the servers *(servitores)* have eaten." [21]

Just as the use of the word " *servitor* " in the Rule has been interpreted as evidence of lay servants in the monastery of St. Benedict, so its use in the Monastic Capitulary of 817 has been accepted as proof that in the Carolingian period the monks were served, not by fellow monks, but by *famuli* who were attached to the monastery in some vague way. In the latter instance, as in the former, the mere words of the passage in question taken in isolation admit of different interpretations; but when read in the light of the contemporary use of the word,[22] are seen to have but one acceptable meaning. Moreover,

18 Paul, pp. 122, 313-314, 373-374; Hildemar, pp. 186, 377, 462-463.

19 Thus we see that the use of " justice " for *mixtus*, common among the Cluny monks, did not originate with them.

20 Hildemar, pp. 462-463; *Cf.* also Paul, p. 381.

21 Paul, p. 373; Hildemar, p. 454.

22 *Cf. supra*, p. 135.

the probable source of this regulation can easily be traced and thus the correct signification can be confirmed.

The disputed passage, the twenty-eighth article of the Monastic Capitulary reads: " *Ut servitores non ad unam mensam sed in propriis locis post refectionem fratrum reficiant; quibus eadem lectio quae fratribus recitata est legatur.*" [23] In his erroneous interpretation, De Valous states that the capitulary " very clearly admitted the presence of *famuli* living in the interior of the monasteries, eating in common in a special refectory where the same reading was to be provided for them as for the monks." [24] The more correct interpretation seems to be: The servers are not to eat at one table but in their own places after the brothers' refection; the same reading is to be provided for them as for the brothers [at the community meal].

The similarity of content between the three articles of the capitulary beginning with the twenty-seventh, and the three articles of the Statutes of Murbach beginning with the twenty-third, proves, beyond doubt, a close source relation between the two series.[25] The twenty-fourth and twenty-fifth articles of the Murbach Statutes refer to the " refection of the *ministri* and the food of the lector ";[26] the twenty-eighth article of the capitulary concerns the refection of the *servitores;* the twenty-ninth orders that nothing else but what the Rule enjoins should be given the reader.[27] Now if *servitores* is merely a synonym for *ministri,* as it appears to be in this use of the word as well as in the instances cited above, the presumption is strong in favor of the servers referred to in the capitulary being monks and

---

23 *MGH, Cap. reg. Franc.,* I, 345.

24 *Op. cit.,* p. 45.

25 *Cf.* O. Seebass, " Ueber die Statuta Murbacensia," *Zeitschrift für Kirchengeschichte,* XII (1891), 322-332.

26 Albers, III, 90: " Vigesimoquarto et quinto capitulis, *quae de lectoris cibo et ministrorum refectione* descripta sunt, statim observata sunt."

27 *MGH, Cap. reg. Franc.,* I, 346. This appears to have originated from the passage above quoted from Hildemar's commentary (*cf. supra,* p. 136).

not laymen. Moreover, if the capitulary had referred to lay servers, it would, doubtless, have prescribed that they eat in the same room—*in proprio loco,* not in *propriis locis.* With reference to the monk servers, the preferred translation given above should suffice.

As reflected in the commentaries, all the monks of the community, excepting the officials, were of equal status. There are no indications of the later medieval distinctions of lay brother and choir monk, notwithstanding the opinion of some writers that the origin of these institutions dates from the early ninth century.[28]

That our commentaries and contemporary accounts evidence the employment of lay persons in certain departments of the monastery as well as on its tributary lands during the Carolingian period was noted in the closing pages of the second chapter. Our somewhat lengthy *excursus* on the *servitores* was introduced to establish the point that laymen were not employed in the domestic services of the monastery proper. From the economic point of view it would make little difference whether laymen were employed in the garden or in the kitchen; from the monastic point of view, however, it would not be the same. The reason is to be found in Warnefrid's explanation as to why laymen may not fill the office of infirmarian. He asks, as already noted, how a lay person who is not a member of the monastery can serve a monk any more than an eye or a foot can serve the body if not of it?[29] Only members of the family may participate in its internal affairs.

Moreover, it is a religious family; its head, the father of the monastery, is to take the place of Christ. This ideal is found in the Rule (c. 2, 63), but it makes so strong an appeal to Warnefrid that he repeats it seven times within two pages (51, 52). He would see in the relation which should exist between the abbot and his monks a replica of that which existed between Christ and His disciples. " The abbot should love and

28 Cf. De Valous, *op. cit.,* p. 45; Delatte, *op. cit.,* pp. 364-365.
29 Paul, p. 340; Hildemar, p. 407.

teach his monks as Christ loved and taught His disciples, and the monks should love and obey their abbot as the disciples loved and obeyed Christ." [30]

Fraternal charity should dominate the relations between monk and monk. Not for the sake of some important work, for gold or any temporal thing, or even out of false zeal for God, as it were, should monastic charity be sacrified.[31] The brother who is weak should be given help,[32] and when seriously ill he should be visited by the others.[33] Paul intimates that in some monasteries a certain hour was appointed in which the brothers might freely visit the infirm.[34] Before a brother goes on a long journey he takes affectionate leave of all the brethren in the chapter; upon his return, he greets, with equal affection, those whom he meets.[35]

Warnefrid enumerates the following reasons why a strong spiritual affection should exist among the members of the monastic family:

It is well that he [St. Benedict] ordered them to be called *fratres* because they have been reborn in the same sacred font of Baptism, they have been sanctified by the same Spirit, they have pledged the same profession, they hope to attain to the same reward, and are all sons of Holy Mother Church. It is to be noted that this spiritual brotherhood is greater than that of the flesh.[36]

The importance of the individual, so well outlined in the Rule, is likewise emphasized in the commentaries. Whether in things spiritual or material, no two individuals are compelled or even expected to conform to type. We have already noted

30 Paul, p. 51; Hildemar, p. 87.
31 Paul, pp. 284, 330-331; Hildemar, pp. 351, 395, 398.
32 Paul, p. 136; Hildemar, p. 203.
33 Paul, p. 103; Hildemar, pp. 150-151.
34 *Loc. cit.*
35 Paul, pp. 497-498; Hildemar, p. 612. *Cf.* also Albers, III, 18.
36 Paul, p. 469; Hildemar, p. 579.

the reservations to be considered in administering penalties, particularly corporal punishment, because of differences in dispositions. The abbot is reminded that, like the Good Shepherd, he should leave the care of the good monks to devote himself with all solicitude to recall the "infirm" brother; thus will he place this erring one on his shoulder and carry him back to the flock when with compassion he zealously exhorts him to follow the ways of salvation.[37] Not satisfied with admonishing all the monks in general concerning the more perfect motives which should animate them in their service, the abbot should confer with each one privately on the subject.[38] Especially when a brother is seen to be tepid or his obedience ill motivated, the abbot should privately exhort and instruct him in spiritual motives.[39]

The sentence of the Rule (c. 40), "It is with some hesitation, therefore, that we determine the measure of food for others," is enlarged by the commentators as follows: "Therefore, we cannot determine the measure of food for others more specifically, because all do not have the same characteristics; no mortal being can arrange satisfactorily that all receive equally in matters of food, drink, or clothing."[40] Applying this principle, they recommend that if the appointed measure of wine be insufficient for individuals, the allowance should be increased; if it be superfluous for some, it should be diminished.[41] Likewise, if a monk cannot eat of the two common foods served at table, he should be given cheese, or an egg, or something which he can eat.[42]

If the abbot see that an infirm brother, who has been confined to bed for four or five days, is growing weaker he

---

37 Paul, p. 294; Hildemar, p. 359.

38 Paul, p. 124; Hildemar, p. 189.

39 Paul, pp. 129, 130; Hildemar, pp. 195-197. For these motives see *infra*, p. 183.

40 Paul, p. 364; Hildemar, p. 444.

41 Paul, pp. 364-365; Hildemar, pp. 447-448.

42 Hildemar, pp. 436, 440.

should order that meat be given him.[43] Should the ascetic-minded brother at first be unwilling to accept the meat, the abbot will convince him that it is preferable to receive this nourishment now so that he may recover and perform his service; otherwise a greater loss will result when later, because of more serious illness, it will be necessary to eat meat for a longer time.[44]

Hildemar relates that it is customary in *Francia* for the infirm brother to receive meat from the time his recovery begins until he has regained his former strength. Upon returning to the refectory for his meals, he will be provided better food than that given to the community for a few days because it would be injurious to descend abruptly to the common food. With approval, he adds: " Thus will the brother have greater love for the father of the monastery and speedily gain in bodily strength." [45]

The care of the infirm has already received some attention in previous discussions. The frequent mention of blood-letting in the commentaries as well as in contemporary literature indicates that it was a remedy commonly used at the time.[46] We have noted earlier the unrestricted use of the bath permitted the infirm;[47] also that the cellarer was expected to visit the infirmary frequently and correct any negligences he might observe.[48] In fine, both commentators remark that St. Benedict spoke with all emphasis possible regarding the care of the infirm.[49]

The various concessions granted the boy oblates, as also the exactions required of them, offer items of considerable interest

43 Paul, p. 343; Hildemar (p. 412) would extend the time to six or eight days.

44 Paul, *loc. cit.*; Hildemar, pp. 412-413.

45 Pages 412, 417.

46 Paul, pp. 136, 313, 380; Hildemar, pp. 203, 377, 463; Albers, III, 86, no. 12; *MGH, Cap. reg. Franc.*, I, 344, no. 11.

47 *Cf. supra*, p. 37.

48 *Cf. supra*, p. 63.

49 Paul, p. 340; Hildemar, p. 407.

from the social viewpoint. As Butler observes, " St. Benedict does not distinguish between ' children ' *(infantes)* and ' boys ' *(pueri)*, but groups them together up to the age of fifteen (c. 70) ; with Paul, however, they are children up to seven, boys from seven to fourteen, and from fourteen to twenty-eight they are youths *(adolescentes)*. It is a surprise to find definite provision for children of five, four, and even three." [50] The abbot is to provide the boys with good clothing and food; the latter may consist of fish, milk, or eggs, and on certain major feast days, such as the Nativity and Easter, fleshmeat may be given them; moreover, if a boy is seen to be weak, he should be given meat more frequently because of this infirmity. " Thus all their needs are to be satisfied, so that, having been reared with plentiful nourishment, they will not require it when they are older." [51]

The commentators make the observation that the amount of meat to be given the children should vary inversely with their age, beginning at three. At this age they have the greatest need of meat; at four years they have less need, and at five, still less. From five until ten or eleven they should have some meat; from ten until fifteen they should be given a substitute for meat except in case of special infirmity. After fifteen they are not to " anticipate " the community refection.[52]

Thus it appears that the special food is to be given at the anticipatory meal, and that at the common table they are to share in the common food; the portion, however, as ordered in the Rule (c. 39), is to be moderated by the cellarer, for "children ought to eat often but not much [at a time]." [53] Since Warnefrid makes no statement to the contrary, we are inclined to think that he intended this special food to precede all meals. We learn from Hildemar, however, that it is not to pre-

---

50 *Benedictine Monachism*, p. 323.

51 Paul, p. 346; Hildemar, p. 419.

52 Paul, pp. 346-347; Hildemar, *loc. cit.* As here used, "anticipate" signifies to eat in advance of the community.

53 Paul, p. 362; Hildemar, p. 439.

cede the evening repast: " In summer the children are not to anticipate the evening meal as they generally anticipate the midday meal, unless perchance some are so small that such anticipation is necessary." [54]

In the concession which follows, we welcome the principle on which it is based but regret that it is granted in such stinted measure. We should like to think that the connotation of the time units as then understood, or the option left to the master, permitted a less rigid application of the concession. It provides that each week or each month, as it seems best to the master of the boys, he should take his charges out to the meadow or some like place and dismiss them for an hour's play, " because of human nature, lest it be broken." [55] The commentators recommend that during this occasional play time as at all other times, by day or by night, the boys are to be under immediate supervision. In winter, when they enter the calefactory, their masters should be present to prevent their romping or playing about.[56] In church they are to chant and pray, standing with their masters; this applies to the night Office as well as to the Hours of the day.[57]

It is at night that the commentators would enforce custody with special rigor. When leaving the oratory to go to the dormitory, the boys are to be accompanied by their several masters. When the boys have retired, their masters are to be relieved by other brothers who will take turns in keeping watch during the night.[58] As a basis for this regulation, the precept

54 Page 420.

55 Paul, p. 346; Hildemar, p. 419.

56 Paul, p. 136; Hildemar, p. 203.

57 Paul, p. 273; Hildemar, p. 334. Butler writes that among the various regulations for the *oblati* prescribed by Paul, " the only thing that seems to us unreasonable is that these children were present at the night Office; but a passage in Aelfric shows us that this was the general practice " (*Benedictine Monachism,* p. 324).

58 Paul, pp. 272-273; Hildemar, pp. 334-335. Calmet notes in his commentary on the Rule (p. 437 of 1732 edition) that the anonymous *Regula magistri* recommends that two religious keep watch through the night and

of the Rule (c. 63) which orders that " the smaller boys and youths should always be under custody and discipline wherever they are until they reach the age of understanding " is combined with a precept of another chapter (22) which prescribes that " the brothers sleep in tens or twenties with the seniors who have charge of them."

The commentators insist that if these and like precepts of the Rule be observed, the sin of immorality against which these precepts are directed can never be committed; and if custody is exercised, the sin will never, or only with difficulty, be perpetrated. They add that if the boys are reared as St. Benedict orders, the abbot need never have suspicion concerning them; those, however, who have come to the monastery at an older age may be regarded with mistrust. Custody should therefore be extended to those who, although older in age, understand less well and need custody.[59]

In concluding the discussion, Hildemar insists that the recommendations he has just enunciated are based on the Rule; that he is not teaching new things, but rather, that he understands the commands of the Rule properly and has even seen them put into practice in the manner he has described.[60]

A careful study of the instructions given by the commentators relative to the supervision and correction of the boys shows a comparatively lenient and intelligent attitude. The passage in the Rule (c. 63) which orders the boys to be kept under discipline at all times by everyone is explained as follows. Only those brothers who are not lacking in discipline themselves, may exercise supervision over the boys. Such as do not " know discipline " ought never be permitted to rebuke or punish the

waken the brothers at the appointed hour, and that the Second Council of Tours (can. 14) prescribes that there shall be always two or three religious who read in turns, keeping watch until the time of Matins. " But it is scarcely believable," Calmet concludes, "that St. Benedict, full of wisdom and discretion as he was, had wished to subject the deans to this fatigue."

59 Paul, pp. 272, 283; Hildemar, p. 333.

60 Page 337. Cf. Albers, III, 15, 16, 38.

children, because if these stupid and negligent ones were allowed to do this they would, through terror, make the children worse instead of better.[61] The master should be solicitous in exercising a thorough custody but is to deal temperately with them, neither beating them to excess nor ill-treating them. When those brothers who are under custody fail, they should be subjected to severe fasts or flagellation; but the smaller boys are not yet old enough to be dealt with severely. Only if they oppose supervision are they to be soundly whipped.[62]

If the master who is truly solicitous for the welfare of the boys should at some time be so incensed as to punish one of them beyond measure, he is to be corrected and admonished lest it happen again; nevertheless, for this incident he is not to be removed, but should be kept in office because of his general solicitude.[63]

Here and there the commentator drops a hint as to the philosophy of his methods. Continuous custody is regarded as a preventive: " Flagellation and excommunication will avail nothing unless custody is exercised; because immediately after the beating or discipline they [the *pueri*] will return to their vanities." [64] The period of boyhood is seen to be one of formation and dependency. " Since this age is weak and unable to help itself, it is necessary that it be helped by others; if thus the boy is aided while in these weaker years, he will become a stronger character and be more solicitous in the service of God. But if he is not helped while young, he will always be tepid and negligent." [65] Incentives should be offered to spur on the good to better things, and to move the negligent to imitate the good:

61 Paul, p. 468; Hildemar, p. 578.

62 Paul, p. 346; Hildemar, pp. 418-419. The discrepancy between the two texts at this point indicates plainly a scribal error; since Hildemar's fails to make sense, Paul's has been considered the more authentic and has been followed.

63 Paul, p. 508; Hildemar, p. 622.

64 Paul, p. 346; Hildemar, p. 419.

65 Hildemar, p. 578.

If the abbot observes a boy who conducts himself religiously and is of good life, he ought to speak of him with praise in the chapter, so that after the boy shall have heard this, he may learn to love the way of sanctity. In the refectory the abbot ought occasionally to offer him of the guest's food, that he may learn to love the norm of righteousness, and be persuaded in this way, as it were, to advance to better things. When the abbot gives the delicacy to the good youth, however, he should subtract from the food of that boy whom he sees given to worldliness, so that the latter, seeing himself contemned, as it were, and the other honored, may be ashamed of his misconduct and be persuaded to love restraint as he has seen the other love it.[66]

The principle contained in this passage constitutes plainly a substitute for—or perhaps it would be better to say a supplement to—custody and coercion; in itself, this is a feature worthy of note. The incentives mentioned are not the most elevated, but if, from a desire to win the good will and favor of his superiors, the Lombard youth acquires refinement of manners and learns to love right conduct, the commentator's purpose in this passage will, doubtless, be achieved. He speaks elsewhere and forcibly of the highest spiritual motives.[67]

Thus far the custody spoken of has related to the boy oblates. For the monks in general, the precepts of the Rule (c. 48, 56) which provide that a few seniors be present always to preserve discipline when the brothers assemble in the refectory, or during the time of spiritual reading, are repeated in somewhat different words but with little substantial change. In addition, the commentators recommend that after the signal has been given for the Office, the *circator* go through the monastic cloister if it is daytime and correct any negligent brother whom he may find there; likewise at night when the signal has been given for Matins, he should go through the dormitory and arouse the sleeping and the lazy. Warnefrid observes that if this is done

---

66 Hildemar, pp. 419-420. Paul's account (p. 347) is the same except for the omission (apparently by the scribe) of a brief phrase.

67 Cf. *infra*, pp. 190-191.

it will rarely happen that a brother must do penance for being tardy.[68]

The question of silence, i. e., the extent to which it was to be observed, has its social as well as ascetical implications; nevertheless, since the latter seem to outweigh the former, it will be treated in a subsequent discussion. At this point, then, it must suffice to state briefly the norm recommended. Although absolute silence was not exacted, neither was there a fixed daily period of recreative conversation. It was permissible for the brothers to speak in a low voice to one another while occupied in their work; during the time devoted to reading and during the night, however, silence was not to be broken except for grave necessity.[69] These regulations are presented by the commentators, not as adjustments or developments in monastic practice, but rather as the currently recognized interpretation of the various admonitions and precepts on silence given by St. Benedict in the Rule.

The final point to be considered in connection with the social aspects of the monasticism represented by our commentaries is hospitality—the reception of guests, lay and ecclesiastical, and the charity extended to the poor.

In commenting on the precepts of the Rule relative to hospitality, our expositors are confronted with some difficulty due to the increased number of guests who then frequented the monastery. Hildemar quotes Cassian as saying that guests were few in his time; although the commentator admits that at the time of St. Benedict, " guests were never lacking in the monastery," he concludes that " they were surely less numerous then than now." He cites Theodulf, a contemporary, on the subject: " *Per Deum,* if St. Benedict were living now, he would close the door against them." [70] The Rule prescribes that all guests be received as Christ, he observes, but since this is

68 Paul, p. 379; Hildemar, p. 460.

69 *Cf. infra,* pp. 178-179.

70 Page 501. Theodulf was a noted scholar of Charlemagne's school and later, bishop of Orléans; he died in 821.

possible for comparatively few, the precept may be fulfilled by receiving all in spirit as Christ would be received.[71]

To accommodate the numbers, two brothers should be appointed to answer the door and report the arrivals to the abbot, as previously noted. In this way one can always be on duty while the other goes to Office, to meals, or is detained with a guest. If a poor man comes, he should be directed to the *hospitale,* or almshouse.[72]

In this distinction between the hospitality shown the wealthy and that extended to the poor, the commentators appear to be conscious of some departure from the letter of the Rule. Instead of recognizing that changed conditions demand an alteration in the practice, they attempt to explain the words of the Rule in the light of current practice; the result is somewhat strained and superficial.

Thus they comment that the words of the Rule (c. 66)— " When anyone knocketh or a poor man calleth, let him [the porter] answer ' *Deo gratias* ' or invoke a blessing "—are well written, for the poor man calls and the rich man knocks, and again, the *'Deo gratias "* refers to the poor and the *benedicat* to the rich and the powerful.[73]

In the following excerpt, the commentators give an interesting account of theory blended with practice. On second thought, the principle underlying the practice appears to be based largely on good sense; and allowing for altered times, the practice is not greatly out of harmony with the Rule.

Beautifully does he [St. Benedict] prescribe that *due honor be shown,* for it is not fitting that an equal reception be given to all; it is not right that the same things, in kind and in quantity— delicate food and abundance of drink—be prepared for the poor as for the rich. It would be more a sin [than an act deserving reward], because the poor man knows not moderation; if he were to eat all the food available as he has been accustomed to do, he

71 Hildemar, p. 501; *Cf.* also Paul, p. 417.
72 Hildemar, p. 605; *Cf.* also Paul, pp. 492-493.
73 Hildemar, pp. 605-606; *cf.* also Paul, p. 493.

would feel surfeited, and the sin would redound to us who occa-sioned it . . . Likewise it is not right that we prepare for the rich man those things which should be prepared for the poor; e. g., if we set before him only beans or a similar food, or should we wish to wash his feet [as it is done for the poor] it would be an insult, and considered foolishness, and it would cause a loss [to the monastery]. Therefore in saying *let due honor be shown* to all, he said that a guest should be received according to the quality of his person.[74]

The more specific directions for the care of the guests fall into three general classes: those for the nobility, those for the guest monks, and those for the poor.

In providing lodging for the rich it is necessary to receive also as many of their followers as come.[75] We have already noted that the food for the lay guests is to be prepared in a kitchen distinct from the monastic kitchen and also from that of the poor.[76] Both commentators state specifically that laymen are not to be admitted to the monastic refectory,[77] If the guest is a bishop or a count, or anyone of power who would take offense at being left alone were the guestmaster to go to the Office when the signal is given, the latter is to remain with the guest to avoid scandal.[78] This quasi-fear of the powerful was noted in the discussions of a suitable location of the mon-astery,[79] and in the question of the permissibility of a monk eating outside the monastery.[80]

74 Paul, p. 417; Hildemar, p. 502. The translation is based on Paul's text; the phrases enclosed in brackets are taken from Hildemar.

75 Paul, p. 420; Hildemar, p. 507.

76 Cf. *supra*, p. 134.

77 Paul, p. 419; Hildemar, *loc. cit.* The same prohibition is contained in the Capitulary of 817 (*MGH, Cap. reg. Franc.*, I, 347, no. 52).

78 Hildemar, p. 466. Scandal is here used in the sense of giving offense, or of arousing the ill-will of the nobleman.

79 Cf. *supra*, p. 27.

80 Cf. *supra*, p. 89. It is reflected, too, in the eighteenth article of the Statute of Risbach in which laymen are forbidden to enter the monastic cloister and disturb the silence of the monks, unless, perchance, they are

For the guest monks, a special dormitory should be arranged near the oratory. It should be separated from that of the lay guests because these latter " can remain up till midnight and talk and laugh, whereas the monks ought rather to keep silence and pray . . . Their vassals, however, should be in the other division with the laymen." [81] This dormitory of the guest monks appears to have been within the guest department, which was near the gate of the monastery; the brother of the monastery who should happen to return late is to be lodged here for the night, because, Hildemar observes, " the monks are all one." [82]

Guest monks and clerics should eat in the monastic refectory.[83] They should be served promptly so that the brethren suffer no delay in leaving the refectory.[84] Hildemar relates with approval that in *Francia* if a brother is entertaining a guest who is a monk or one to whom the " regular " order is known, the brother will leave the guest to repair to the Office when the signal is given; if fitting, he will return to the guest after the Office is completed.[85]

The number of poor to be received was restricted only by the number of beds available.[86] That this number did not always

persons of distinction who cannot be altogether avoided (*MGH, Cap. reg Franc.*, I, 228).

81 Hildemar, pp. 611-612.

82 *Loc. cit.*; *cf. supra*, pp. 27-28; Delatte, *op. cit.*, p. 339.

83 Paul, p. 419; Hildemar, p. 507. The Monastic Capitulary (*MGH, Cap. reg. Franc.*, I, 345, no. 27) specifies that bishops, abbots, canons, and nobles should eat with the abbot in the refectory. It grants power to the abbot to increase somewhat the customary allowance of the brethren when a guest is present. The twenty-third article of the Statutes of Murbach permits the monks to rejoice at the coming of other brothers and to relax the rule of abstinence (Albers, III, 89-90).

84 Paul, p. 420; Hildemar, pp. 507-508. Albers (III, 133, n. 1) sees in this admonition of Paul the implication that lay guests were admitted to the refectory; however, in view of what the commentator writes elsewhere, it would seem that this reference is to clerical or monastic guests.

85 Page 465.

86 Paul, p. 420; Hildemar, p. 507.

satisfy the demand is evident from the following remarks of Hildemar:

There should be this discretion in receiving the poor: if two or three come, some weak and others in health, you ought rather to help the weak, if it is not possible to help both the weak and the strong. With us, the guests are admitted at the ninth hour; but if a poor man come later, those already received are not to be ejected to make room for him. If possible he will be received, but if not, he is to be told to find another lodging since ours is filled to capacity.[87]

Although the ceremony of washing the feet of the poor seemed to concern primarily the wayfarers, Hildemar teaches that it should include even those from nearby who are in the *hospitale,* for it is not the distance to the place from which they come but the fact that they now reside in the *hospitale* that entitles them to participation in the ceremony; moreover, those to whom the monks give food and who live daily in the monastery should also be included.[88] Apparently, the *hospitale* was a sort of almshouse in which some poor men lived continually.

87 Page 508.
88 *Loc. cit.*

CHAPTER VII
LITURGY AND SPIRITUALITY

The most important corporate work to which Benedictine monks are devoted—and this applies to all ages since the founding of the Order—is the *Opus Dei,* the Divine Office. St. Benedict admonishes his followers to " let nothing be preferred to the work of God." [1] and he devotes eleven of the seventy-three chapters of the Rule to the subject.

In the Carolingian period some monasteries chanted the Roman Office instead of that outlined in the Rule.[2] There are several explanations for this lack of uniformity. The continuity of the Monte Cassino tradition was broken with the destruction of that monastery by the Lombards in the late sixth century. In its restoration nearly a century and a half later, it was only through the Anglo-Saxon monk Willibald who assisted Petronax of Brescia that it had even a roundabout connection with the first Monte Cassino.[3] The basilican monasteries in Rome and in Gaul originally chanted the Roman Office; gradually they adopted the Benedictine Office but often with modifications.[4] In the seventh century there were a number of Columban foundations which had not yet assumed the Rule, much less the Office, of St. Benedict.[5] Finally, the attitude of the bishops and of Charlemagne seemed to favor the Roman breviary as the subsequent discussion will show.

According to the commentaries, opinion was not of one cast even within some Benedictine monasteries. The indecision

1 *Regula,* c. 43 : " Ergo nihil operi Dei praeponatur."

2 *Cf. Statuta Murbacensia,* no. 3 (Albers, III, 81-82) ; letter of Paul to Charlemagne (*ibid.,* III, 54).

3 *Cf.* Butler, *Benedictine Monachism,* pp. 354-356.

4 *Cf.* Berlière, *L'Ascèse bénédictine,* pp. 42-45 ; Leclercq, " Office divin," *Dictionnaire d'archéologie chrétienne et de liturgie,* XII, 1962 ff., especially 1976-77.

5 *Cf.* C. Selmer, *Middle High German Translations of the Regula Sancti Benedicti,* p. 1, n. 4.

arose from the passage of the Rule (c. 18) which reads: "If perchance this distribution of the psalms displease anyone or he judgeth another better, let it be followed if, in any case, the whole psalter of one hundred fifty psalms be recited each week." Both commentators personally feel that St. Benedict wished his arrangement to be followed, but lest they might appear arbitrary in their explanation, they argue the question from both sides. To those who see in this passage of the Rule permission to say the Roman Office, they explain that St. Benedict spoke these words, not as a concession, but out of humility. Some may dissent, saying that his words offer proof of the concession, whereas proof that he spoke out of humility is lacking. In reply to this objection, the commentators insist that in the apparent concession, St. Benedict merely imitated the manner of the great and learned doctors who, when they have so thoroughly propounded a cause that nothing more can be added, say: "If another can explain it better, let his interpretation be followed." They point out that the Office was sung in his time and in his monastery as he explains it in the Rule, for St. Gregory writes that as he taught so he lived.[6]

To this, Hildemar adds the authority of St. Gregory, who, he notes, is said to have formulated the Roman Office. He praised the Rule, and in praising it, praised the Office described therein; on the basis of his authority, then, the monastic Office cannot rightly be considered inferior to the canonical Office.[7]

As to the Offices themselves, Hildemar explains that both are holy, for they are composed of holy and divine words; the same words are to be found in the monastic as in the Roman Office, the order alone being different. Likewise both are chanted by holy and devout men who are wholly pleasing to God in the singing of their respective Offices.[8]

In the weeks following Easter and Pentecost, according to Hildemar, the whole psalter was not sung in the Roman Office.

6 Paul, pp. 252-253; Hildemar, pp. 310-312.
7 *Loc. cit.*
8 *Ibid.*

For monks this would show, in the words of the Rule, "too slack a service in their devotion," especially since monks ough to devote more effort than the canons to the Offices; for a times the latter are burdened with the care of the faithful from which hindrances monks are free.[9]

Before analyzing what the commentators have to say con cerning conciliar and imperial regulations relative to certain parts of the Office, we shall note the attitude of the councils and the capitularies relative to the monastic Office as a whole.

The Council of Aachen held in 789 confirmed a number of articles which were contained in Charlemagne's capitulary of the same year.[10] The eightieth article of this documen /orders "that the Roman chant be taught everywhere as pre scribed by our father Pepin when he abolished the Gallicar chant."[11] Although this legislation is addressed to the eccles iastical order, it is not followed by a parallel command to the monastic order. It appears that Charlemagne's zeal in the matter of the Office centered only on the Roman chant.[12]

Seebass discounts almost totally the statement in the Chronicle of Moissac to the effect that the Synod of 802 re quired the monks to perform the Office according to the Rule he fails to find the demand in any preserved capitulary of Charlemagne, and concludes that it "originated only in the unreliable *Chronicon Moissiacense.*"[13]

9 Pages 312-313.

10 Hefele-Leclercq, *Histoire des conciles,* III, ii, 1027.

11 *MGH, Cap. reg. Franc.,* I, 61; A. Amelli has edited and analyzed the verse written by Paul Warnefrid commemorating the Roman Synod of 78 which decreed the discontinuance of the Ambrosian chant: "L'epigramma d Paolo Diacono intorno al canto Gregoriano e Ambrosiano," *Memori storiche Forogiuliesi,* IX (1913), 153-175.

12 *Cf.* O. Seebass, "Ueber die Statuta Murbacensia," *Zeitschrift für Kirchengeschichte,* XII (1891), 329.

13 *Ibid.,* 328, n. 1. Perhaps the chronicler based his statement on the mor general regulation constituting the twelfth article of the capitulary; it reads "Where there are monks, the abbots should live with their monks in stric accordance with the Rule" (*MGH, Cap. reg. Franc.,* I, 91). This genera command, after its first appearance in the capitulary of Karlmann in 74

Coming to the time of Louis the Pious and Benedict of Aniane, we find the emphasis shifted to the monastic Office. The Annals of Lorsch record for the year 816 that the Aachen Synod of that year commanded all the monks to sing the *cursus* of St. Benedict in the regular order.[14] Furthermore, the Murbach Statutes, which are based on the decrees of this synod, order that all the monks perform the Office of St. Benedict. In commenting on the decree, the compiler makes an interesting reservation: Those things concerning the distribution of the psalms which have been added from the Roman Office are to be retained at Murbach until such time when, by " the advice of our betters, either they will be dismissed or more definitely ordered to be retained."[15] Finally, the Monastic Capitulary of 817 orders that the monks celebrate the Office in the manner prescribed in the Rule of St. Benedict.[16]

Paul Warnefrid makes a vague reference to a council which should have enjoined that the Office for the days of Holy Week, beginning with Holy Thursday and including Easter Sunday, should be sung wholly as it was done in the Roman Church, and not according to the Rule for monks.[17] Hildemar apparently relates this council to that of Aachen held in 817.[18] " The pious Emperor Louis," he writes, " wished that the monks perform the Office according to the Rule, but because the bishops said it was not well that on these days [of Holy Week] the monks differ from the Roman Church in singing the Offices, certain abbots agreed with them." The result, according to Hildemar, was that the bishops prevailed in so far that the decree which

ibid., I, 25), was frequently repeated, at least in substance, in later Carolingian capitularies.

14 *MGH, SS*, I, 122. This chronicle, unlike that of Moissac, is reliable; *f*. Seebass, *op. cit.,* XII, 329.

15 Albers, III, 81-83 (article 3).

16 *MGH, Cap. reg. Franc.,* I, 344, no. 3.

17 Page 239.

18 In the record of the Aachen Council there is nothing which corresponds to Hildemar's report. *Cf.* also Traube, *Textgeschichte,* p. 104.

was drawn up ordered the Roman Office to be chanted during
the last three days of Holy Week, but the regular Office was to
be sung on Easter Sunday.[19]

Hildemar's personal sympathies are with those who pre
ferred to follow the monastic Office throughout; as a defense
of his view, he cites St. Gregory as saying that " varied customs
do no harm to the Catholic faith or to good morals." [20]

It is difficult to say just how much accuracy these reports
of Paul and Hildemar possess. Traube suggests that Paul'
mention of an otherwise unknown Lombard council might refer
to the Synod of Pavia which, according to a poem that is its
only witness, was held about 698 and dealt with the schism of
Aquileia.[21] He raises a question as to the historicity of the
detailed additions to Paul's statement which Hildemar offers
suggesting that the latter wished to bring the views of his
predecessors into agreement with the only report which he had
to give from decrees relative to the manner of performing the
Office in the monasteries.[22] Hildemar's statement that the pur
pose of the Frankish synod was to effect that the monks chan
the Office of the Roman Church during Holy Week is far from
accurate if, as it appears, he refers to the Aachen Council of
817; and it tends to arouse suspicion regarding the accuracy of
his entire account.

The question of accretions to the liturgy in the course of the
centuries is one which has considerable interest for Benedictines
in particular and for liturgical scholars in general. It was long
held that many additions and innovations originated with
Cluny. More recently, a number of these changes have been
traced to the time and person of Benedict of Aniane. Thus the
introduction of the daily Office of the Dead and the *trin*

19 Page 302.
20 Pages 301-302.
21 *Op. cit.*, p. 105.
22 Page 104.

oratio have been ascribed to him by recent Benedictine scholars.[23]

In his commentary, however, Paul Warnefrid mentions both of these additional devotions in a way which implies acquaintance with their use. He takes occasion to speak of the Office of the Dead in commenting on that chapter of the Rule (c. 52) in which St. Benedict prescribes that all leave the oratory in silence when the *Opus Dei* is completed unless a brother desires to pray alone in private: " He [St. Benedict] does not say that the Office of the Dead should not be celebrated there if it is done in community; likewise if one wishes, he may recite a second Office if this is done by all in common. To an individual, however, it should not be permitted to pray aloud if the whole congregation does not pray."[24] From these explanations, it does not follow that the Office of the Dead was recited daily; nevertheless, they seem to offer a precedent to the usage of Aniane.

Another reference to an additional Office is made in describing the order to be followed when the feast of a saint occurs on a Sunday. In this case, Paul explains that the Laudes should be those proper to the feast; if the brothers have another church, they may go there and chant the Laudes proper to

---

23 Butler, *op. cit.*, 295; Berlière, *op. cit.*, 48; Leclercq, *op. cit.*, XII, 2006 ff. These writers are inclined to think that under Benedict of Aniane the Office of the Dead was recited daily, but they recognize that the sources do not warrant absolute surety on the subject. Gougaud (*op. cit.*, pp. 58-59) is the only one to observe that the practice of making visits to the various altars is mentioned in the *Vita* of St. Pardulf who died *ca.* 737.

24 Paul, p. 413; Hildemar, p. 500. Butler (*op. cit.*, p. 294) writes that in this mention of an Office of the Dead by Warnefrid " there is no ground for supposing it was said otherwise than when a death occurred in the community." However, the equal mention of duplicating the Office in this passage, as also in the one referred to in the text which follows, does not seem to bear out Butler's opinion. The words of the text are: " non enim dicit ut ibi Officia Mortuorum non agantur, si generalitas est; similiter si duplicare vult officium, potest, si generalitas hoc agit. Verum non licet quemquam, si non generaliter hoc facit Congregatio, voce orare." In Abbot Angilbert's ritual *Ordo* for St. Riquier (*ca.* 800) it is prescribed that the monks recite Vespers, Matins, and Laudes of the Dead daily (Bishop, *op. cit.*, p. 328).

the Sunday.[25] This, Hildemar adds, is a matter of option and, therefore, need not be observed as if a law.[26] Furthermore, some additions were made to the various hours as originally outlined in the Rule. Paul points out that " the verse and the *Miserere* said in church are not ' regular,' for they are not prescribed in the Rule but are of monastic custom." [27] Apparently the psalm *Miserere* was chanted at the close of the canonical hour, for he writes in another connection that when the *Miserere* is begun at Sext the servers leave to put the food on the table. This same psalm is listed as a part of the Hours in the Codex St. Gall 914, the famous ninth-century manuscript which also contains the exemplar of the Rule.[28]

The *trina oratio* of Benedict of Aniane was not, strictly speaking, so much a liturgical function as it was a semi-private devotion which all the monks were exhorted to perform; later in the consuetudinaries of Cluny it became universally established. In the time of Benedict it consisted in chanting from five to fifteen psalms and visiting the altars of the church three times a day: before Matins, before Prime, and after Compline.[29]

This custom of visiting the altars was likewise known to Paul Warnefrid; moreover, he associates it with the same three times of the day. His remarks on the subject, however, are less precise, being made more or less indirectly.[30] He speaks of the custom, not as a precept to be followed, but rather as a practice already in vogue. In referring to the interval between Laudes and Prime he comments that " if you do not go chanting psalms

25 Page 225; *cf. ibid.*, p. 228.

26 Page 291.

27 Page 381; Hildemar, p. 463.

28 Albers, III, 172-173. Although this list is doubtless of a date somewhat later than that of Paul's commentary, it verifies for the later time the practice given by Paul for his time.

29 *Cf. Vita Benedicti abbatis Anianensis et Indensis auctore Ardo, MGH, SS,* XV, i, 216-217.

30 Paul, pp. 232-233, 261, 272; Hildemar, pp. 296, 322, 333. *Cf.* also *supra,* p. 115.

you do not act contrary to the Rule; although I have spoken of the practice, I neither encourage nor discourage it." [31]

Thus Paul seems quick to observe and point out customs which are not contained in the Rule. He does not easily approve of, much less enforce, innovations. At the same time he does not limit his interpretations to the letter of the Rule. The following instance will, perhaps, illustrate clearly his attitude on the subject. It concerns the provision of the Rule (c. 10) which prescribes that during the night Office in summer only one lesson is to be recited from memory in place of the three lessons and responsories which are "read from the book in winter." Paul writes that St. Benedict did not wish that there should be no reading from the book, but for the sake of discretion "he condescended to the pusillanimous," lest, because of the brevity of the nights and the heavier work of the day during the summer season, an occasion be given to murmuring. But, "since truth is not bound up in words, i. e., one ought not to interpret according to the letter, but according to the intention with which the holy doctor spoke," he concludes that if the labor is not strenuous and the congregation wishes to read in order to show greater devotion to God, it should be so done.[32]

Some years later at Monte Cassino, Paul writes to Charlemagne in the name of Abbot Theodemar, and among other things discusses the subject of the lessons for Matins in summer. He explains that at the time of St. Benedict the Roman Church did not read the three lessons, for that practice was introduced later by Pope Gregory or Honorius. In order that the monks might not appear to differ from the Roman Church, according to the letter, the predecessors at Monte Cassino instituted that the monks should likewise read three lessons from the book.[33] Even in this apparently different explanation, the

---

31 Paul, p. 233; Hildemar, p. 296. A custom, essentially the same although performed more as a public devotion, is contained in Angilbert's *Ordo* (Bishop, *op. cit.*, pp. 238-239).

32 Paul, p. 218; Hildemar, pp. 283-284.

33 Albers, III, 52-53.

implication is that under the current circumstances, St. Benedict would have legislated that the lessons be read in the summer Matins; to fulfill the spirit of the Rule appears to be Paul's goal.

The content of the Office as outlined in the Rule (c. 9-14) varies according as it is celebrated on week days, Sundays, or days of the solemnities and festivities. The commentators observe that the " solemnities " pertain to Christ and are preferred to the " festivities of the saints,"[34] Among the saints' days they distinguish those of first rank *(praecipua)* and those of lesser rank. The feasts which are observed throughout the " whole world " are considered the principal festivities;[35] likewise the feasts of those saints whose bodies are interred in a certain locality and whom the region particularly honors are to be ranked as major festivities for that place, e. g. Saints Ambrose and Victor for Milan.[36]

To the feasts of the first rank only, the commentators apply the precept of the Rule (c. 14) relative to the festivities of the saints. It provides that Matins should be proper to the feast but

34 Paul, p. 237; Hildemar, p. 299. The commentators enumerate the following solemnities of Christ: the Nativity, Circumcision, Apparition, Presentation, the Last Supper, Good Friday, Holy Saturday, Easter, Ascension, and Pentecost.

35 Those specified are: the feasts of the twelve apostles, the Assumption of the Blessed Virgin, the feasts of Saints John the Baptist, Lawrence, Benedict, Martin, Caecilia, Agatha, Agnes, and All Saints in November. Concerning the introduction of the last feast, see P. Paschini, " Paolo Diacono e la sua *Expositio super Regulam sancti Benedicti*," *Memorie storiche Forogiuliesi*, XXV (1929), 84.

36 Paul, pp. 237-238; Hildemar, p. 300. Other Milanese saints named are Saints Protase, Gervase, Nabor, Felix, Nazarius, Celsus, and Simplicianus. Paschini *(loc. cit.)* notes that all the feasts except the last are to be found in the Cassinese calendars of the eighth and ninth centuries. Three of these calendars were published and analyzed by E. A. Loew: *Die ältesten Kalendarien aus Monte Cassino*, Quellen und Untersuchungen zur lateinischen Philologie des Mittelalters, III, iii (1908). By way of a supplement to this study, G. Morin published, along with the calendars given by Loew, a fourth calendar contemporary with the other three: "Les Quatres Plus Anciens Calendriers du Mont-Cassin (VIIIe et IXe siècles)," *Revue bénédictine*, XXV (1908), 486-497.

should be arranged as on Sundays, i. e., it should consist in the chanting of three nocturns of psalms and canticles, twelve lessons with their responsories, and the Gospel. The commentators point out that the other Hours of the Office and the Mass should likewise be those of the feast. Moreover, the Vespers of the preceding day, beginning with the *capitulum,* should also relate to the feast.[37]

The saints' feasts of lesser rank, even though they are important enough to have a proper Mass, are not to be observed as the Sundays. If they were, the commentators observe, the greatness of their number would render the celebration of all of them difficult and little else could be done.[38] Instead, at Matins three lessons with their responsories will be read proper to the feast; likewise, the Laudes and the Mass will be those of the feast; but all the other canonical hours will be taken from the ferial Office.[39] Hildemar notes that the Vespers of the preceding day, beginning with the *capitulum* should be proper to the feast of the day. Both commentators speak of this manner of observing the lesser feasts as "making a commemoration of the saints." [40] This terminology as also the *ordo* for the lesser feasts, when compared with that of the current *memoria* and *duplex maius* Offices, presents a tradition which has suffered little alteration in the course of a thousand and more years.

The commentators discuss with equal clarity another point regarding the content of the Office. It is not treated in the Rule, and yet it is a matter which would demand a solution in practice, namely, the procedure to be followed when a saint's feast falls on a Sunday. The passage in Paul's account reads:

If it is one of the principal festivities, i. e., of St. John the Baptist, of the Apostles, of St. Martin, or any feast universally

37 Paul, p. 238; Hildemar, pp. 300-301. To conform to current usage, the *lectio* of Vespers is denoted as the *capitulum.*

38 Paul, p. 237; Hildemar, p. 299.

39 Paul, p. 238; Hildemar, pp. 300-301.

40 Paul, p. 237; Hildemar, p. 299.

considered of first rank, the entire Office of the saint should be sung: the twelve lessons with their proper responses and the whole of Laudes including the psalms and antiphons. The day Hours are to be sung with antiphons,[41] and the psalms and antiphons of Vespers are to be those of the feast. The morning Mass should be that of the Sunday and the major Mass that of the feast. If, however, it is the festivity not of St. John . . . or any feast of first rank, but one of lesser importance, then eight of the lessons and responsories ought to be proper to the Sunday, and the four remaining lessons and responses should be read from the Office of the saint. The entire Laudes should be from the feast, . . . but the *alleluia* is to be sung at Tierce, Sext, and None. The Mass of this lesser feast should be sung in the morning, and the major Mass should be that of the Sunday.[42]

The precision with which these expositions are expressed gives the impression that the commentator has directly transmitted to writing the practice of his time; its resemblance to current usage is surprisingly striking.

Further discussions on the content of the Office, such as those regarding the *alleluia*,[43] the doxology,[44] the *capitulum* for Laudes on week days,[45] the choice of lessons for Matins according to the season,[46] even to the special arrangement for an early morning Mass on Christmas Day,[47] should be of interest to the liturgist but seem superfluous for this study.

The commentaries tell us only a little concerning the external execution of the Divine Office; of the attitude and spirit in which it should be performed they tell more. The little which

41 The "day Hours" signify Prime, Tierce, Sext, and None. In saying that they are said with antiphons, the commentator implies that the antiphons are proper to the feast; for the Sunday Office they would be said with *Alleluias.*

42 Paul, p. 225; Hildemar, pp. 290-291.

43 Paul, pp. 227-228, 243; Hildemar, pp. 293, 303-304.

44 Hildemar, pp. 302-303.

45 Paul, pp. 227, 232; Hildemar, pp. 292-293, 295-296.

46 Paul, p. 216; Hildemar, p. 281.

47 Hildemar, p. 287.

is related relative to the outward form, however, is sufficient to indicate that this public prayer was conducted in a dignified and orderly manner. A brother is appointed to write out the names of those who are to read or chant on Sunday and feast days, and to list also what they are to read or chant.[48] The brothers who intone the verses are appointed by the abbot.[49] They are to stand in the first place in choir if worthy; if not, those who are first among the boys are to intone the verses.[50] For the sake of learning the chant and for propriety, the eldest of the boys should sing the antiphons if they can.[51]

The Rule (c. 11) prescribes that when the lessons have been read and the cantor begins the *Gloria Patri* of the response, all should rise at once with reverence. The commentators explain that the brothers are not to rise hastily but reverently with bowed heads; they are to remain inclined until the words *Spiritui Sancto* have been sung. This bow should be uniform and sufficiently deep that the brothers may place their hands on their knees; likewise they are to rise in unison.[52]

Passing from the externals to the spirit, we find the commentators admonishing the cantors that when they sing they should desire to please the people, not with their voices, but with the words they sing, for thus will they seek the advance-

---

48 Hildemar, p. 475; Paul (p. 390) speaks only of the names of those who read or chant.

49 Paul, p. 386; Hildemar, p. 469.

50 Hildemar, p. 475; Paul (p. 390) differs slightly on this point.

51 Hildemar, *loc. cit.* This sentence is ungrammatical but has been translated in the light of a preceding sentence: ". . . debet ille, qui in capite infantum est in choro, prehendere versum." The text reads: "Antiphonas autem propter cantum discendi et ad honestatem priorum infantes, si posunt, dicere debent." In the commentaries as in the Rule, *dicere* and *canere* are used interchangeably in connection with the Office. A monastic document, thought to be contemporary, legislates similarly regarding verse intonation: "Those begin the verse, who, in comparison with the rest, can be the more useful, so that after the first or second syllable the rest can join in. And those youths should always pronounce the verse in a high voice" (Albers, III, 43-44).

52 Paul, p. 224; Hildemar, p. 289.

ment and salvation of the people; if, however, they were to de
sire to please only with their voices, they would be seeking no
the salvation of others but the vanity of their own glory.[53]

In spiritual things such as prayer and fasting, Hildemar
writes, he builds on a rock who, for the love of Christ, performs good works and has Christ as his foundation, i. e., as
the motivation of his work; and he builds on sand who does
any good work with the intention of receiving human praise.[5]
Mere lip service is not sufficient; only he chants wisely and
offers praise to God who meditates in his heart what he speaks
with his lips.[55] "But," Hildemar asks, "what of a simple
brother who does not know the meaning of the verse he sings?"
He answers his own question: So long as his mind is occupied
not with some person or thing of the world, but with God
through a more or less imperfect grasp of what the versicle
connotes, he fulfills the precept.[56]

The attitude of mind in which the psalms are to be chanted
is described by way of a gloss on the pertinent words of the
Rule. The following paragraph gives, in a slightly condensed
form, the interpretation of the commentator, together with the
passages of the Rule on which it is based.

When St. Benedict reminds us that the Prophet saith, "Serve
ye the Lord with fear," he wishes to explain that at no other
time can we so well contemplate God as at the time of prayer.
And therefore when we assist at that Divine Work, i. e., at the
time of the psalmody, we should stand before God with fear,
but with a chaste fear, such as that with which a son comes
before his well-loved father; thus should we come before God,
seeking, in so far as human frailty permits, to realize and understand His presence. When he says, "Especially when we assemble for the *Opus divinum*," it is not meant that we come
nearer to God by approaching in space, but by thinking upon

53 Paul, p. 256; Hildemar, p. 316.
54 Pages 56-57.
55 Paul, pp. 245, 256; Hildemar, pp. 308, 316.
56 Pages 317-318.

Him and devoting ourselves to Him as much as human frailty permits. For although He is wholly in the house, in the church, in Heaven, and everywhere, the more we meditate upon Him in any place whatsoever, the more we know and feel His presence.[57]

The commentators observe that he whose devotion is always based on God offers continual praise to Him in his heart whether he sleeps or keeps vigil; but St. Benedict, knowing that vocal praise cannot be offered to God without intermission as can the praise of the heart, appointed stated hours so that at least at these times praises would be offered to God also in words.[58]

Thus far, liturgical prayer, or the public prayer of the Church, has been the subject of discussion. The Rule (c. 52) provides also for private prayer, and the commentators make some interesting remarks on the same. Why, they ask, does St. Benedict speak of praying privately or in secret, when he has allowed no time for such prayer? Since, during the entire day the monks are to be devoted to reading, or are to work, or eat, or sleep, how can one remain in the oratory or enter there to pray? The implication in the answer is that since contemplation is the gift of only the few, it was not included in the general disposal of the monk's day. The answer then states clearly that although contemplation pertains to only a few, these few are not to be deprived of the tears of devotion; for St. Benedict did not prefer reading or work to contemplation. Therefore one so gifted may dispense with reading or work to go into the oratory to pray.[59]

In another passage, Hildemar appears to contradict what has just been said regarding the number who are inclined to contemplation; he states that there are many who are given to contemplation and who experience such good thoughts that they

[57] Hildemar, pp. 315-316; Paul's account (p. 255) is not so complete.

[58] Paul, p. 244; Hildemar, p. 306.

[59] Paul, pp. 412-413; Hildemar, p. 500. *Cf.* also Paul, p. 402, and Hildemar, p. 492.

would find it impossible to express them in words.[60] In this passage, however, Hildemar is not speaking exclusively of private prayer.

In commenting on the precept of the Rule that prayer should always be short,[61] our expositors point out that the reference is not to the prayer said in the Office, but to that prayer which each monk makes by himself.[62] So long ought one remain in prayer as, with the Lord's help, he can repress vain thoughts. If, however, he sees himself overcome by distractions, and that he no longer delights in prayer, he should rise up and apply himself to reading, to the psalmody, or to work. And since St. Benedict understood that because of its infirmity the human mind cannot continue long in prayer without distractions, he recommended that prayer be short.[63]

In a brief passage Paul Warnefrid strikes a mystical note which echoes the strains of St. Gregory relative to contemplative prayer:

Moreover, the Lord gave us the words with which to pray, and those same words are few, so that when we stand to pray before God, our mind, by dwelling on the meaning of the words, may tranquilly and serenely enjoy that Invisible Light to the extent that human nature permits; for we cannot always see God because of the various terrestrial preoccupations with which our mind is impressed and made to reflect, and our vision is not receptive solely to the things of God.[64]

The brief glimpse of the Light Invisible is particularly characteristic of St. Gregory's mysticism, and is very probably traceable to the influence of his writings.[65]

60 Page 243.
61 *Regula*, c. 20.
62 Paul, p. 260; Hildemar, p. 321.
63 Paul, pp. 258-259; Hildemar, p. 320.
64 Paul, p. 255; Hildemar, p. 315.
65 *Cf.* Butler, *Western Mysticism, passim.*

In his discussion of private prayer, Hildemar inserts a few words regarding the manner of assisting at the Sacrifice of the Mass. Although this instruction doubtless reflects the ancient practice, it may well have been written by an exponent of the modern liturgical movement exhorting the faithful to follow the prayers of the Mass rather than some pious devotions contained in a prayerbook. We shall quote the passage.

The better [method of] prayer, it seems to me, is as follows: when the priest recites the Lord's Prayer and other prayers aloud, you should not pray anything else, but in spirit follow that prayer [of the priest]; and so follow it that when he says *per omnia saecula*, you may answer, *Amen*. If, however, the priest says the Lord's Prayer or other prayers in secret as at the Mass over the oblation, you may pray either in words and in the heart, or in the heart only, as you wish; but you should so end your prayer that when the priest says *per omnia*, you may be prepared to respond *Amen*.[66]

Although the commentators state that the contemplative life consists in reading and prayer,[67] it does not appear that the time of reading was generally considered to be one of contemplative prayer. It is true that, as we noted earlier, the commentators would have the monks sit apart during the time of reading so that one inclined to contemplation and tears would not be impeded by others.[68] But we also observed in a passage above that when a monk ceases prayer he is to apply himself to reading or the chant, thus distinguishing *lectio* from *oratio*. It seems more correct to conclude that the hours of reading were regarded as a time in which the monk familiarized himself with spiritual writings so as to widen his spiritual horizon and thus prepare himself for the more intensively spiritual exercises. Delatte has neatly expressed this idea in saying that " the name *lectio* is only

66 Page 321.
67 Paul, p. 394; Hildemar, p. 478.
68 *Cf. supra*, p. 118.

the first moment of an ascending series: *lectio, cogitatio, studium, meditatio, oratio, contemplatio.*" [69]

An adequate estimate of the deep spirituality which underlies the commentary cannot be formed without a careful reading of the entire work. The prologue of the Rule, however, containing as it does the philosophy of the Rule, lends itself more readily to the development of the more spiritual phases of monastic thought. From our Carolingian interpretations of the prologue, therefore, we shall select a few characteristics of this spirituality.[70]

In general, its essence arises in the relations which the commentator sees to exist between God, the Creator, and man, the creature. On the part of man there is original sin in general and the personal sin of the individual; on the part of God there is the " loving kindness of His mercy " and the Redemption of His Cross. It is well, Hildemar observes, that St. Benedict speaks of God's loving kindness, " for no one is saved by his own merit; after we were all expelled from Paradise in the person of Adam, the whole human race fell. Therefore when one is saved, it is not by his own merit, but through the kindness and mercy of God . . . He shows us the way of life by which we may return to life." [71] In another passage the commentator explains that according to the sacred Scriptures, God rarely looks upon the bad, but he does see the good. He looks upon those of the good who are in sin that they may be corrected, and upon the just that they may become more perfect.[72]

Paul sees in the phrase of the Rule, " the Lord Christ, the true King," words weighty with meaning.[73] We shall paraphrase a part of what he gives regarding the name of Christ,

---

69 *Op. cit.,* p. 306.

70 In Hildemar's version, seventy-two pages are devoted to the Prologue; in Paul's only twenty-six, covering less than one-fourth of the Prologue. Traube (*Textgeschichte,* p. 102) states that this brevity is due to defects in the *Vorlage* on which it was based.

71 Page 43.

72 Hildemar, p. 39.

73 Page 17.

for he associates it with the mystery of the Redemption. Whenever one hears mention made of the Son of God—and "Christ" is appellative of the Son—he ought to recall to mind the mystery of his own redemption and that of the whole human race; for although man's redemption is related to the operation and mercy of the undivided Trinity, nevertheless, it is related in a special manner to the Son, for He only assumed flesh and shed His blood. For this reason, so Paul interprets, St. Benedict added the name of Christ to that of Lord, to recall the mystery of the Redemption. As above he spoke of Him from Whom man had departed by disobedience, i. e., the sin of Adam,[74] so now he adds the name "Christ" to make it plain to his followers that it is particularly through Christ's Redemption that they are recalled.[75]

The commentators continually insist on properly comprehending the spiritual significance of the words of the Rule, and, for that matter, all religious literature. To this end they frequently compare and contrast the faculties "of the interior man" and "of the heart" with the external senses, e. g., they explain that the words of the Gospel, "who has ears to hear, let him hear," is paramount to saying, "I speak to those who hear with the ears of the heart." [76] In the following passage, Hildemar continues this comparison of the exterior and interior faculties and gives also a contrast of the present and future life.

As our exterior man when walking in darkness needs a temporal light, because without it he cannot make his way in the dark, so also our interior man, walking the dark way of this present life, which, when compared with the eternal life, should rather be called death than life, needs a spiritual light, namely, the word of God, in order that he may pass through this present life without offense; for without this light, i. e. the word of God, he errs in this present life just as the exterior man errs who walks in the dark without a lamp.[77]

74 Paul, pp. 13-14. 75 Paul, p. 18; Hildemar, p. 13.
76 Paul, p. 10; Hildemar, p. 5. *Cf. ibid.,* Prologue, *passim.*
77 Pages 45-46.

The commentator's remarks on the beatific vision illustrate an equal grasp of the spiritual. Although this vision is not granted equally to all because of dissimilar merits, nevertheless it is one and the same vision just as it is enjoyed in the one kingdom of Heaven. Nor is God seen with the eyes as some material thing is seen; for "to see " in this usage means to comprehend. Furthermore, this vision will never become tiresome, but will ever be desired; the Apostle Peter testifies to this in speaking of God as " Him whom the angels desire to gaze upon." To the saints, this vision will be nourishment, brilliance, and power.[78]

Finally, the question is raised as to how the precept of the Rule, to serve God continually *(omni tempore)* can be fulfilled.[79] This is an unusual admonition, the commentators remark, to serve God continually; for man's service cannot be continuous but only through an interval of time. The solution lies once more in the distinction drawn between the spirit and the externals. The *"omni tempore"* applies not to the external man but to the interior; for the exterior man must also engage in worldly occupations without which he cannot subsist.   The interior man can offer continuous service to God, because through his intention he can serve God at all times although he is occupied with the cares and solicitudes of subsistence.[80]

78 Hildemar, p. 47.
79 *Regula,* Prologue.
80.Paul, pp. 25-26; Hildemar, pp. 22-23.

CHAPTER VIII
ASCETICISM AND IDEALS

THE concept of asceticism reflected in the commentaries accords well with the Christian principles of asceticism. Abstinence, fasting, and like practices are not to be performed for their own sakes, but as a means to an end; this end is the advancement in spiritual perfection, or as the commentators express it, the performance of "perfect works," i. e., the exercise of "faith, hope, and charity." [1]

To present this teaching in a manner in which it could be grasped by readers less learned and, perhaps, less spiritual than himself, Paul develops the thought by way of a simile: Just as the smith fashions a sword or a lance with his proper tools such as the hammer and the forceps, as the physician performs healing by means of his knife and book of herbs, and as the scribe writes a book with his pen and parchment, so the servant of God performs such works as faith, hope, and charity by means of prayer, fasting, and the like. And as it would be folly for the smith to fashion a sword in order that he might possess the tools, so would it be folly for the servant of God to exercise faith, hope, and charity in order to possess the "instruments of the spiritual art." [2]

Furthermore, these "instruments" constitute a necessary means without which the perfect works cannot be effected. [3] The explanation is to be found in the fact and effects of original sin. Man is weak in body by nature; but weakness of the soul is to be deputed rather to man's tainted state, for God created

1 Hildemar, pp. 139-140. Paul's explanation (pp. 97-98) is basically the same.

2 Hildemar, p. 139. In comparing the text of this passage in Paul's work (p. 97) with that of Hildemar, it becomes evident that the apparent contradiction in the former is due to a scribal omission of what follows in Hildemar's version between the phrase *his similia* and its repetition a few lines further on.

3 Hildemar, p. 140; Paul, p. 98.

the soul good; wherefore if it had remained in the dignified state of its creation it would not be deficient in goodness; but because man fell from this dignified state, he cannot, without labor, attain to the goodness which he formerly possessed without effort.[4]

The commentators present this teaching more specifically in relating the difficulty man experiences in obedience, to the sin of Adam. Adam, when in Paradise, obeyed God without effort; but since man has been expelled from Paradise and sent into exile he cannot obey God without labor. His inclination to disobey God's commands arises in the disobedience of Adam.[5]

They explain that in self-denial man rejects that which exists in him through sin, not what he is by nature; " We are one thing fallen through sin, and we are another as founded by nature. What we have done is distinct from what we were made . . . Therefore, we should deny ourselves inasmuch as we have acted through sin and we should remain ourselves inasmuch as we have been formed through grace." [6]

Self-abnegation may consist in corporal or in spiritual austerities; both are treated by the commentators. In discussing the former they insist on the necessity of discretion, as the following lines indicate:

Great discretion is necessary in bodily chastisement lest it be insufficient or overmuch—lest when one wishes to smite the enemy, the citizen be struck. For if the chastisement be too severe, one will not be able to fulfill the service of God; if it be insufficient, one will be led into the abyss. For example, the slave, if not constrained, will murmur and rise up against his master; if constrained he will, likewise, murmur. It is better that he murmur under constraint than dissolutely. So it is with the body: if chastised, it will murmur because it always thinks in the manner of the world; and if not chastised, it will fall into the abyss. It is better that it

4 Hildemar, pp. 63-64.
5 Paul, pp. 13-14; Hildemar, pp. 8-9.
6 Hildemar, pp. 146-147; cf. also Paul, p. 101.

should find fault under constraint, than that it should go wantonly into the abyss.[7]

The leading corporal austerities commented upon by our expositors are fasting and abstinence. The former, they observe, leads man to the mortification of the vices.[8] In this and similar uses of the word "vices," it evidently signifies the passions or inclinations to sin; for example, the commentators explain that the vices are so closely a part of human nature that one is not able to be wholly free from them, although all are not of equal force; therefore, those which cannot be entirely removed, may at least be controlled and repressed;[9] and again, "we ought to acquire such contrary virtues as will repress the vices from which we cannot be wholly free".[10]

Fasting should be performed so discreetly and temperately that the monk does not thereby become unable to fulfill his obedience, nor that he becomes so weak as to require fleshmeat or another special food; rather he should so fast that if perchance he become weakened, he can regain his strength from the measure of food prescribed in the Rule.[11] This admonition is given with reference to the Lenten fast which each individual is voluntarily to assume over and above the fast of the Rule. The latter consists in the restriction of the food to one refection daily during the winter and on the Wednesdays and Fridays of the summer season. The Wednesday-Friday fast, according to the commentators, originated with the Fathers, although there was also a Jewish custom of fasting on these days.[12]

7 Hildemar, p. 148. In copying the corresponding passage in Paul's account (pp. 101-102), the scribe has erroneously written *minimum* for *nimium*. It is evident from the context that *nimium* was the word used by the author: "In castigatione enim corporis, magna discretio necessaria est, ne aut minus, aut nimium [not minimum as in Paul] castigetur, . . . Si enim nimium [Paul: minimum] castigaveris corpus, Dei servitium operari non potes . . ." (Hildemar, *loc. cit.*).

8 Paul, pp. 206-207; Hildemar, p. 269.

9 Paul, p. 401; Hildemar, p. 490.   10 Paul, p. 444; Hildemar, p. 541.

11 Hildemar, p. 492; *Cf.* also Paul, p. 403.

12 Paul, p. 367; Hildemar, p. 449. Gougaud (*op. cit.*, pp. 144-145) writes

Concerning the precept of abstinence from the use of flesh-meat, there is evidence of a disputed point in the interpretation of the commentaries and contemporary literature. The indecision and divergent opinions center around the question as to whether or not the Rule, by implication, forbids the flesh of fowls; in one passage it expressly forbids the flesh of quadrupeds.[13] Both commentators would answer the question in the affirmative, and they cite various reasons for their view.

Perhaps the reason which would possess greatest weight today is that given by Hildemar, namely, that St. Benedict did not specify the kinds of meat, but under the general term " carnes," forbade the eating of meat not only of quadrupeds but of fowls as well. In support of his view, he cites Cassiodorus, St. Augustine, and St. Jerome.[14] Both commentators argue that since the meat of fowls is sweeter than that of quadrupeds, and since the latter is forbidden, there is all the more reason that the former should likewise be forbidden.[15] Again, they admit that a solution of the matter cannot be derived conclusively from the wording of the Rule; the proper method to follow, therefore, is to dismiss the doubtful and accept the certain. In the case in point, one would not sin were he to abstain from the meat of fowls even though St. Benedict had intended it to be eaten, whereas one would sin were he to eat

that this fast was legislated for in the monastic Rules of Macarius and Columban, was prescribed by Bishop Perpetuus of Tours for his flock, and, according to Cassian, was observed by the monks of Egypt and long practiced in the Orient where it seemed to have been of precept for the faithful. About the year 800, it was decreed by the Councils of Risbach, Freising, and Salzburg that it be observed by all the clergy (*MGH, LL,* III, *Concilia aevi Karolini,* I, i, 208, 214, 216).

13 *Regula,* c. 39: " Carnium vero quadrupedum omni modo ab omnibus abstineatur comestio, praeter omnino debiles aegrotos." The Rule of St. Caesarius of Arles, a contemporary of St. Benedict, specifically prohibits the use of the flesh of fowls along with that of quadrupeds: " Pullos et carnes numquam sani accipiant " (*Regula ad monachos, PL,* 67, col. 1103).

14 Page 414.

15 Paul, p. 342; Hildemar, pp. 409-410.

the meat which the lawgiver had intended to forbid. Therefore, the former course should be followed.[16]

Turning to contemporary regulations and practice, we find the seventh article of the Murbach Statutes forbidding use of the flesh of fowls to all except the infirm.[17] In explanation, the compiler states that although the authority of the Rule does not forbid the use of fowls, but, as it were, leaves it to one's choice either to eat or abstain, the synod (on which the Murbach Statutes are based) has decreed that monks, who have chosen the more religious discipline of life, should abstain from such viands.[18]

The same interpretation of the precept of the Rule regarding the use of meat is to be found in Paul Warnefrid's letter to Charlemagne, namely, that St. Benedict so prudently arranged the matter that, when it is opportune, the monks may eat the flesh of fowls, if they wish, without being subject to fault. It is not to be understood, however, that the brothers may demand it as if it were a right. The practice was never to eat the flesh of fowls except within the octave of the Nativity and on the Paschal days.[19]

The eighth article of the Aachen Capitulary (817), like the seventh article of the Murbach Statutes, forbids the use of the flesh of fowls except to the infirm. The seventy-eighth article of the capitulary corresponds to Paul's letter in providing that the flesh of fowls, if available, may be eaten on the Nativity and within Easter week, but it is not to be regarded as a right which may be demanded.[20]

16 Paul, pp. 342-343; Hildemar, pp. 410-411. To say that it would be sinful to eat the meat under the circumstances given, is not, of course, morally sound. The doubt may be resolved in favor of him who is unable to obtain more precise knowledge.

17 It implies, of course, that the prohibition of the flesh of quadrupeds, as expressed in the Rule, also obtains.

18 Albers, III, 84-85.

19 Paul's letter Charlemagne, Albers, III, 57-58.

20 *MGH, Cap. reg. Franc.*, I, 344, 348. This seventy-eighth article is not given in all the manuscripts of the capitulary, and since it partially contradicts the eighth article, it is probably an interpolation (*Cf.* Albers, III, xxi-xxiii).

Thus, although the commentators would interpret the Rule as excluding all fleshmeat from the monastic table, out of deference to the current interpretation they do not dismiss the subject without presenting various arguments on both sides. Butler intimates that at Monte Cassino the interpretaion permitting the use of fowls arose during the break of over a hundred years in the Cassinese traditions;[21] he also notes that " a distinction between the flesh of animals and of birds is not one that would appeal to the modern mind." [22]

Hildemar offers reasons why all forms of fleshmeat should be excluded from the monastic fare: it is not read of the Lord that, after his resurrection, he ever ate any meat but fish; nor is it read of the Apostles or the monastic founders that they ever ate fleshmeat; finally, as the meat of fowls, through its sweetness of taste, is wont to stimulate the passions, so also the flesh of quadrupeds, through its greater strength, confers power to these passions; for the repression of the same, therefore, neither kind of meat should be eaten.[23]

The commentators point out that if delicate foods are placed before a monk, he may eat them for the sake of hospitality or necessity. They explain that the sin does not consist in the food itself, but rather in an unlawful desire for it. Thus many have sinned in desiring only common food as did the sons of Israel when in the desert they yearned for onions and melons, whereas others have eaten meat without sin as did the prophet Elias to whom ravens supplied meat morning and evening.[24]

Hildemar even makes reference to a conciliar decree directed against the Manichaean heresy of dualism; the decree threatened with anathema anyone who abhorred the use of fleshmeat. The commentator explains that those who abstain

21 *Benedictine Monachism,* p. 44, n. 1.

22 *Op. cit.,* p. 308.

23 Pages 441-442. In 1336 the Bull "Benedictina" granted the general dispensation whereby meat was permitted to be eaten on four days a week. Most of the Benedictine congregations today observe the rule of abstinence on one or more days of the week, over and above the Friday abstinence.

24 Hildemar, p. 149. *Cf.* also *ibid.,* p. 152; Paul, pp. 102, 105.

from meat for the sake of restraint do not violate the decree; but those who " abominate the flesh " should eat herbs in which meat has been cooked.[25] The context of this sentence, as also the foregoing paragraphs, indicates clearly that the doctrines of Gnosticism find no place in the commentaries under study nor in the ascetic literature of the period. In the light of this fact, some sweeping statements made by certain writers on monastic asceticism need revision; for example, Mr. H. B. Workman speaks of the " half-veiled Gnosticism throughout the vast literature of monasticism," [26] and he states that " not only the wilder hermits of the East, but monks of culture and influence—for instance, St. Bernard—sought to reduce it [the body] to ruin. They made pain an end in itself." [27] Some pages further on in his study, the same writer contradicts the last sentence, at least in part, and in doing so he agrees better with our commentary literature. He writes: " For the more reasonable monk asceticism was but a means to an end, rather than an end in itself. A St. Benedict or St. Bernard strove to get this world beneath his feet that he might the better see the other world above his head." [28]

The following passage from Hildemar's commentary presents a forcible statement of his attitude toward the excessive practice of corporal austerities.

Is the censure of the silent to be preferred to the edification of many, or is abstinence from food to be preferred to patience, or vigils to reason?   For he does not err lightly who prefers a lesser good to a greater good. Does not rational man lose his dignity when he prefers fasting to charity or when he so prefers the keeping of vigils to the integrity of reason that he incurs the mark of madness or sadness through the immoderate and indiscreet chanting of psalms or the Offices?   Can God be bent by a multitude of words as man can be?   For not only in words but also in deeds

25 Page 411.
26 *The Evolution of the Monastic Ideal*, p. 63.
27 *Ibid.*, p. 324.
28 *Ibid.*, p. 339.

should God be implored, for He asks not for many words but for purity of heart . . . Therefore, let him who deprives the body of what is necessary hear what the Lord has spoken through the Prophet: " I am the Lord that love judgment, and hate robbery in a holocaust."[29]   Now he offers to God a holocaust of robbery who indiscreetly deprives himself of food, clothing, sleep, and the like, without which human infirmity is not able to subsist.[30]

In passing on to the ascetic practices which pertain more to the spiritual than the material life, we observe that the admonitions of the commentators to use discretion and moderation are replaced by exhortations to more intensive application.

The many references in the Rule to the subject of silence have occasioned many comments on the subject by our glossators. That the Rule does not demand absolute silence is evident from two brief passages: " Let permission to speak be seldom given " (c. 6) and " Let not brother join brother at unsuitable hours " (c. 48). From the latter, modern commentators infer that " suitable hours " during which the monks are permitted to converse are implied.[31]

Paul Warnefrid explains that the " unsuitable hours " (*horae incompetentes*) are those hours which the brothers devote to reading. During this time a brother ought not to join another nor speak with him without necessity. The hours of work are also " unsuitable," if to speak with another it would be necessary to leave one's work. But if all the brothers work together at the same task of obedience, it is permitted, Warnefrid writes, for one to speak with another, notwithstanding the opinion of some to the contrary.[32] In another passage, the " suitable hours " are identified with " those hours in which they ought to speak, as are those hours of the day in which they are not to read or to keep silence . . . The time is *in-*

29 Isa. 61 : 8.
30 Page 566.
31 *Cf.* Delatte, *op. cit.,* p. 316; Butler, *op. cit.,* pp. 288-290.
32 Paul, pp. 396-397; Hildemar, p. 483.

competens during the night, and during the time which should be devoted to reading." [33]

These remarks are not sufficiently explicit to warrant the conclusion that there was a daily fixed period of recreative conversation. Although they do seem to indicate that some speaking beyond what necessity would demand was permitted, there are other references in the commentaries which would give a contrary opinion. [34] At Corbie in the early ninth century, the brothers were permitted to assemble each day and converse freely, after the *horae incompetentes* had passed. [35] An eighth-century document thought to have originated at Monte Cassino reports that it was customary for a certain verse to be said at chapter as a signal for the breaking of silence, which had been carefully preserved until that hour. The authority was given the abbot to say the verse again after None to permit conversation if he saw fit. [36] In view of these customs, the attitude of our commentators regarding silence is seen to be quite conservative. [37]

In order to preserve silence the better during the "unsuitable hours," the commentators prescribe that a place in the monastery be appointed in which one may speak when necessary without hindrance to those who read or chant. [38] A similar provision is reported for Monte Cassino in the eighth century. [39] The commentators interpret those passages of the Rule

33 Paul, p. 318; Hildemar, pp. 384-385.

34 For example, Paul, p. 135; Hildemar, p. 202.

35 Levillain, *Les Statuts d'Adalhard pour l'abbaye de Corbie*, p. 32.

36 Albers, III, p. 16.

37 G. Morin ("La journée du moine," *Revue bénédictine*, VI [1889], 352) writes that a daily period for conversation was universal in the monasteries as early as the ninth century.

38 Paul, p. 135; Hildemar, p. 202.

39 Albers, III, 17-18. Evidently the custom at Monte Cassino was to set aside two places in which speaking was permitted. The sentence in which this is reported is ungrammatical, and has been wrongly interpreted to mean that certain brothers, "desiring to come to the perfection of silence, were permitted to speak only to two brothers appointed for the purpose" (G. Falco, "Lineamenti di storia Cassinese," *Casinensia*, II, 508).

in which the word " silence " is modified by some such adjective as *"summum"* or *"omne"* to refer to complete silence, whereas those in which no adjective is used, signify merely the suppressed tone of voice.[40] The former relate to the hours of the night, the time devoted to reading, and to the refectory. The latter, i. e., the subdued tone of voice is proper at all times in order not to disturb others, for in the monastery things should be conducted in a becoming manner and without hindrance to anyone.[41]

In concluding the discussion, Hildemar points out that St. Benedict placed great stress on the observance of silence; just as he emphasized the renunciation of one's own will, so he emphasized the observance of silence, for it, too, signifies mortification.[42]

The renunciation of personal ownership—later known as the vow of poverty—is treated in three several chapters of the Rule.[43] In their explanation of these, the commentators, like the author of the Rule, do not use the term " poverty." [44] The entire emphasis is not on getting along with little or less than necessary in matters of worldly goods, but on the inability of the monk to appropriate anything as his own, and on the necessity of his receiving permission for the things which he uses. Why, they ask, does St. Benedict say that a monk is not to have anything whatever as his own, when further on, he orders that all things necessary be given him by the father of the monastery? The answer follows that whatever is given him, is for his use and not to be considered his property; furthermore, should the abbot, prior, or dean request the things

40 Paul, p. 353; Hildemar, pp. 424, 453, 457.

41 Paul, p. 199; Hildemar, p. 264.

42 Hildemar, p. 457.

43 Chapters 33, 54, 55.

44 As Butler (*op. cit.,* p. 159) observes, St. Benedict "never speaks of ' monastic poverty'; the word ' paupertas' occurs only once in the Rule, and then of a case regarded as abnormal, a monastery so poor that the monks should have themselves to gather in the harvest (c. 48)."

given him, such as a tablet or a pen, the monk ought to part with them readily.[45]

Hildemar explains that the words of the Rule (c. 33) which forbid a monk to give or receive anything without the permission of his abbot, refer to private ownership, but do not mean that one should not assist another by offering him a knife, a tablet or the like; for this he may do without permission, because it is an act of charity, and it was the intention of St. Benedict, not to exclude charity, but to confirm it.[46]

Chapter fifty-five of the Rule prescribes that " the beds be frequently examined to prevent personal goods from being found." The commentators describe the manner in which this precept is to be fulfilled. About three times a year when the community is assembled for the morning chapter, the abbot will send several of the brothers to inspect the beds. If anything questionable be found, it is to be brought to the chapter and placed before his feet, at or near whose bed it was discovered. He is then required to account for it; if it was obtained with permission, the brother is exonorated; if not, he is penalized in a manner dependent on the conditions under which the object was retained among his effects.[47]

Thus the poverty explained by the Carolingian commentators was a personal poverty consisting in the inability of the individual to possess property in his own name or receive goods for his own use without permission. There is no mention of corporate poverty which, in the organization of the Franciscan Order, became a subject of considerable importance.[48]

Chastity, like poverty, was not included formally among the vows prescribed in the Rule. But unlike poverty, it is not the subject of even one chapter of the Rule; it was so generally

45 Paul, p. 322; Hildemar. pp. 388-389.

46 Page 387.

47 Paul, pp. 428-429; Hildemar, p. 517.

48 Workman (*op. cit.,* pp. 220-224) seems to confuse some fundamental notions regarding monastic principles. According to him, monasticism was founded on renunciation; renunciation consists chiefly in the practice of poverty; and personal poverty cannot exist long without corporate poverty.

regarded as a requisite of the monastic life at the time of St. Benedict that he took it for granted. Consequently it is not discussed in the commentaries.

According to both Paul and Hildemar, the spiritual renunciation which is first in the order of time and importance, is obedience. They write that, just as the faithful are not admitted into the Church unless they renounce the devil and his works, and the world and its pomps, so is it required of those who are received into the monastic life to renounce their own wills.[49] The same thought is expressed in a second passage with greater emphasis: " As in the beginning of the conversion from the cult of idols to God, it is required of those who receive the Sacrament of Baptism to renounce the devil and the idols, so also is it required in the beginning of the monastic life that those who are admitted to its discipline make the renunciation of their own wills, which is obedience." [50] Hildemar points out that the chief teaching of the Rule is obedience, for it is the first precept which St. Benedict addresses to his disciples.[51] Paul writes that the monk places his faith in doing the will of another, whereas the hermit devotes himself to contemplation.[52]

It is recognized by the commentators that the practice of obedience is difficult, especially to the beginner. Hildemar observes that St. Benedict spoke well in using the expression, " about to do battle," for obedience requires effort and struggle. This is particularly true with reference to the beginners; to the perfect, however, that sentence of the Gospel is applicable, " My yoke is sweet and my burden light." [53] Again, in commenting on the words of the Rule (Prologue), " The beginning of the way of salvation cannot but be narrow," Hildemar explains that by the " narrow beginning " is to be understood the renunciation of one's own will. " Indeed," he writes, " it is very

49 Paul, p. 16; Hildemar, p. 11.

50 Paul, p. 20; Hildemar, p. 15.

51 Page 542.

52 Paul, p. 41; Hildemar, p. 81.

53 Page 63.

narrow to those who have lived for many years according to their own wills, and who later submit themselves to the rule and power of another . . . Such as these, St. Benedict encourages, saying, ' As we advance in the religious life and faith, we shall run the way of God's commandments with expanded hearts and unspeakable sweetness of love.' " [54] If a monk is seen to be slothful in obedience, the abbot should remind him that the obedience which is offered to his superiors is offered to God. Therefore, realizing this, he ought to obey without tepidity or slothfulness, and without murmuring or a word of unwillingness.[55]

In one of his comments on obedience, Warnefrid is apparently so eager to impress his readers with the idea that it is necessary to obey not only in things pleasant and agreeable, but also in things adverse and disagreeable, that he somewhat overshoots his mark. He writes that " he, who is truly obedient, receives worldly honor, delight, or prosperity, unwillingly, and he accepts the sorrow, dishonor, and adversity of the world, willingly; for if one receives joys and prosperity gladly he is not obedient; nor is one who meets sorrow and trials unwillingly, obedient." [56]

In theory, a monk should be so obedient, according to the commentaries, that if he were required by obedience to pass through death, he would not withdraw. In practice, however, this situation is not to be expected. If the abbot sends a monk on a task of obedience which involves serious danger unknown to the abbot, the monk should inform him of the danger; or if on the way he should foresee a danger which would threaten him were he to continue, he should return to the abbot and report the situation; for, in obeying, a monk should regard the intention, not the words, of him who commands.[57]

54 Page 69.
55 Hildemar, pp. 195-196; Paul, p. 129.
56 Paul, p. 444; Hildemar, p. 541.
57 Paul, p. 163; Hildemar, pp. 226-227.

Should a situation arise in which a monk has been given a command, to fulfill which would involve sin, the procedure to be followed by the monk, as given by Warnefrid, is not morally sound. He would have the brother compare the evil in the act commanded with that of disobeying the command; should the former outweigh the latter, the brother is to refuse obedience. But should he consider the evil in the act commanded equal to or less than the evil of disobedience, he is to fulfiull the command.[58] To the commentator it is a question of choosing the lesser of two evils. His entire discussion of the matter is morally wrong, being vitiated by the false assumption that there can be any sin in refusing to obey an unlawful command. We noted the same error, though not stated so directly, in his discussion of the relation between the abbot and the cellarer.[59]

The commentators, like the author of the Rule, do not treat the two remaining Benedictine vows, stability and the conversion of morals, at such length as they treat poverty and obedience. To historians of the Order, however, it has always been of interest to note the manner in which the vow of stability has been interpreted in the course of the centuries—chiefly whether it signifies local stability, i. e., adherence to the house of profession, or merely stability in the monastic state.[60]

Our commentators, apparently unconscious of more than one signification, take local stability for granted, and look beyond the external stability in the monastery to the inner spirit. Both expositors relate stability to perseverance.[61] Paul adds that one's conversion is as it should be if he perseveres to the end;[62] Hildemar comments that if one fails to fulfill in part, or in *toto,* a good work or desire begun, he does not possess stability before God even though before men he remains in the

---

58 Paul, pp. 113-114; Hildemar, pp. 175-178.

59 *Cf. supra,* p. 56; *cf.* also Hildemar, p. 326.

60 Butler (*op. cit.,* pp. 123-134, 403-404) cites the views of the leading writers who have discussed the subject.

61 Paul, p. 444; Hildemar, p. 540.

62 *Loc. cit.*

monastery.[63] We noted in an earlier chapter that a monk may leave his monastery only when sent on a mission by his superior or if he is thereby enabled to live a better life in another monastery or in the desert.[64]

The promise of conversion of morals, according to the commentators, consists in the eradication of vices and in the implanting of virtues. The one without the other is not sufficient.[65] Hildemar observes that he who does neither, is worse than a pagan or a man of the world; because in as much as one assumes the obligations of the monastic state, in so much the greater danger is he if he does not live accordingly.[66] Thus by his profession, the monk is seen to have assumed higher obligations than the average Christian, and consequently is held to a more severe reckoning.

Our commentators recognize clearly that St. Benedict required less austerity in the matter of exterior mortifications than did his predecessors, such as St. Basil and the Fathers about whom Cassian writes in his *Institutes* and *Conferences*. For the mortification of the interior man, however, they judge that " nothing more nor better could be found " than that prescribed in the Rule.[67] The similarity between this comment on the asceticism of the Rule and that of one of its most recent commentators, Dom Butler of Downside Abbey, is striking. He writes that St. Benedict " places his asceticism primarily in the renunciation of self-will, and on this he is as insistent, as uncompromising, as in matters of corporal austerity he is indulgent." [68]

Hildemar paraphrases the admonition of St. Benedict, " to do nothing but what is sanctioned by the examples of the elders,"

---

63 Page 541.

64 *Cf. supra*, p. 87.

65 Paul, p. 444; Hildemar, p. 541.

66 *Loc. cit.*

67 Hildemar, pp. 254-256; Paul (pp. 187-188) writes in much the same tone.

68 *Op. cit.*, p. 49. *Cf.* also *ibid.*, pp. 391-392.

as follows: "If anyone shall have mortified the interior man in the manner I have described, and he shall have wished to restrain the exterior man more than I have disposed, namely, that he drink no wine and eat no cooked food—concessions which I have granted—then let him follow the example of the elders." [69] Since the "example of the elders" suggests the lives of the desert Fathers, the question is raised as to whether or not St. Benedict intended that the monks retire into the desert after learning to live according to the Rule. In the discussion, the commentators relate this mention of the "example of the elders" to the last chapter (73) of the Rule in which St. Benedict, by way of retrospect, speaks of "this least Rule written for a beginning," and of the "teaching of the holy Fathers, the observance of which leadeth a man to the height of perfection."

These words of the Rule do not present the attitude of their author with sufficient clarity that from them one can conclude whether or not St. Benedict favored the cenobitical or the eremitical form of life as the ideal. Indeed, there are writers today who hold "that St. Benedict kept the eremitical life within the scope of his Rule, as being the consummation to which a term of cenobitical life under the Rule might be hoped to lead." [70]

Our commentators hesitate to take a definite stand on the question. Although they are personally inclined to favor the cenobitic form, they direct the discussion toward an investigation of the mind of St. Benedict on the subject. They marshall all the evidence available from various passages of the Rule, [71] and present the current views for both sides. Some think that chapter seventy-three of the Rule in which St. Benedict speaks of "this least Rule written for a beginning" was written out of humility; others see in it a concession—the authority on

69 Page 256. Paul (p. 188) likewise speaks of the "example of the elders" being imitated only after the fulfillment of the Rule.

70 Butler, *op. cit.*, p. 392

71 Paul, p. 189; Hildemar, p. 257.

which a monk may withdraw to the desert.[72] A discussion of the same subject evoked by the first chapter of the rule, ends with dissimilar conclusions on the part of our two commentators.[73] Both begin by noting that St. Benedict spoke of those monks who go from the monastery to the desert—apparently with approval, for " it is the custom of preachers always to exhort their hearers to advance from lesser to greater things." Next they observe that in his speaking of the cenobites as the most valiant kind of monks (*fortissimum genus*), St. Benedict preferred them to the anchorites. At this point the two lines of argument take different directions. Paul explains that although St. Benedict advised that anyone after having been well trained in the monastery should go into solitude if this seemed best he did not say this by preference, as if it were better to leave the monastery to set out for the desert; rather, he spoke with reluctance, as if to say that only for some cause whereby a brother cannot remain in the monastery, should he, with the consent of the abbot, retire into the desert.[74] Hildemar, at the point of departure from Paul's line of reasoning, comments that as it cannot be said that Peter or John excelled the one the other, for the former is a figure of the active life, and the latter, of the contemplative, so it cannot

72 Paul, pp. 188-189; Hildemar, p. 257. It is interesting to note the explanation of this passage given by a recent commentator, Abbot Marmion of Maredsous (*Christ the Ideal of the Monk*, p. 83, n.). He writes: "We must not take these words of the holy Patriarch too literally. Here we certainly have an expression of humility, but there is something more. The Rule of St. Benedict contains both relatively slight material observances and very lofty ascetical directions. In this place, he is only considering the first; he draws a comparison between what he regulates in the way of common ordinances and what was done by men such as Antony, Macarius, and even Pachomius."

73 This is one of the few instances in which the two commentators differ in thought, although it frequently happens that one omits a point treated by the other, or develops it more briefly. Even in this particular case, there is not so much a contradiction of thought, as a shift in the point of view; Hildemar is no longer trying to determine which type of life St. Benedict considered ideal, but is weighing the merits of the types themselves.

74 Paul, pp. 43-44.

be said that the life of the anchorite excels that of the cenobite, or *vice versa*.[75]

All this discussion seems to indicate that current opinion was divided as to the relative merits of the cenobitic and eremitic form of life. That the commentators favor the former, however, is evident not only in the foregoing but also in remarks concerning the advantages of the cenobitic life. They see the monk in a community aided by his companions through prayer, consolation, and exhortation—help which is not possible in the "single-handed combat." [76] Again, they would put into the mouth of the monk these words of gratitude for his calling: "We give thanks to Thee, O God, because when we were in the world we did not know nor learn Thy commands; now however, placed in the monastery and subject to the rule of others, by hearing, reading, and seeing good example we learn Thy will." [77]

This thought indicates briefly the essence or ideal of the monastic life as viewed by the commentators. The monastery constitutes the place, obedience and the imitation of good example, the means whereby the monk learns to fulfill God's will—His service. The same idea is set forth at greater length in the following excerpts, explanatory of the phrase, "the school of divine service," used in the Prologue of the Rule:

Therefore, if in this present world we are to do good which will profit us in eternity, a place should be established in which without worldly impediment we ought to perform that good. In this passage he [St. Benedict] speaks of monastic discipline as a school; for there are other schools, such as that of the ecclesiastical discipline, of the liberal arts, and of any art whatsoever in which anything is learned . . . It is well that he called it a school of *divine service,* because there are also schools of human service, and there is a great difference between the two. In the school of human service men fight for a king and learn the ways of warfare, the chase, and all things which pertain to the proper culture of the age; they perceive with likesome eye whatever concerns

75 Pages 84-85.   **76** Paul, pp. 37, 39; Hildemar, p. 77, 79.
77 Paul, p. 185; Hildemar, pp. 253-254.

their service, and for its sake endure all things—famine, tribulation, and the like. Those in the school of the Lord's service, on the other hand, fight for a celestial king, they learn the salvation of their own souls, and they perceive with the spiritual eye the heavenly beatitude for which they endure all evils and hardships.[78]

In commenting on the passage of the Prologue in which St. Benedict speaks of the " Lord seeking his workman in the multitude of his people," Hildemar takes occasion to view the religious life in a world-wide setting. If, in this quotation, the " multitude " refers to the human race, then, according to our expositor, the Lord's workman is the Church considered as one man; but if the " multitude " signifies the Church—which Hildemar considers the more fitting interpretation—the Lord's worker is the order of apostolic followers. He explains that the Lord does not abandon the rest to seek out one workman, but He does as a king who chooses from among the great multitude of his people some for particular offices, and others as counsellors. The Lord chooses from among his Church that order of men who accept the word spoken to the rich man : " If thou wilt be perfect, go sell what thou hast . . . and come follow me." While preaching here on earth He chose twelve from among the multitude of his disciples. Nor is it to be wondered at, that He did this while in the flesh, or that He continues to do it daily in the Church, since even from the beginning of the world, He acted thus in choosing Noah, Abraham, Moses, and other holy persons.[79]

Thus the life of the monk is viewed by our commentators as one of more intimate service than that expected of the average Christian; the emphasis is on the service—the life of devotion to God, not merely on the practice of one or other virtue or renunciation. It is on this point that some writers make a fatal mistake. In attempting to define a force which is essentially spiritual, they take into account only the external manifestations and ignore the spiritual element. Moreover, the invitation which the religious answers in assuming the monastic state is not complete with the words: " Go sell what thou hast, and give to the poor "; it includes " and come follow me."

In what has been said, it is obvious that the monastic ideal did not consist in the practice of any one virtue, but rather in the more intensive service of God—in becoming a more perfect Christian than was possible for one living in the world. The various ascetical practices, we recall, are but a means to the end.[80] If, however, it were desired to point out from among these practices the one on which the commentators placed most emphasis, it would, doubtless, be obedience—the renunciation of one's own will. This is applicable, also, to the Rule itself, and to the Order in general. Poverty, particularly corporate poverty, was never the Benedictine ideal. It received its first emphasis in the Cistercian reform. It is difficult to understand, therefore, why Mr. Workman, even though he made no use of the commentaries, should write that at the time of the Cistercians " the center of emphasis in renunciation was being slowly changed. Hitherto ' poverty ' had been supreme, but the experience of centuries has shown that poverty as an ideal defeated itself. But ' obedience ' had in it latent possibilities as yet little exploited." [81]

The degree of perfection to be found in the service rendered by the monk is dependent on the motives with which it is performed. The commentators enumerate, in ascending order, four several motives whereby a monk may be actuated in his service. They explain that " those who serve God out of fear of punishment are not good in comparison with those who serve because of the promises made in their profession; again, those who serve for the love of their heavenly inheritance are better than those who serve in order to fulfill their promise; finally, those who serve solely for the love of God are better than those who serve for the love of their celestial country." [82]

To elucidate the import of all this to his readers, Paul Warnefrid makes use of the following figure:

80 Cf. supra, p. 171.   81 Op. cit., p. 245.

82 Hildemar, p. 188; in Paul's version (p. 124), one item of the series has evidently been omitted by the scribe.

For example, there is a slave, a vassal, and a son. The slave obeys because of fear, lest he be beaten; the vassal serves because of the word which he has given, lest he be found false. The son may be one of the two kinds: one obeys his father lest he be disinherited—he is indeed a mercenary; another serves only out of love for his father, lest he offend him. This son has no anxiety about the possession of his inheritance—rather he would be willing to lose it so long as he is in his father's favor and enjoys his happiness. Such a one is a true son. So it is with the monk: if he serves God from fear of punishment, lest he be excommunicated or beaten, he is a slave; if he serves God because of the profession which he has promised, he is, as it were, a vassal; if he serves God in order to receive the inheritance of the heavenly country, he is a mercenary; if he serves God only to possess His good pleasure and not to know His anger, he is a perfect son.[83]

The monk's service, therefore, which is motivated by the fear of eternal punishment is not perfect; nevertheless, according to the commentators, his " conversion is sound." They observe, however, that some come to the monastery for a still less worthy motive—out of necessity for the material things of life. Such as these, although their "conversion is not right," will in time and through the Lord's mercy, be transformed, i. e., they will begin to fear, and will pass on to the higher degrees, even to love.[84]

A final point, and one which has been the subject of particular interest among recent Benedictine writers, remains. Assuming that the cenobitical form of life is the ideal, and assuming that the cenobite aspires to the perfection of the pure love of God, is he to devote himself equally to manual work and to spiritual activities as the casual reading of the Rule would seem to imply, or is the contemplative life to be preferred to the active?[85]

The commentators discuss the question from the viewpoint

---

83 Paul, p. 124; Hildemar, pp. 188-189.

84 Paul, pp. 121, 172; Hildemar, pp. 185, 242-243.

85 For an excellent analysis of this question with reference to the Rule, see Justin McCann, *St. Benedict,* pp. 168-189.

of one trying to ascertain the mind of St. Benedict on the subject, and on the merits of the question itself. Their conclusion in the first case is that St. Benedict recommended both the active and the contemplative occupations, but with the implication that the latter is the ideal or end, and the former is a necessary means to that end. In his writing that the monks should not be saddened if the circumstances require them to gather in the harvest themselves, for then are they true monks indeed, he spoke by way of consolation, " not that those who are free to read are not *true monks.*" And again, if they devote themselves solely to reading, they would experience tedium, and could not, therefore, fulfill the spiritual exercises properly.[86]

The same conclusion is reached in the second discussion, i. e., the one based on the merits of the two types of life.[87] The proper procedure to follow, therefore, is to strike a balance between the two, for although contemplation is the desired goal, it can best be attained through a limited devotion to the active life.[88]

The following quotation expresses the attitude of the commentators regarding the practical and the ideal, as well, perhaps, as any which could be cited.

The disposition of human and of divine things should be both separated and combined: they should be separated in dignity, inasmuch as the disposal of divine things should hold first place, for there is, indeed, great difference between the good which should be desired and the necessary which must be undertaken. They should be combined so that God be sought for Himself, and these temporal things be foreseen and obtained, not for themselves, but for that one and only Good. Thus those who in these things have but one purpose, i. e., zeal only to please God, are able praiseworthily to serve both, so that neither the divine things are neglected, nor the human things improperly done.[89]

86 Paul, p. 395; Hildemar, pp. 479-480.

87 Butler (*op. cit.,* p. 101) points out that the allegory on which this passage of the commentary is based, is taken from the writings of St. Gregory who in turn took it from St. Augustine.

88 Paul, p. 394; Hildemar, pp. 477-478.   89 Hildemar, pp. 136-137.

CONCLUSION

THE historical importance of the commentaries selected for the present study lies chiefly in the aggregate of details which, when pieced together, form in mosaic an interesting and somewhat intimate picture of Carolingian monasticism. Particularly when compared with the meager glimpses available from contemporary chronicle literature and from legal documents, the picture loses, in large measure, the sketchiness it might appear to have on the first reading of the commentaries. Moreover, the information which they yield correlates well with the pertinent material in current conciliar and imperial decrees, and with the few scant monastic consuetudinaries of the period, thus adding weight and authority to the literature of the commentaries.

The fact that Paul Warnefrid's commentary is, after the Rule itself, the earliest extant account of any size pertaining to primitive Benedictinism, contributes special interest. This interest extends in two directions. On the one side, it is noteworthy to observe the manner in which the Rule, written more than two centuries earlier, is interpreted and applied in Carolingian times. In this respect, the historical developments in the interim, such as the introduction of daily Mass, the tendency of an ever increasing proportion of the monks to advance to Holy Orders, and the employment of laymen in the monastery are reflected in the adjustments to the Rule made by the commentators.

On the other side, it is interesting to note the various institutional features of later monasticism, particularly that of Cluny, and, chronologically nearer, that of Benedict of Aniane, which are traceable to our commentaries; in this respect, certain liturgical developments and devotional practices, as well as numerous social customs, might be cited as illustrations. Moreover, these features are reported by the commentators, not as innovations, but as practices already in vogue; frequently they are merely mentioned in passing. The question at once suggests itself as to the actual time and place of their origin.

It is in this respect, too, that Warnefrid's commentary tends to diminish considerably the importance hitherto ascribed to the Carolingian reform, accredited by many writers to Benedict of Aniane, and by others to Louis the Pious. The famous document which serves as the chief basis of our knowledge of this reform is the Monastic Capitulary of 817 containing eighty-two articles relative to the monastic life. A large proportion of these coincide closely in substance, some even verbally, with our commentaries; a considerable proportion are to be found in previous canonical and imperial decrees. Thus the contribution of Benedict of Aniane and the Aachen Council is seen to consist not so much in their originality as in the confirmation and codification of the regulations and discipline already contained in Warnefrid's commentary and in current legal literature.

More important than the comparative study which the commentaries make possible with reference to primitive Benedictinism and its later history, is the picture of contemporary monasticism which they present. Certain disputed questions regarding particular elements of monasticism can be solved for the Carolingian period on the basis of the treatment given them in the commentaries; for example, the relation between the monastic and the canonical penances and the irrevocability of the oblate's promise made by proxy. This statement is limited, of course, to the extent that the commentators base their remarks on current practice. Again, other elements are observed to be in a state of development not sufficiently advanced to warrant their acceptance as general, although the commentators indicate their preference in the matter. As belonging to this category, we might suggest the discussions relative to the use of fleshmeat, the superiority of the cenobitical to the eremitical form of life, and the use of the Roman or the monastic breviary.

The details concerning social and religious institutions afford worthwhile material for students of the respective fields. As might be expected from the amplification of a monastic rule of life, the most important results of the study, however, concern the constitutional and ascetical phases of monasticism. The former presents a somewhat rigorous and legalistic impression of the institution; the spirit of custody and the ever ready penalty for violations of observance stand out in clear form. The latter, i. e., the ascetical phase, indicates little departure from fundamental Christian principles of asceticism and the spirit of the Rule; spiritual austerities take precedence over the corporal, and all renunciation is subsidiary to the more positive ideal of a deep devotion to the service of God.

APPENDIX
SURVEY OF THE MEDIEVAL COMMENTARIES

THE bibliographies of the commentaries on the Rule are not satisfactory. The most complete ones are now long antiquated; they are to be found in Calmet's commentary [1] and in Ziegelbauer's literary history of the Benedictine Order.[2] Some of the commentaries in manuscript form have since been removed to libraries other than those indicated; some of the items listed are vaguely given, lacking precise title and date; others are editions of the Rule with a few scattered comments; still others are notices from chronicles for which there is no corresponding literature.

Abbot Butler sketched briefly in his *Benedictine Monachism* sixteen of the leading commentaries, including those of the modern period; [3] Dom Berlière devoted a few pages of his *L'Ascèse bénédictine* to the commentaries written before the thirteenth century.[4] Both of these accounts have been used in preparing the following survey of the medieval commentaries. It is by no means exhaustive; current conditions in Europe render it extremely difficult to verify the location of the commentaries still in manuscript. All of the published Latin commentaries originating before 1500, however, are available in the university and monastic libraries of this country and have been examined.

After the commentary of Paul Warnefrid which is first in the order of time, and perhaps the best of the medieval commentaries viewed as an historical source, the next works on the Rule to merit our attention are those of Benedict of Aniane, who died in the year 821. His name is vitally associated with

1 French edition (1734), pp. 73-90, 592-597.

2 M. Ziegelbauer, *Historia rei literariae ordinis S. Benedicti*, III (Augsburg, 1754), 12-24.

3 Pages 177-183.

4 Pages 19-23.

the Carolingian reform movement which had for its purpose
the uniformity of observance and practice among the monasteries of the empire. Although the two works he compiled on
the Rule are not commentaries in the full sense of the word,
they are so closely related to the commentaries that we must
needs point them out. He collected into one volume entitled
Codex regularum all the Latin Rules prior to the ninth century; this was edited by L. Holsten in Rome, 1661, and its contents have since been reprinted in various volumes of Migne's
Latin Patrology.[5] The second work, entitled *Concordia regularum,* is a quasi-commentary in which Benedict reorganized
the contents of the *Codex regularum* in the following manner: the Rule of St. Benedict is presented, a passage at a time;
after each of these passages, there follows the pertinent passage
from one or more of the twenty-six Rules from which he
quotes. The originality of the work lay chiefly in the novel
idea of the compilation; it rendered not only possible but easy
the study of the sources of the Rule and the comparison of its
general tenor with that of the Rules which preceded and followed it. The *Concordia* was first edited by the Maurist Ménard
in 1638, and has been reprinted in Volume 103 of Migne's
collection.

Shortly after the death of Benedict of Aniane, Smaragdus,
abbot of St. Michael's at Verdun, wrote a commentary entitled *Expositio in regulam B. Benedicti.* This was first published at Cologne in 1575, and has been reprinted in Migne,
Volume 102. Having in view not the learned but the simple,
as he himself writes in the *prooemium,*[6] Smaragdus devotes
considerable space to the literal interpretation of the Rule. Being quite void of historical details, his treatment, in general,
might apply equally well to another age. The entire work is
interlarded with quotations from the Scriptures, the Fathers,
and, in particular, from the various monastic Rules; the last

5 Volume 103 contains a number of the Rules and it indicates the volumes
in which the others may be found.

6 *PL,* 102, col. 691.

named source indicates, doubtless, a generous use of the *Concordia regularum*.

The next commentary, chronologically, is the enlarged version of Warnefrid's *Expositio* made by Hildemar about the middle of the ninth century. As this was discussed in the Introduction, we shall note here only the further versions which derive from this revision of Warnefrid's commentary. Two manuscripts, originating in Reichenau and now preserved at Karlsruhe, contain a slightly modified version of Hildemar's work. One of them, MS. Augiensis 203, dating from the ninth century, contains chapters one to thirteen of the commentary; the other, Augiensis 179, written in the early tenth century, contains chapters fourteen to sixty-one of the commentary. The latter is attributed, by an eleventh-century hand, to an Abbot Basil. Alfred Holder [7] and, after him, L. Traube [8] discount entirely this attribution, and maintain that the two manuscripts supplement each other in presenting the *Expositio* of Warnefrid in the enlarged edition given it by Hildemar. Traube explains that varying versions may have arisen either as copies of the original draft written at Hildemar's dictation, or as the notes of different pupils from the same series of lectures.[9] Two ninth-century copies of this "Basil" commentary are extant: Engelberg 142, and Einsiedeln 253.[10]

The surviving fragment of a second version of Hildemar's commentary was edited and analyzed by C. Cipolla in 1894.[11] It dates from an eleventh-century manuscript thought to have originated at the monastery of Novalese and is now preserved

7 *Die Handschriften der grossherzoglich badischen Hof- und Landesbibliothek in Karlsruhe*, V, *Die reichenauer Handschriften*, I, 418, 464.

8 *Textgeschichte der Regula S. Benedicti*, p. 44.

9 *Ibid.*, p. 43.

10 *Ibid.*, n. 5.

11 *Ricerche sull' antica biblioteca del monastero della Novalesa*, Turin, 1894; this was reprinted in large part in *Memorie della reale accademia delle scienze di Torino*, XLIV (1894), 71-88, 115-150, 193-242, 243-319. The fragment of the commentary is edited on pages 219-224. See also Cipolla, "Brevi appunti di storia Novaliciense," *Ibid.*, XLV, 150-166.

in the state archives of Turin.[12] Traube sees it to be essentially Hildemar's work to which additions have been made by some monk living after him.[13] Berlière suggests that it is a manuscript of this kind which Trithemius attributed to Ruthard, a ninth-century monk of Hirschau, since the *incipit* which Trithemius gives corresponds to that of Paul and Hildemar.[14]

Two ninth-century manuscripts, Codex 278 of Valenciennes and Codex n. a. lat. 763 of the Bibliothèque Nationale, Paris, are entitled *Glose de diversis doctoribus collecte in Regula S. Benedicti;* this composition is thought to have been made by Hucbald of St. Amandus in the diocese of Tournai, Belgium.[15]

A commentary ascribed to one Remigius was seen by Bernard of Montfaucon in the library of the Camaldolite monastery of Our Lady of the Angels in Florence. Bernard would identify the author with Remigius of Auxerre who died in 908.[16]

Theuzo, an eleventh-century monk of St. Marys, Florence,[17] composed a commentary on the Rule. A thirteenth-century manuscript of this work was preserved in the monastery of St. Mathiae de Murano, Venice, in the eighteenth century.[18] In 1810-1811, however, the manuscripts of this monastic library, except those codices which were deposited in the library of St. Gregory on Monte Coelio, Rome, were transferred to the

12 Traube, *Textgeschichte,* pp. 44-45.

13 *Ibid.,* p. 45.

14 *L'Ascèse bénédictine,* p. 20. Berlière also notes that Trithemius attributes to Rudiger of Echternach (10th century) and to Marquard, monk of St. Burchard of Würzburg (11th century) commentaries which are nowhere else indicated (*Ibid.,* p. 20, n. 4).

15 Berlière, *op. cit.,* pp. 21-22.

16 *Diarium Italicum* (Paris, 1702), p. 354.

17 *Cf.* U. Chevalier, *Répertoire des sources historiques du moyen âge: Bio-bibliographie,* II (new ed., 1905), col. 4397.

18 The dedicatory letter associated with this commentary is given in *Annales Camaldulenses* (1755-1773), II, 156, and is reprinted in *PL,* 143, col. 846.

library of St. Mark's, Venice.[19] Since the manuscript catalogue of the latter does not list Theuzo's commentary, it is possible that it was among the codices later removed to Rome. Berlière reports a second manuscript (sixteenth century) of this commentary preserved at La Badia of Florence.[20]

Another Theuzo of the same century is likewise associated with an exposition of the Rule.[21] In his bibliography of the commentaries, Calmet reports that Theuzo, disciple of St. John Gualbert and abbot of Saint Paul of Raggiolo, wrote a commentary which is preserved in manuscript in the library of the grand duke of Tuscany, Florence.[22]

Three of the four twelfth-century commentaries have been printed but no one of them is a complete and orderly exposition of the Rule. The title of the one written by Rupert of Deutz indicates that it treats only of certain points of the Rule.[23] It is divided into four books: the first concerns theological controversies; the second, the order of the psalms chanted in Matins and Laudes; the third, the ordination of monks, the black color of their habit, and the use of fur garments in winter; the fourth, the preëminence of the state of the monks as compared with that of the canons regular. The author died in 1135.

Contemporary with Rupert of Deutz lived Peter the Deacon of Monte Cassino. His exposition of the Rule is a very uneven piece;[24] instead of following the order of the Rule by chapters, it is divided into three books. The first of these is devoted to

19 J. Valentinelli, *Bibliotheca manuscripta ad S. Marci Venetiarum,* I (Venice, 1868), pp. 127-128.

20 *Op. cit.,* p. 22, n. 8.

21 Chevalier (*op. cit.,* col. 4397) places his death in 1095. The editors of the *Annales Comaldulenses* caution against confusing this Theuzo with the one previously mentioned: see *PL,* 143, col. 843.

22 *Op. cit.,* bibliography, pp. 73-90.

23 It reads: *Super quaedam capitula regulae Divi Benedicti abbatis*; it is printed in *PL,* 170, cols. 477-538.

24 It is published in *Bibliotheca Casinensis,* V, 82-174. Peter the Deacon also wrote an epitome *Super regulam* of three folio pages; cf. *ibid.,* pp. 73-76.

the Prologue of the Rule; the second and a great part of the third are abstract rhetorical treatments of subjects remotely connected with the Rule. Peter also wrote a brief commentary, entitled *Explanatio brevis*. It starts from the beginning of the Rule and gives a strictly literal interpretation of terms used in the first twenty-eight chapters. Then follow three columns of terse rules, customs, and penances. The author lifted bodily the whole of Smaragdus' *Expositio*, Gregory's *Cura pastoralis*, and a great part of Smaragdus' *Diadema monachorum* into his major work. These borrowings he broke up into sections which he interspersed with his own discussions. He seems not to feel responsible for giving a thorough treatment, for he refers on several occasions to the work already done by his predecessors;[25] on the other hand, he states that he has tried to cull from the writings of certain Fathers the sentiments which seem to agree with those of the Rule.[26]

The third twelfth-century commentator was Stephen of Paris, about whom little else is known than what is related in the autobiographical notes contained in his work. Judging from the title, *Tractatus magistri Stephani Parisiensis in Regula S. Benedicti*,[27] Stephen was a teacher in a school of Paris. In the course of the commentary, he relates that he was an eye witness to the elevation of Pope Eugenius III in 1146 and that he visited Monte Cassino. His treatment in general is less literal than moral; he passes over in silence nearly all of the chapters of the Rule relating to the Divine Office.[28] His commentary has not been printed, but is extant in two manuscripts: at Melk in the fifteenth-century MS. 12 of Epinal, once at Sens, and at Munich in the fifteenth-century MS. clm., 3029, once at St. Ulric of Augsburg.[29]

25 *Ibid.*, pp. 82, 111, 137, 165; among the names cited, that of Paul the Deacon (Warnefrid) is the only one mentioned in all these references.

26 *Ibid.*, p. 83.

27 Berlière, p. 23, n. 2.

28 *Histoire littéraire de la France*, XII, 260.

29 Berlière, *loc. cit.*

St. Hildegarde, abbess of the convent of Bingen, who died in the year 1189, has left a brief explanation of the Rule. It was written at the request of the convent of Huy, Belgium, and constitutes, as it were, one item of her extensive correspondence, rather than a commentary properly so-called. It is not a complete treatment, since it covers only thirteen columns in Migne's *Patrology*.[30] In so far as it goes, it is more liberal than our Carolingian commentaries in the interpretation of the Rule.

Bernard of Monte Cassino wrote an *Expositio in regulam St. Benedicti* which was edited by Dom Caplet in 1894. Bernard died in 1282, having been abbot at Monte Cassino during the twenty years preceding his death. His commentary is complete and systematic, and is practical and descriptive of contemporary life and thought. Although it contains more than sixty direct references to the exposition of Warnefrid and reflects his influence almost continually, it does not thereby lose its title to originality; the author does not hesitate to disagree with Paul or others whose opinions differ from his own.

The next three commentaries, chronologically, are preserved in manuscript at Monte Cassino. Nicholas de Fractura, also known as Nicholas of St. Germain, wrote, according to a contemporary scribe who copied the *Chronicle of Volturno,* an exposition of the Rule in 1299. In the list of abbots appended to the chronicle, the scribe writes: "Nicholas de Fractura, monk of Cassino was a Doctor of Canon Law. In 1299 he wrote an exposition of the Rule of St. Benedict which I have copied."[31] Martène cites Arnold Wion as his authority for the explanation that Nicholas wrote the commentary at Monte Cassino before he was made abbot of St. Vincent's monastery at Volturno.[32] The manuscript of this commentary is No. 445 in the Monte Cassino collection.[33] Richard of St. Angelo, also a

30 Vol. 197, cols. 1053-66.

31 *Chronicon Vulturnense* in Fonti per la storia d'Italia, LX, 106. The quotation reads: " Nicolaus de Fractura monacus Casinensis. hic Decretorum doctor fuit. 1299 exposuit regulam sancti Benedicti, apud me manuscriptam."

32 *Commentarius, PL,* 66, 209.

33 *Bibliotheca Casinensis,* I, Appendix, lxvii. Unfortunately this manu-

monk of Monte Cassino, is the author of a commentary of which only chapters eight to nineteen have survived in a manuscript fragment preserved in Codex 441 at Monte Cassino.[34] Finally, the fourteenth-century Codex 412 at Monte Cassino contains, among other works ascribed to an Antoninus, a commentary entitled *In regulam S. Benedicti*.[35]

Peter Bohier, a French monk, who later became abbot of St. Anianus (near Narbonne), and bishop of Orvieto in 1364, wrote two commentaries on the Rule. The first was written from the viewpoint of the canonist in 1361 while Bohier was abbot. The second he wrote as bishop of Orvieto at the request of the monks of Subiaco, completing it in the year 1373.[36] It was published in 1908 at Subiaco. The method employed, of explaining the Rule word by word or phrase by phrase instead of by sentences or passages, tends to detract from the interest it might otherwise have. The purpose, indicated in the preface and pursued throughout the work, of illustrating the Rule from the writings of Jerome, Cassian, Basil, and Pachomius directs the attention of the author away from the practice and thought of the time in which he lived.

Toward the close of the fourteenth century, John of Kastel in the Upper Palatinate composed a commentary which, according to Calmet, who wrote in the eighteenth century, was preserved in the library of St. Peter at Salzburg.[37] John Keck of Tegernsee, who was present at the Council of Basel, was likewise the author of an exposition of the Rule. It was preserved in manuscript in the library of Tegernsee at the time

script catalogue (*Bibl. Casin.*) is incomplete, MS. 358 being the last manuscript analyzed in Vol. V. The 3d volume of the later manuscript catalogue, *Codicum Casinensium manuscriptorum catalogus*, is scheduled to describe codices 400-500, but is still in preparation.

34 *Cf.* Martène, *loc. cit.; Bibliotheca Casinensis, loc. cit.*

35 *Bibliotheca Casinensis,* I, Appendix, lxvi-lxvii.

36 L. Allodi, *Petri Boherii in regulam Sancti Benedicti commentarium* (Subiaco, 1908), xx-xxi.

37 *Commentaire,* Bibliog., pp. 73-90.

Martène wrote his commentary (1690).[38] Martène also reports that in the library of Weingarten is preserved the manuscript of a commentary written by John Vlitpacher, monk of Melk, Austria, after the reform of his monastery in 1420.[39]

Cardinal John Turrecremata (Torquemada), a Dominican and an eminent ecclesiastic at the time of the Councils of Constance and Basel, wrote a commentary about 1441 which went through three printed editions before the close of the following century.[40] Butler considers it a commentary of great excellence. " Its interest lies in the fact that it reflects the ideas of the reforming efforts associated with the two Councils aforesaid." [41]

John of Trittenheim, known also as Trithemius, wrote a commentary shortly after becoming abbot of Spanheim in 1484. A phrase following the title indicates that the work was divided into two books but, unfortunately, only the first one has survived. This was published among his works in 1605 and separately in 1608.[42] It covers only the Prologue and the first seven chapters of the Rule, and is concerned chiefly with religious discipline and fervor.

Before the close of the fifteenth century, Christian of Salzburg wrote a commentary which, according to Calmet [43] and at the time he wrote, was extant in manuscript in the monastery of St. Blaze, Vienna.

38 Martène, *Commentarius, PL,* 66, col. 210.

39 *Ibid., loc. cit.* Martène also mentions a commentary in the library of Tegernsee written by another monk of Melk, John Schlippacher *(loc. cit.).* Calmet *(loc. cit.),* however, thinks this author to be the same as the one above called John Vlitpacher.

40 The edition examined by the writer is bound with several other works in a volume entitled *Regula S. Benedicti cum doctiss. et piiss. commentariis Joannis de Turre Cremata, S. R. E. cardinalis, et Smaragdi abbatis. . .* (Cologne, 1575).

41 *Benedictine Monachism,* p. 180. The councils are those of Constance and Basel.

42 *Cf. ibid., loc. cit.* The earlier edition forms a substantial part of the volume entitled *Joannis Trithemii . . . opera pia et spiritualia, . . . a R. P. Joanne Busaeo, . . . et in unum volumen, mendis expurgatis redacta* (Maintz, 1605).

43 *Loc. cit.*

BIBLIOGRAPHY

Alamo, M., "La Règle de Saint Benoît éclairée par sa source, la Règle du Maitre," *Revue d'histoire ecclésiastique*, XXXIV (1938), 740-755.

Albareda, A. M., *Bibliografia de la regla benedictina*, Montserrat, Abbey press, 1933.

Albers, Bruno, *Consuetudines monasticae*, 5 vols. in 4; Vol. I, Stuttgart, 1900; Vols. II-V, Monte Cassino, 1900-1912.

Allodi, Leo, *Petri Boherii in regulam Sancti Benedicti commentarium*, Subiaco, Abbey press, 1908.

Altaner, Berthold, "Zur Geschichte der mittelalterlichen Orden," *Zeitschrift für Kirchengeschichte*, XLIX (1930), 54-64.

Amann, É., "Pénitence public et pénitence privée à l'époque de la réforme carolingienne," *Dictionnaire de théologie catholique*, XII, 862-879.

Amelli, A. M., *Ars Donati quam Paulus Diaconus exposuit*, Monte Cassino, Abbey press, 1899.

——, "L'epigramma di Paolo Diacono intorno al canto Gregoriano e Ambrosiano," *Memorie storiche Forogiuliesi*, IX (1913), 153-175.

Antiquiores consuetudines monasterii Cluniacensis Udalrici, ed. Luc d'Achery in *Spicilegium*, I (Paris, 1773), 639-703; reprint in PL, 149, cols. 635-778.

Baluze, Étienne, *Capitula regum Francorum*, Vol. II, Paris, 1780.

Balzani, Ugo, *Chronicon Farfense di Gregorio di Catino*, 2 vols., Rome, 1903; Fonti per la storia d'Italia, XXXIII-XXXIV.

Benedict of Aniane, *Codex regularum monasticarum et canonicarum*, PL, 103, cols. 393-702.

——, *Concordia regularum*, PL, 103, cols. 702-1380.

——, *Excerptus diversarum modus poenitentiarum a Benedicto abbate [Anianensi] distinctus de regula sancti Benedicti abbatis*, PL, 103, cols. 1417-1420.

Bernard de Montfaucon, *Diarium Italicum*, Paris, J. Anisson, 1702.

Berlière, Ursmer, *La Familia dans des monastères bénédictins du moyen âge*, Brussels, 1931; Memoires de la classe des lettres de l'Académie royal de Belgique, XXIX.

——, *L'Ascèse bénédictine des origines à la fin du XIIᵉ siècle*, Bruges, Desclée, 1927.

——, "Les Coutumiers monastiques des VIIIᵉ et IXᵉ siècles," *Revue bénédictine*, XXV (1908), 95-107.

——, "Les Écoles abbatiales au moyen âge," *ibid.*, VI (1889), 499-511.

——, "Le Nombre des moines dans les anciens monastères," *ibid.*, XLI (1929), 231-261; XLII (1930), 31-42.

——, "Les Oblats de Saint Benoît au moyen âge," *ibid.*, III (1886-1887), 55-61, 107-111, 156-160, 209-220, 249-255.

——, *L'Ordre monastique, des origines au XIIᵉ siècle*, 3d ed., Lille, Desclée, 1924.

Bernard, P., "Confession (du concile de Latran au concile de Trente)," *Dictionnaire de théologie catholique*, III, 894-926.

Bethmann, L., "Paulus Diaconus, Leben und Schriften," *Archiv der Gesellschaft für ältere deutsche Geschichtskunde*, X (1849), 247-334.

Bibliotheca Casinensis seu codicum manuscriptorum qui in tabulario Cassinensi asservantur, 5 vols., Monte Cassino, Abbey press, 1873-1894.

Bilfinger, Gustav, *Die mittelalterlichen Horen und die modernen Stunden*, Stuttgart, Kohlhammer, 1892.

Bishop, Edmund, *Liturgica historica: Papers on the Liturgy and Religious Life of the Western Church*, Oxford, Clarendon press, 1918.

Butler, Cuthbert, *Benedictine Monachism*, 2d ed. with supplementary notes, London, Longmans, Green and Co., 1924.

——, "The Cassinese Manuscripts of the Rule," *Casinensia*, I, 124-127, Monte Cassino, Abbey press, 1929.

——, *Sancti Benedicti regula monasteriorum*, 3d ed., critico-practical, Freiburg im Breisgau, Herder and Co., 1935.

——, *Western Mysticism: The Teaching of SS. Augustine, Gregory, and Bernard on Contemplation and the Contemplative Life*, 2d ed. with after thoughts, London, Constable, 1927.

Calmet, Augustin, *Commentaire littéral, historique et moral sur la règle de Saint Benoît*, 2 vols in 1, Paris, Emery, 1734.

Capitula regum Francorum, Vol. I, ed. A. Boretius, MGH, LL, II, Hannover, 1883.

Caplet, A. M., *Bernardi I abbatis Casinensis in regulam S. Benedicti expositio*, Monte Cassino, Abbey press, 1894.

Chronicon Salernitanum, ed. G. H. Pertz, MGH, SS, III, 467-561.

Cipolla, Carl, "Brevi appunti di storia Novaliciense," *Memorie della reale accademia della scienza di Torino*, XLV (1896), 150-166.

——, "Notizia di alcuni codici antica biblioteca Novaliciense," *ibid.*, XLIV (1894), 193-242.

——, "Note bibliografiche circa l'odierna condizione degli studi critici sul testo delle opere di Paolo Diacono," *Miscellanea di storia Venetia*, ser. 2, VIII (1902), 1-43.

Clark, J. M., *The Abbey of St. Gall as a Center of Literature and Art*, Cambridge, Cambridge University press, 1926.

Codex diplomaticus Langobardia, Monumenta historiae patriae, XIII, Turin, 1873.

Codicum Casinensium manuscriptorum catalogus, 2 vols., edited by the Benedictine monks of Monte Cassino, Monte Cassino, 1915-1934.

Concilia aevi Karolini, Vol. I, i-ii, ed. A. Werminghoff, MGH, LL, III, Hannover, 1906.

Consuetudines Hirsaugienses, PL, 150, cols. 923-1146.

Cottineau, L. H., *Repertoire topo-bibliographique des abbayes et prieurés*, 2 vols., Macon, Protat, 1935-1938.

Delatte, Paul, *Commentary on the Rule of St. Benedict*, trans. from the French by J. McCann, London, Burns, Oates and Co., 1921.

Deroux, M. P., *Les Origines de l'oblature bénédictine*, Vienne, 1927; Les editions de la Revue Mabillon, I.

Dolhagaray, B., " Confession (science acquise en)," *Dictionnaire de théologie catholique*, III, 960-974.

Dopsch, Alfons, *Wirtschaftliche und soziale Grundlagen der europäischen Kulturentwicklung aus der Zeit von Caesar bis auf Karl den Grossen*, 2 vols., 2d ed. revised and enlarged, Vienna, 1923-1924.

Doren, Alfred, *Italienische Wirtschaftsgeschichte*, Jena, G. Fischer, 1934.

Dulcy, Suzanne, *La Règle de Saint Benoît d'Aniane et la réforme monastique à l'époque carolingienne*, Nimes, A. Larguier, 1935; Thesis, University of Montpellier.

Ermini, Filippo, " La poesia enigmistica e faceta di Paolo Diacono," *Memorie storiche Forogiuliesi*, XXV (1929), 97-110.

Evans, Joan, *Monastic Life at Cluny, 910-1157*, London, Oxford University press, 1931.

Falco, G., " Lineamenti di storia cassinese nei secoli VIII e IX," *Casinensia*, II, 457-548, Monte Cassino, 1929.

Federici, V., *Chronicon Vulturnense*, 3 vols, Rome, 1925-1938; Fonti per la storia d'Italia, LVIII-LX.

Frank, H., *Der Klosterbischöfe des Frankenreiches*, Münster in W., 1932; Beiträge zur Geschichte des alten Mönchtums und des Benediktinerordens, XVII.

Formulae Merovingici et Karolini aevi, ed. K. Zeumer, MGH, LL, V, Hannover, 1886.

Gougaud, Louis, *Anciennes Coutumes claustrales*, Ligugé (Vienne), 1930.

——, *Dévotions et pratiques ascétiques du moyen âge*, Paris, Desclée, 1925.

Grasshoff, Hans, *Langobardish-fränkisches Klosterwesen in Italien*, Göttingen, E. A. Huth, 1907; Dissertation, University of Göttingen.

Hannay, J. O., *The Spirit and Origin of Christian Monasticism*, London, Methuen, 1903.

Harnack, Adolf, *Das Mönchthum: Seine Ideale und seine Geschichte*, 5th ed., Giessen, Ricker, 1901.

Hauck, Albert, *Kirchengeschichte Deutschlands*, Vol. II, 3d and 4th ed., Leipzig, Hinrich, 1912.

Hefele, K. J., *Histoire des conciles d'après les documents originaux*, transl. from the 2d German edition, and augmented with critical and bibliographical notes, by Henri Leclercq, 10 vols., Paris, 1907-1938.

Heimbucher, Max, *Die Orden und Kongregationen der katholischen Kirche*, 2 vols., 3d ed., Paderborn, Schoningh, 1933-1934.

Herwegen, Ildefons, *Geschichte der benediktinischen Professformel*, Münster in W., 1912; Beiträge zur Geschichte des alten Mönchtums und des Benediktinerordens, III, ii.

——, *St. Benedict: A Character Study*, transl. from the German by Peter Nugent, London, Sands and Co., 1924.

Hinschius, Paul, *Decretales pseudo-Isidorianae et Capitula Angilramni*, Leipzig, Tauchnitz, 1863.

Holder, Alfred, *Die Reichenauer Handschriften*, 3 vols., Leipzig, 1906-1918; Die Handschriften der grossherzoglich badischen Hof- und Landesbibliothek in Karlsruhe, V-VII.

Hörle, G. H., *Frühmittelalterliche Monchs- und Klerikerbildung in Italien, geistliche Bildungsideale und Bildungseinrichtungen vom 6. bis zum 9. Jahrhundert*, Freiburg im Breisgau, 1914; Freiburger theologische Studien, XIII.

Koschek, J., *Die Klosterreform Ludwigs des Frommen im Verhältnis zur Regel Benedikts von Nursia, Greifswald*, 1908; Dissertation, University of Greifswald.

Kurtscheid, Bertrand, *A History of the Seal of Confession*, authorized translation by the Rev. F. A. Marks; ed. Arthur Preuss, St. Louis, Herder, 1927.

Labriolle, Pierre de, *Histoire de la litérature latine chrétienne*, 2d ed., revised and enlarged, Paris, Société d'edition " Les Belles-lettres," 1924.

Laistner, M. L. W., *Thought and Letters in Western Europe*, A. D. 500-900, London, Methuen, 1931.

——, " The Christian Attitude to Pagan Literature," *History*, XX (1935), 49-54.

Leclercq, Henri, *L'Ordre bénédictine*, Paris, Rieder, 1930.

——, " Chaussure," *Dictionnaire d'archéologie chrétienne et de liturgie*, III, 1232-1257.

——, " Cenobitisme," *ibid.*, II, 3047-3248.

——, " Oblat," *ibid.*, XII, 1857-1877.

——, " Office divin," *ibid.*, XII, 1926-2017.

Lesne, E., " L'Économie domestique d'un monastère au IXe siècle d'après les statuts d'Adalhard, abbé de Corbie," *Melanges d'histoire du moyen âge offerts à M. Ferdinand Lot*, pp. 385-423, Paris, Champion, 1925.

Levillain, L., *Les Statuts d'Adalhard pour l'abbaye de Corbie* (IXe-Xe siècles), Paris, E. Bouillon, 1900; reprinted from *Le Moyen Age*, XIII.

Linderbauer, Benno, *S. Benedicti Regula monasteriorum*, Bonn, 1928; Florilegium patristicum, XVII.

Lindsay, W. M., *Isidori Hispalensis episcopi etymologiarum sive originum libri xx*, 2 vols., Oxford, Clarendon press, 1911.

Loening, Edgar, *Geschichte des deutschen Kirchenrechts*, 2 vols, Strassburg, Trübner, 1878.

Loew, E. A., *Die ältesten Kalendarien aus Monte Cassino*, Munich, 1908; Quellen und Untersuchungen zur lateinischen Philologie des Mittelalters, III, iii.

Luzzatto, Gino, *I servi nelle grandi proprietà ecclesiastiche italiane dei secoli IX e X*, Senigallia, Marchigiana, 1909.

Lynch, C. H., *Saint Braulio, Bishop of Saragossa* (631-651) : *His Life and Writings*, Washington, 1938; The Catholic University of America Studies in Medieval History, new series, II.

Maassen, Friedrich, *Geschichte der Quellen und Literatur des canonischen Rechts im Abenlande bis zum Ausgange des Mittelalters*, Vol. I, Gratz, Leuschner and Lubensky, 1870.

Mabillon, Jean, *Annales ordinis S. Benedicti,* 6 vols, Paris, 1703-1739.

Manitius, Max, *Geschichte der lateinischen Literatur des Mittelalters,* 3 vols., Munich, 1911-1931.

Mansi, Johannes, *Sacrorum conciliorum nova et amplissima collectio,* 31 vols., Florence and Venice, 1759-1798; new edition and continuation, vols. 32-53, Paris and Leipzig, 1901 ff.

Marmion, Columba, *Christ the Ideal of the Monk: Spiritual Conferences on the Monastic and Religious Life,* trans. from the French by a nun of Tyburn convent, London, Sands and Co., 1926.

Martène, Edmund, *Commentarius in regulam S. P. Benedicti,* Paris, 1690; reprinted in PL, 66, cols. 215-932.

Mayer, H. S., *Benediktinisches Ordensrecht,* Vol. II, Beuron, Hohenzollern, Beuroner Kunstverlag, 1932.

McCann, Justin, *St. Benedict,* New York, Sheed and Ward, 1937.

——, *The Rule of Saint Benedict,* translation with notes, Stanbrook Abbey press, 1937.

McNeill, J. T., and Gamer, H. M., *Medieval Handbooks of Penance: A Translation of the Principal Libri Poenitentiales and Selections from Related Documents,* New York, 1938; Records of Civilization, XXIX.

Mittermüller, R., "Der Regel-Commentar des Paul Diakonus (Warnefrid), des Hildemar und des Abtes Basilius," *Studien und Mittheilungen aus dem Benediktiner- und dem Cistercienserorden,* IX (1888), 394-398.

——, *Expositio regulae ab Hildemaro tradita* (Part III of *Vita et regula SS. P. Benedicti una cum expositione regulae a Hildemaro tradita*). Regensburg, Pustet, 1880.

Morin, Germain, "La Journée du moine, d'après la règle et la tradition bénédictine," *Revue bénédictine,* VI (1889), 72-75, 181-185, 211-216, 309-315, 350-355, 398-401, 458-463; VII (1890), 170-177, 324-327.

——, "L'Ordre des heures canonicales dans les monastères de Cassiodore," *ibid.,* XLIII (1931), 145-152.

——, "Les Quatres Plus Anciens Calendriers du Mont-Cassin (VIIIe et IXe siècles)," *ibid.,* XXV (1908), 486-497.

Mullinger, J. B., *The Schools of Charles the Great and the Restoration of Education in the Ninth Century,* New York, Stechert, 1911.

Narberhaus, Joseph, *Benedict von Aniane: Werk und Persönlichkeit,* Münster in W., 1930; Beiträge zur Geschichte des alten Mönchtums und des Benediktinerordens, XVI.

Neff, Carl, *De Paulo Diacono Festi epitomatore,* Erlangen, 1891.

——, *Die Gedichte des Paulus Diaconus,* Munich, 1908; Quellen und Untersuchungen zur lateinischen Philologie des Mittelalters, III, iv.

Paschini, P., "Paolo Diacono e la sua Expositio super regulam sancti Benedicti," *Memorie storiche Forogiuliesi,* XXV (1929), 67-88.

Paul Warnefrid, *Pauli Warnefridi diaconi Casinensis in sanctam regulam commentarium,* edited by the monks of Monte Cassino, Abbey press, 1880; also published in Bibliotheca Casinensis, IV (*Florilegium Casinense,* 1-173).

Pérez de Urbel, J., "La Règle du Maître," *Revue d'histoire ecclésiastique*, XXXIV (1938), 707-739.

——, "Le Maître et Saint Benoît," *ibid.*, 756-764.

Peter the Deacon, *Petri Diaconi Casinensis explanatio regule sanctissimi patris nostri Benedicti*, Monte Cassino, 1894; Bibliotheca Casinensis, V, 82-165.

Poschmann, Bernard, *Die abendländische Kirchenbusse im Ausgang des christlichen Altertums*, Munich, 1928; Münchener Studien zur historischen Theologie, VII.

Rupert of Deutz, *Super quaedam capitula regulae Divi Benedicti abbatis*, PL, 170, cols. 477-538.

Santi, P. de, "Paolo Diacono," *Civilta cattolica*, series 17, X (1900), 398-415.

Savage, J. J. H., "The Manuscripts of the Commentary of Servius Danielis on Vergil," *Harvard Studies in Classical Philology*, XLIII (1932), 77-121.

Seebass, O., "Benedikt von Aniane," *Realencyklopädie für protestantische Theologie und Kirche*, II (3d ed., Leipzig, 1897), 575-577.

——, "Ueber die Statuta Murbacensia," *Zeitschrift für Kirchengeschichte*, XII (1891), 322-332.

——, "Ueber zwei Turiner Handschriften des Capitulare monasticum," *Neues Archiv der Gesellschaft für ältere deutsche Geschichtskunde*, XIX (1894), 217-220.

Selmer, Carl, *Middle High German Translations of the Regula Sancti Benedicti*, Cambridge, 1933; Mediaeval Academy of America Publications, XVII.

Smaragdus, *Smaragdi abbatis Diadema monachorum*, PL, 102, cols. 593-690.

——, *Expositio in regulam B. Benedicti*, PL, 102, cols. 689-932.

Solmi, Arrigo, *Storia del diritto italiano*, 3d ed. revised and enlarged, Milan, Società editrice libraria, 1930.

Spreitzenhofer, Ernest, *Die historischen Voraussetzungen der Regel des. hl. Benedict von Nursia*, Vienna, 1895.

St. Caesarius of Arles, *S. Caesarii regula ad monachos*, PL, 67, cols. 1098-1104.

St. Hildegarde, *Regula S. Benedicti juxta S. Hildegardim explicata*, PL, 197, cols. 1053-1066.

St. Isidore of Seville, *Sancti Isidori Hispalensis episcopi regula monachorum*, PL, 83, cols. 867-894.

Stosiek, Konrad, *Das Verhältnis Karls des Grossen zur Klosterordnung mit besonderer Rücksicht auf die regula Benedicti*, Greifswald, 1909; Dissertation, University of Greifswald.

Thompson, J. W., *Feudal Germany*, Chicago, University of Chicago press, 1928.

Traube, L., *Textgeschichte der Regula S. Benedicti*, 2d ed. by H. Plenkers, Munich, 1910; Abhandlungen der königlich bayerischen Akademie der Wissenschaften: Philosophisch-philologische und historische Klasse, XXV.

Trithemius, *Joannis Trithemii spanhemensis primum, deinde D. Jacobi in suburbano Herbipolensi, abbatis erudissimi opera pia et spiritualia.* . . ed. Joannis Busaeus, Maintz, Albinus, 1605.

Turrecremata, *Regula S. Benedicti cum doctiss. et piiss. commentariis Joannis de Turre Cremata, S. R. E. Cardinalis, et Smaragdi* . . . Cologne, Calenius, 1575.

Valentinelli, Giusseppe, *Bibliotheca manuscripta ad S. Marci Venetiarum,* Venice, 1868.

Valous, Guy de, *Le Monachisme clunisien des origines au XVᵉ siècle: Vie intérieure des monastères et organization de l'ordre,* 2 vols., Paris, A. Picard, 1935; Thesis, University of Paris.

Vita Benedicti abbatis Anianensis et Indensis auctore Ardo, ed. G. Waitz, MGH, SS, XV, 198-220.

Voigt, Karl, *Staat und Kirche von Konstantin dem Grossen bis zum Ende der Karolingerzeit,* Stuttgart, W. Kohlhammer, 1936.

Volpe, G., "Per la storia giuridica ed economica de medio evo," *Studi storici,* XIV, 145-227.

Workmann, H. B., *The Evolution of the Monastic Ideal,* 2d ed., London, Epworth press, 1927.

Ziegelbauer, Magnoaldus, *Historia rei literariae ordinis. S. Benedicti,* 4 vols., Augsburg, 1754.

INDEX

Aachen, capitulary of, 15n, 41, 42n, 43, 44, 45, 46, 78, 97, 114, 116n, 129, 134n, 136-137, 150n, 155, 175, 194; court of, 22, 23, 46; reform of, 59-60, 128, 194, 198

Abbot, authority of, 55-56, 63, 100; discretion required of, 57, 114; onerous position of, 56-57; as ordained, 57-58; as representative of Christ, 138-139; see also Canonical abbots

Abstinence; see Fleshmeat

Accretions to the liturgy, 156-160

Adalard of Corbie, 23, 44

Admission, of a boy oblate, 76-81; of a monk from another monastery, 73-74; of a lay novice, 66-69; of a priest, 73

Admonitions, 61; secret and public, 92-93, 96; of the abbot, 140

Age periods, 80, 142, 145

Albers, B., 92n

Altars, 27, 114-115, 158

Alcuin, 123

Allodi, L., 204n

Amann, E., 86n, 96n

Ambrose, St., 122, 124

Amelli, A. M., 123n, 154n

Angilbert of Milan, 25

Annals of Lorsch, 155

Antoninus, 204

Ardo; see Smaragdus of Aniane

Arichis, 23

Asceticism, as a means to an end, 171, 177, 195; of the Rule, 185; see also Austerities

Atticus of Constantinople, 76

Augustine, St., 122, 124, 174, 192n

Austerities, 172-186; corporal, 173-178, 185-186; discretion in, 172-173, 177-178; spiritual, 178, 185-186, 195

Basil, St., 78, 185, 204

Bathing, 37-39

Beatific vision, 107

Bede, 122, 124

Benedict of Aniane, 54n, 58, 59, 73, 90n, 92, 114-115, 118, 128, 156, 157n, 158, 193-194, 197; *Codex regularum*, 198; *Concordia regularum*, 16, 198, 199; *Diadema monachorum*, 16, 202

Benedict, St., 5, 153, 186; see also Rule of St. Benedict

Benedictine vows, 68, 70-73, 184; see also Religious profession

Berlière, U., 54n, 70n, 78n, 83n, 107n, 108n, 110-111, 152n, 157n, 197, 200, 201, 202n

Bernard of Monte Cassino, 19, 35n, 203

Bernard, St., 177

Bethmann, L., 19

Bibliographies, 197

Bilfinger, G., 108n

Bishop, E., 157n

Blood-letting, 141

Books (manuscripts), the copying of, 124-125; distribution of, 120-121; preserved when not in use, 40n

Boy oblates, 16; concessions in food of, 141-143; corporal punishment and, 145; courtesy in, 129-130; custody over, 65, 143-145, and the Divine Office, 143, 163; education of, 126-129; and expulsion, 88; how offered to the monastery, 76-81; incentives offered to, 145-146; recreation of, 143

Bread, *libra* of, 32

Butler, C., 5, 27n, 73n, 103n, 107n, 108n, 111, 114, 116n, 142, 143n, 152n, 157n, 166n, 176, 178n, 180n, 184n, 185, 186n, 192n, 197, 205

Calefactorium, 47, 143

Calmet, A., 18, 99, 35n, 143n, 197, 201, 204

Camerarius, 37, 44, 47, 62, 63-64

Canonical abbots, 58-60

Canonical hours, 107, 109, 116; signals for, 109-110, 117-118; see also Divine Office, Prime, Matins, Laudes, Vespers

Canons, 154; see also Clerics

Caplet, A. M., 203

Cassian, 124, 147, 174n, 204; *Institutes*, 102, 185; *Conferences of the Fathers*, 127, 185

Cassiodorus, 124, 125, 174

Cells, 49-50

Cenobitic life, compared with the eremitic life, 186-188; predomi-

BC   OP   £7.99